Raymond Williams

Williams believed that making connections between politics, economics, education and culture was a continuing critical task. John and Lizzie Eldridge adopt this spirit in undertaking a critical exploration of the full range of Williams' work. This book is the fullest and most sustained treatment of his work currently available. It spans his fiction and non-fiction, his contributions to drama, film, literary criticism, sociology, cultural studies, media studies and politics.

Williams was a socialist intellectual with a complex relationship to Marxism. At a time when the socialist project is on the defensive, Williams' own wary utopianism and commitment to an educated, participatory democracy warrants careful re-examination. This book fulfils this task. It also re-examines his sharp critiques of modernity and post-modernity and evaluates the worth of his work on culture and communications.

The book will be of interest to students of sociology, cultural studies, communication studies, politics and anyone interested in the life and work of one of the towering Western intellectuals of the post-war period.

John Eldridge is Professor of Sociology at the University of Glasgow. He is a founder member of the Glasgow University Media Group and contributor to its major publications. **Lizzie Eldridge** is Lecturer in Cultural Studies at the University of Glamorgan with a particular interest in theatre and drama.

Raymond Williams

Making connections

John Eldridge and Lizzie Eldridge

London and New York

First published 1994
by Routledge
11 New Fetter Lane, London EC4P 4EE

Simultaneously published in the USA and Canada
by Routledge
29 West 35th Street, New York, NY 10001

© 1994 John Eldridge and Lizzie Eldridge

Typeset in Baskerville by Mews Photosetting,
Beckenham, Kent
Printed and bound in Great Britain by
T.J. Press (Padstow) Ltd, Padstow, Cornwall

British Library Cataloguing in Publication Data

A catalogue record for this book is available from the British
Library

Library of Congress Cataloging in Publication Data has been applied for

ISBN 0-415-04087-6   ISBN 0-415-04088-4 (pbk)

Contents

Acknowledgements

We are very glad to acknowledge the help and encouragement we have received during the course of this study. At an early stage we went to see Joy Williams. We remember with affection her hospitality, helpfulness and generosity of spirit.

Friends and colleagues have spoken with us about Raymond Williams, made suggestions, drawn our attention to references and relevant material and encouraged us in the project. Whether they agree with what we have written is, of course, quite another matter. Our thanks to: Robin Benson, Phil Cooke, Peter Cressey, David Frisby, Simon Frith, Bridget Fowler, Fred Inglis, John MacInnes, Graham Martin, Theo Nicholls, Greg Philo, Newman Smith, Ian Taylor, Kevin Williams, Brian Winston and Peter Worsley. One of us (J.E.) had the opportunity of spending a sabbatical term in the Department of Sociology, University of Edinburgh, which proved a great help in getting this work started. To colleagues there, and especially Colin Bell and Janet Siltanen, many thanks. Our thanks also to Sheila Lovett for her help with the typing of parts of the manuscript and to Lesley Henderson who prepared the index. Finally, we give thanks to the staff at Routledge for their thoughtful and friendly guidance of this work towards publication. In particular we thank Chris Rojek, Ann Gee, Beth Humphries and Leigh Wilson.

The responsibility for what is written and the opinions expressed remain ours.

John Eldridge
Lizzie Eldridge

Chapter 1

Introduction

Raymond Williams was sixty-six when he died in 1988. In the obituaries that followed, the intellectual left underlined his accomplishments as writer, academic and cultural critic. They also expressed a sense of personal loss – of guide, mentor and inspiration. His long-time friend and colleague, Stuart Hall, wrote:

> In this age of Philistine barbarism over which Mrs Thatcher is pleased to preside, the loss of Raymond Williams is irreparable; and those of us who had the privilege to know him personally, to read his work, to talk and argue with him, to be formed, intellectually and politically, in his shadow, hardly know how to express or where to put our sense of the enormity of that loss.
>
> (Hall 1988a: 20)

Hall went on to celebrate the range and stubbornness of Williams' critical intelligence, the variety of his modes of writing and his seriousness of purpose in seeking to understand and communicate to others the 'central processes of our common life'. For Hall, Williams was a socialist intellectual who refused to be captured by any tendency:

> There wasn't the usual rift between thought and feeling, idea and life, which characterises so much 'politicised' intellectual work. His practice was that of 'dialogue' – with other traditions, positions, other ways of seeing and feeling, as a 'pointed response to a particular orthodoxy' because 'the society of dialogue' was his way of imagining what socialism would be like.
>
> (ibid.: 21)

To lose such a person when New Right ideologues were still rampant following Margaret Thatcher's third election victory and when the socialist project worldwide was looking charmless and shop-soiled and at its worst brutally repressive, was to lose someone who always saw socialism and democracy as mutually inter-dependent if both were to flourish for the common good.

Anthony Barnett who, like Stuart Hall, has been closely associated with the *New Left Review*, wrote in the *Listener*, where in the early 1970s Williams had been the television critic:

> When I try to answer the question of what Raymond Williams was ... my answer is that he was a thinker. When you talked with him, his thinking was almost palpable: a deceptively slow delivery allowed a tremendously impressive body of mental capital to go into action. Above all, he grasped what few of his political associates realised: that we are far from understanding the processes of social change. He proposed a new general approach that he termed 'cultural materialism.'

The significance of this, as Barnett points out later in the piece, was that it required a reassessment of the terms of the argument in which socialism was conducted: 'He insisted that "culture", which was regarded as "superstructure" by Marxists, was in fact central to structures of change, control and democracy' (Barnett 1988: 15).

Whereas Hall drew attention to Thatcherism, Barnett reminds us of the fact that a large part of Williams' life was experience of the Second World War (where he served with a tank regiment in Normandy) followed by the cold war. Williams actively sought to reconstruct the terms of the ideological debate. To oppose anti-communist hysteria in the USA was not to endorse Stalinism; to oppose Stalinism was not to reject socialism. From his egalitarian perspective Williams was suspicious of leadership. Even to talk in those terms could contribute to a politically and culturally subordinated people. Barnett comments: 'He wanted people to be at home with themselves and each other. He knew that this could demand an extremely tough and complex struggle for power, yet people had to undertake it for themselves' (ibid.: 15).

To be an egalitarian among the privileges of Cambridge University was not without its ironies, even contradictions, as Frank Kermode recalled in his obituary of Williams:

He once told me of a preliminary visit to his new college, on a day when a newly-instituted feast was to be held in honour of the patron saint of servants. This seemed an untypical, even a promising development, until he discovered that it was the fellows who were going to feast while the servants waited on them as usual.

(Kermode 1988: 25)

A former student, Terry Eagleton, writing in the *Independent* on the same day, referred to the range and versatility of Williams' writings and the originality and independence of his thought and claimed that 'Almost single-handedly, he transformed socialist cultural studies in Britain from the relative crudity of the 1930s Marxism to an impressively rich, subtle and powerful body of theory' (Eagleton 1988: 25).

There was more in this vein, notably from Fred Inglis, who wrote explicitly about the loss of a father-figure for British socialists. What he particularly emphasizes is Williams' hope for a socialist future despite all the forces ranged against it and the sectarian, sometimes self-destructive politics of the left itself:

In Britain, Williams was a singular figure, a socialist intellectual whose beliefs and whose work came together in an extraordinary integrity. The only other figure of that same stature with the same features is Edward Thompson. Both men are striking in that they command a wide, popular affection. The conditions for socialist parties being presently so unpropitious, it is no surprise that their conduct is marred by rancorous differences. Williams and Thompson alike stand outside these, and yet both men address themselves straightly, passionately and in the real language of men to the fretting, chafing and usual uproar of everyday politics.

(Inglis 1988)

Yet it is notable that the obituaries refer to the loss of the intellectual left. Michael Rustin, writing for the periodical *Radical Philosophy* (Summer 1988) drew attention to the gap between theory and practice in the politics of the left, as reflected in the differing responses to Williams' death:

Looking back, one can see now that the mainstream Labour tradition in Britain should have embraced Williams as the central figure of his generation, as it had been earlier able to acknowledge G.D.H. Cole and R.H. Tawney. T.H. Marshall's trilogy of citizenship rights – civil, political, social and economic – has its proper extension in Williams' idea of a cultural entitlement, and it is an index of the deep failure of British labourism that it has so far been unable to recognise this, or to absorb Williams' work in any significant way into his politics. It is notable that while his death has been widely mourned by intellectuals – and not only of the left – it seems to have been scarcely noticed publicly by any figure from Labour's mainstream political institutions.

(Rustin 1988: 47)

This leads Rustin to conclude that Williams' central concern with a democratic culture seems far from realization:

The distance between a vigorous practice of cultural criticism and dissent, on which Williams has had a great influence, in education and elsewhere, and a still predominantly utilitarian politics, remains seemingly as wide as ever.

(ibid.)

In *Politics and Letters* (1981a) Williams referred to what he called a comic episode. When the Labour government was elected in 1963 the *Sunday Times* ran a feature on 'The New Establishment' including photographs of Peter Townsend, Richard Hoggart, Brian Abel-Smith and Raymond Williams:

These were supposed to be the people who would be giving the intellectual orders to the Labour Ministers. In reality, throughout the entire six years of Labour Government in the sixties, I never had one enquiry, formal or informal, private or public, one invitation to a committee or conference, from anybody in the Labour government or Labour machine. Not one line. On the other hand, following a private leak from a man in the Civil Service, Hoggart and I and the Musicians' Union had to fight a plan by Benn to set up a reported chain of commercial radio stations. In the case of the Open University, which combined my interest in communications and in Adult Education, there was no consultation whatsoever.

(Williams 1981a: 37)

So all was not sweetness and light. On the academic front, Williams was no stranger to hostile criticism. Let us recall some examples:

Mr Williams is a dull writer who expresses himself in a tone of heavy and persevering piety.

(Anthony Quinton, review of
Culture and Society, *Spectator*, 26 May 1961)

It is easy to get irritated with Raymond Williams. His politics, as revealed in the last 50 pages of the book, seem to me to be mostly wishful thinking and romantic fervour. He describes himself as having been 'absolutely solid' with the May events in 1968, as if anyone *can* be absolutely solid with something as frothy and insubstantial as that insurrectionary carnival.

(Alan Ryan, review of *Politics and
Letters*, *New Society*, 20 September 72)

The most interesting feature of Mr Williams' writing is its violence. He seems incapable of talking of any change, move-ment or effort, except in violent language. Tightening, breakthrough, crisis, struggle, revolution, pressures, drives, forces, tensions, stresses: these are the descriptive words which come naturally to him; and to anyone who is used to reading social and political theory, they are warning signals. Those who habitually see political or social situations, or political or social movements in such terms usually end as either apostles of despair or apologists of authoritarianism. Mr Williams is a knotted figure, greyer than most of them, and his argument, certainly, is not a blueprint for an authoritarian regime. But it is a hand knitting pattern for it.

(Henry Fairlie, review of *Communications*,
Encounter, August 1962)

We may pause a little longer with Henry Fairlie. Later in the review he contrasts a 'great academic sociologist like Professor Morris Ginsberg' with the 'easy sensationalism which is accepted as serious criticism'. Here, Williams is placed with the latter:

It is sensationalism which is the mark of the quasi-sociologist or quasi-social critics who today are so quickly translated into paperback pundits. We are not, as yet, so infested with them as America, but it cannot be long before others realise that, like Mr Wright Mills or Mr Vance Packard in America, Mr Raymond Williams and Mr Richard Hoggart have cottoned on to a good thing. As sociologists they do not qualify, because they observe no strictness in the use they make of sociological methods, even when equipped to use them; as social critics they do not qualify, because they ignore the diversity of human experience, so that they may concentrate on aspects of it which will serve for their sensational generalisations and ignore also the different depths of different kinds of experience, so that they may convince us that anything which happens to anybody in this long night of the 20th century is a matter for alarm if not despondency, and certainly matter for a book.

(ibid.: 84)

We will take one more illustration for our present purposes. Two years after Williams' death a clutch of books by or about him appeared. These were reviewed in the *London Review of Books* (8 February 1990) by R.W. Johnson, who referred to them as 'essentially fan club books'. In the review, Johnson claims that Williams was not a major or even a very coherent theorist and that his political writings represented what Michael Walzer had called the failure of English political writing. In Johnson's opinion, Williams 'never actually spells out what socialism is for him. It seems, in the great tradition of British wooziness, to be all about values and community and wholeness; in a word, Christian socialism and brown bread.' The review essay is consistently hostile to Williams throughout. We get the measure and tone of it from the last paragraph:

I must confess that I simply do not understand the claims made for his political writings, which seem to me to be repetitive, ritualised, empty and downright evasive. Their significance surely lies in the exemplary way in which they display the exhaustion of a tired political tradition, a final anguished charge into a cul de sac. There is a very real sadness to this but it is better to be frank. In the new, post-Communist world of the 1990s the Left has much hard thinking to do – about its own roots and identity as well as about where it goes from here. The inspiration that can be gained from a backward look to the heroes of the Sixties has now a merely nostalgic quality to it. A whole new intellectual beginning is required and the greatest danger to that process will be to get trapped within the rhetoric of an exhausted tradition.

(Johnson 1990: 6)

Let us recall the scope and nature of Williams' work. He wrote six novels. *Border Country* (1960), *Second Generation* (1964) and *The Fight for Manod* (1979), which constitute a trilogy; as well as *The Volunteers* (1978), *Loyalties* (1985) and *People of the Black Mountains*. The last of these was published posthumously in two volumes, *The Beginning* (1989) and *The Eggs of the Eagle* (1990). Novel writing was a continuing and for Williams a significant part of his work. In response to a question, in *Politics and Letters* (1979; Williams 1981a) – 'Is there a major difference for you between discursive and fictional works in your practice as a writer?' – he replied:

> It is certainly true that I have given relatively more time, in comparison with what became visible and valued, to fiction, than to any other forms of writing. In the late forties, I regarded the novels as the work which I most wanted to do. Now I feel differently about them. All along there have been certain things pressing on me, which I could simply find no alternative way of writing; today, however, fiction is something I'm prepared to work on a long time without feeling any urgency to finish quickly.
>
> (Williams 1981a: 271)

The non-fictional work does not easily fit into conventional disciplinary categories. Still, Williams was closely associated with English at Cambridge as both a student and a teacher, and some of his books focus more closely than others on issues of literary theory and criticism. These include *Reading and Criticism* (1950), *Drama from Ibsen to Eliot* (1952) later extended to *Drama from Ibsen to Brecht* (1968), *Modern Tragedy* (1966), *Drama in Performance* (1954), *The English Novel from Dickens to Lawrence* (1970), *The Country and the City* (1973), *Marxism and Literature* (1977) and *Writing in Society* (1983). This last was a collection of essays culled from published papers and lectures. There is another group which deals centrally with issues of cultural change and communication. Among these can be numbered *Preface to Film* (with Michael Orrom) (1954), *Culture and Society* (1958), *The Long Revolution* (1961), *Communications* (1962), *Television: Technology and Cultural Form* (1974), *Problems in Materialism and Culture: Selected Essays* (1980), *Keywords: A Vocabulary of Culture and Society* (1976), *Culture* (1981) and *Towards 2000* (1983). There were two short monographs, *Orwell* (1971) and *Cobbett* (1983), both authors who had been discussed in *Culture and Society*. Perhaps his most explicit political writing was *May Day Manifesto* (1967). This he co-edited with Stuart Hall and Edward Thompson, but the Penguin version of 1968 was produced under his editorship.

After Williams' death a number of edited books were published containing papers, lectures and reviews that had been written throughout his life and published in a wide range of places. These were *The Politics of Modernism* (1989) edited and introduced by Tony Pinkney, *Resources of Hope* (1989) edited by Robin Gable with an introduction by Robin Blackburn, *What I came to say* (1990b) edited by Neil Belton, Francis Mulhearn and Jenny Taylor, and *Raymond Williams on Television*, edited by Alan O'Connor (1989).

Williams did not publish an autobiography, but in 1977 and 1978 he was interviewed by three members of the *New Left Review* (*NLR*) board (Perry Anderson, Anthony Barnett and Francis Mulhearn). The results of this were published as *Politics and Letters* (1981). The interview format was maintained although for reasons which are not clear the identity of the individual asking the question or making comments is not. However, what we have is a kind of autobiography, albeit structured by the questions put to Williams. The book is organized in five sections (preceded by a helpful chronology of dates relating to his life and activities); Biography, Culture, Drama, Literature and Politics. It is an indispensable resource for students of Williams. We should recall the point of entry for *Politics and Letters* as indicated in the Foreword. First there is a very high opinion of his standing as a socialist intellectual:

> Raymond Williams occupies a unique position among socialist writers in the English speaking world today. No contemporary figure of the Left has so extensive an oeuvre to their credit. The range of this work, moreover, is probably unprecedented in either England or America, including political intervention, cultural theory, history of ideas, sociology, literary criticism, analysis of drama, semantic inquiry, novels, plays and documentary film scripts.
>
> (1981a: 7)

But how does Williams' work relate to Marxism? In 1959 Victor Kiernan had reviewed *Culture and Society* (Kiernan 1959), and in 1961 Edward Thompson wrote an extended two-part review of *The Long Revolution*. These were both from avowedly Marxist standpoints. But it was Terry Eagleton, a former pupil of Williams, who really set the cat among the pigeons. His *New Left Review* article 'Criticism and politics: the work of Raymond Williams' (1976), which can also be found as the opening chapter of his *Criticism and Ideology* (1976), was a fierce critique of the Williams corpus and provoked a strong response from Anthony Barnett – 'Raymond Williams and Marxism: a rejoinder to Terry Eagleton' (Barnett 1976). At about the same time Williams wrote *Marxism and Literature* (1977). All this then persuaded the *New Left* editorial committee of the timeliness of exploring with Williams the significance of his work and activity in relation to Marxism. It was also the recognition of an omission. The *New Left Review* had, as a matter of policy, explored and evaluated the work of a range of European Marxists – Lukács, Sartre, Gramsci, Althusser, Adorno and Della Volpe – yet Williams, whilst a contributor to the pages of the *NLR*, had not been so evaluated. This might be considered alongside a comment by Perry Anderson, which touches on the difficulties of labelling Williams, whilst admiring his contribution to socialist thought:

> Perhaps the most distinguished socialist thinker to have so far come from the ranks of the Western working class itself has been a Briton, Raymond Williams. Yet Williams' work, while it has corresponded closely to the pattern of Western Marxism in its typically aesthetic and cultural focus, has not been that of a Marxist. However, its class history – steadily and confidently present throughout Williams' writings – has conferred on his work certain qualities which cannot be found anywhere else in contemporary socialist writing, and which will be part of any future revolutionary culture.
>
> (Anderson 1976: 105)

This is a footnote to a comment on Gramsci suggesting that the 'organic intellectuals', who he envisaged coming from the ranks of the proletariat, have not so far played the role in revolutionary socialism predicted by Gramsci. Yet Anderson still thought that 'in the long run' the future of Marxist theory would lie with such people 'as they steadily gain in cultural skill and self-confidence'.

Williams' relationship to Marxism is an issue which, not surprisingly, comes up in a number of contexts in this book. There were changes in his intellectual position, as we shall see. There were also changes in his personal commitments: the pacifist of 1938 became the soldier in Normandy in 1944. In the politics of the left neither Stalinism nor Fabianism were, for him, acceptable: the one was an outrage to the socialist tradition and the other simply became incorporated into the capitalist society it was supposed to transform.

Those who felt like him, although like most such movements it was variegated, became members of the New Left. Although Williams was not a contributor to *Out of Apathy* Thompson (1960), that volume expresses the energy and political thinking of the New Left. Williams, for his part, outlines his position in a 1977 essay with the teasing title, 'You're a Marxist aren't you?' (reprinted in Williams 1989c). Incorporation, for him, had to be seen as a process of social and cultural incorporation and, in this respect, Gramsci's concept of hegemony was instructive. Class dominance could thereby be seen as based not just on naked power and force but on the saturation of habits, experiences and outlooks into the lived order of culture. The question is whether we recognize it and if we do whether we struggle against it. In a characteristically personal passage (Williams moves from the abstract to the personal in many places throughout his work) he writes:

> Can I put it this way? I learned the experiences of incorpora-
> tion, I learned the reality of hegemony. I learned the saturating
> power of the structures of feeling of a given society, as much
> from my own mind and my own experiences as from observing
> the lives of others. All through our lives, if we make the effort,
> we uncover layers of this kind of alien formation in ourselves,
> and deep in ourselves. So then the recognition of it is a recognition
> of large elements in *our own* experiences, which have to be – shall
> we say it? – defeated. But to defeat something like that in yourself,
> in your families, in your neighbours, in your friends, to defeat
> it involves something very different, it seems to me, from most
> traditional politics.
>
> (Williams 1989c: 75)

This, at the time, he himself thought, was different from Marxism, and Marxists like Anderson clearly thought so too. Yet his position was also that the general approach of historical materialism as found in Marx was true. The difficulty was to work out in detail what was meant and implied by it – only gradually did he work out his own position of cultural materialism, although the sense of cultural hegemony was clearly an important constituent of this approach. But there was an underlying value position that permeated his work:

> I believe that the system of meanings and values which a capitalist
> system has generated has to be defeated in general and in

detail by the most sustained kinds of intellectual and educational work. This is a cultural process which I called 'the long revolution' and in calling it 'the long revolution' I meant that it was a genuine struggle which was part of the necessary battle for democracy and of economic victory for the organised working class.

(1989c: 76)

In the end, given his commitment to socialism and his growing sense that contemporary Marxism could contain undogmatic, even at times meditative, people like him, he was able to establish what he meant by and what it meant for him to make connections:

we have to learn and to teach each other the connections between a political and economic formation, a cultural and educational formation and, perhaps, hardest of all, the formations of feeling and relationship which are our immediate resources in any struggle. Contemporary Marxism, extending its scope to this wider area, learning again the real meanings of totality, is, then, a movement to which I find myself belonging and to which I am glad to belong.

(ibid.)

This theme of making connections has guided our approach to Williams' work. We begin with a review of some available perspectives, taking as our point of departure the hints available in Williams' *Keywords* as to what is entailed in making connections. We then offer an expository account of the main corpus of Williams' fiction and non-fiction, which, taken together, Williams himself liked to call 'the work'.

Chapter 2

Perspectives on Williams

There are, at the time of writing, four book-length studies which deal with aspects of Williams' work. J.P. Ward's *Raymond Williams* (1981) is a short monograph of 79 pages published by the University of Wales Press, and rather overlooked. It is a continuous text without chapter divisions but lucid, accessible to the reader and much to be commended. Compared to Henry Fairlie's strictures on Williams' vocabulary, noted earlier, Ward is interestingly different. In his comments on *Keywords* he writes:

> The words are seen to be quietly energised, and to move, if very slowly and gently, through history, not having constant meanings, still less 'correct' ones, but yet not arbitrary either, for they have a logical and understandable continuity which, even with internal surprises, can be traced.
>
> (Ward 1981: 63)

Indeed, Ward takes the view that, given Williams' preoccupation with the wholeness and integration of culture as a way of life, he is deeply ambivalent about the desirability of the revolutionary rupture. This, he feels, is evident even in the extended discussions found in *Politics and Letters*:

> There is almost an equilibrium of despair, as the absence of illusion about revolution's possible outcomes is balanced against the sense that only something fairly uncompromising will ever alter the chief features of our system which for Williams, are its vice and tragedy. These, he frequently says, are its endless capacity to incorporate, to cover up, to win every round by the pre-emptive political manoeuvre, to let opponents expend their energy, and so on . . . the emphasis to be made here is that his

careful qualifications, the distanced generalising, the equivo-
cations about change and reformism, the admissions of change
from his own earlier positions, seem to come from a position
still held open.

(ibid.: 70–1)

Given the Welsh imprint, it is not surprising to see that Ward
makes clear the importance to Williams of Wales, the land of his
birth. He does this in the context of writing about Williams' mild
pragmatic utopianism. Nostalgia for the past or a yearning for easy
futurist utopias are sentimentalist responses to the problem of
analysing cultural totality. Ward suggests:

> In the Welsh context this is illustrated by the way Williams,
> eschewing a generalised and diluted picture of his country, has
> referred to it and its past piecemeal, or periodically. He is
> sensitive to the archaeological layering of the land; to the varia-
> tions between its earlier Ages (such as that of Methodism; the
> Tudor Age; the earlier Celtic); to the far-from-simple position
> of language; to the industrial thirties and the not always successful
> attempts to deal with that period in fiction; to the old grammar-
> schools and universities in Wales, the almost colonial relationship
> of the former to Oxbridge requirements and the latter's strong,
> perhaps unique, democratic basis of original foundation.
>   All this is to say that even a small country must be seen in
> its complexity, its own cultural particularity, if it is ambitious
> to throw off its constraints and make its own future.

(ibid.: 74)

That, after all, was what the novel *The Fight for Manod* in part
addressed, and on a much grander historical canvas what *People
of the Black Mountains* accomplished. But Wales also served as a
symbol for, an expression of the possibilities of a socialism that
emphasizes the importance of devolution and small-scale autonomy.
It is the connection between these local autonomous groupings,
where people share power and experience to control the conditions
of their work and environment, and the global internationalized
world of which they are a very small part that points to the
complexity of working through to a democratic future.

A recurring word in the Williams vocabulary is *complexity*. It
functions as a cautionary word and is applied to both the theory
and the practice of socialism. It is contrasted, for example, with the

notion of social simplicity. In *Politics and Letters* Williams was asked whether he would respond differently to socialist writers like Christopher Caudwell and William Morris than he did in *Culture and Society*. In both cases he refers to the problem of simplification of the future found in these writers. Caudwell, he suggests, in *Studies in a Dying Culture* and *Further Studies* fails to separate 'the generic notion of what is exploited and what is alienated within present society from simplified projections of future man' (Williams 1981a: 127). And Morris also, he thinks, lapses into simplicities when writing about the future; this indeed is a general problem of emphasizing discontinuity in social change:

> Because what the representation of discontinuity typically produces is a notion of social simplicity which is untenable. The extent to which the idea of socialism is attached to that simplicity is counter-productive. It seems to me that the break towards socialism can only be towards an unimaginably greater complexity.
>
> (ibid.: 128)

Moving from the present to a possible socialist future is the issue raised again at the very end of *Politics and Letters*. Out of current working and social experience, Williams argues, definitions of problems and modes of solution can indicate shapes of specific practicable futures:

> Left to itself, the present crisis of capitalism – and specifically of industrial capitalism – can only destroy us. We want more, much more, in its place than a chaotic breakdown or an imposed order or the mere name of an alternative. The challenge is therefore to a necessary complexity. I've been pulled all my life ... between simplicity and complexity, and I can still feel the pull both ways. But every argument of experience and of history now makes my decision – and what I hope will be a general decision – clear. It is in only very complex ways that we can truly understand where we are. It is also only in very complex ways, and by moving confidently towards very complex societies, that we can defeat imperialism and capitalism and begin that construction of many socialisms which will liberate and draw upon our real and now threatened energies.
>
> (ibid.: 437)

If moving from the present to the future in a socialist direction is complex in a practical way, then any Marxist theory that purports to analyse and explain social change will also be complex. In a passage that speaks of Althusser in all but name, Williams' own language takes on a tortuous complexity:

> The short-cut solution, in one powerful variant of Marxism, has been to unify these theories within a theory of Ideology, but the only thing right about this is the realisation that the theoretically separated 'areas' have to be brought within a single discourse. The main error of this solution is that it substitutes Ideology (a general, coherent and monopolising practical consciousness, with its operative functions in institutions, codes and texts), for the complex social relations within which a significant (including alternative and oppositional) range of activities, is a significant (including dominant, subordinated but also contesting) range of situations were being at once expressed, produced and altered, in practice in contradictory as well as in coherent, directive ways. These could in any case not be seen as a superstructure, or as a simple ideological manipulation, in a period in which the process involved quite large-scale primary production, in publishing and broadcasting, and in which, also, what was seen by capitalist institutions as a market often contradicted what was seen by bourgeois ideologists as a culture. Moreover, it was impossible, looking at the new forms of broadcasting (especially television) and at formal changes in advertising and the press, to see cultural questions as practically separable from political and economic questions, or to posit either second-hand or dependent relations between them.
> ('Notes on Marxism in Britain since 1945', Williams 1980: 245)

There is in Williams a continuing struggle to find a space between the experience of late capitalism and the rigid and undemocratic command economies of Eastern Europe which can be advocated on socialist grounds. This value position and the practical inferences he chooses to make comes out very clearly in *Towards 2000* (Williams 1985b). There he tells us that socialism emerging out of bourgeois democratic countries will have to be rooted in new forms of communal, cooperative and collective institutions. But if this is the only way forward for socialism, it is then necessary to begin a very open and practical discussion about the relations between such institutions and the undoubted need for larger-scale institutions, whether in the struggle against major capitalist or external resistance, or in the actual working of a complex and modern industrial society. 'The existing dominant formula of the tight party government which will deliver self-management, seems to be at best a pious hope, at worst a pathetic delusion' (Williams 1985b: 123).

Williams is, of course, well aware that most of what is done in the name of self-management is small scale. The problem for the socialist thinker is to work a way through the connections between these activities and the larger sphere without returning to the concept of the common economy or assuming if not stating the good will of the larger spheres of action – political and economic. It has to be said that he does not deal in the detail which he insists is required. On the principle he is clear enough: 'The socialist intervention would introduce the distinctive principle of *maximum self-management*, paired only with considerations of economic viability and reasonable equity between communities, and decisively breaking with the new dominant criterion of administrative convenience to the central-ised state' (1985b: 125). In his essay, 'Walking backwards into the future' (1985) (reprinted in Williams 1989c), Williams pivots his discussion around ideas of despair on the one hand and confidence on the other. There is a clear statement of this theme at the outset:

> The morale of generations of struggle was sustained by the belief that the *future was ours*. It is not often like that today. Actual majorities, including very many young people, have lost this conventional hope, from the experience of repeated political failures and long term economic decline. Our future is now regularly defined in terms of *dangers*; the threat of nuclear war; the probability of large-scale structural unemployment; the steady working through of ecological crisis. Many of us still respond actively, and propose different ways forward. But this change in thinking about the future is taking its toll. Fear and apathy breed in these shadows, and are the grounds for a politics of hard and selfish competitive advantage: the propaganda of the ruling hard Right.
>
> (Williams 1989c: 281)

Williams contrasts what he regards as the despairing gravity of some of the best voices with the chirpy optimism of consumer jingles. Where does this leave the idea of progress, and is there any basis upon which a confidence in socialism can be renewed? Character-istically, he invites us to consider the connection between the words 'socialism' and 'society'. The idea of a society, understood as a definite form of human relationships in certain specific conditions at a particular moment in history, is comparatively modern. From his discussion of the term in *Keywords* (1983a: 243–7), Williams sees the eighteenth century as the decisive period, when society as referring to the company of fellows is being replaced by society as a system of common life. When such an idea is in place then the long standing problems of virtue and happiness can be considered by looking at the precise forms of society in which people live and what kind of changes could or should be made, rather than by starting from assumptions about human nature or the inevitable conditions of existence. And here Williams makes the connections with socialism:

> The first uses of *socialism*, as a way of thinking, were in deliberate contrast to the meanings of *individualism*: both as a challenge to that other way of thinking, in which all human behaviour was reduced to matters of individual character, and more sharply as a challenge to its version of human intentions. Was life an arena in which individuals should strive to improve their own conditions, or was it a network of human relationships in which people found everything of value in and through each other?
> (Williams 1989c: 282)

Part of the faith which sustained many socialists was simply that at the end of the capitalist phase, whose demise was routinely assumed and sometimes predicted (in the name of 'scientific socialism') socialism would be ushered in. This has not happened. Yet in the wealth-creating capitalist societies, based on competitive individualism, a great deal of poverty still remains. Modernization, in itself, does not provide for the reasonable basic needs of all members of a society which enjoys the benefits of technology and increased production. At the same time those societies labelled socialist have had problems of production alongside experiences of repression. Where does this leave socialism as a valid and possible alternative for the future? This is where the paradox of Williams' essay title come into focus. He takes us back to what he sees as the central socialist value of sharing. He points to popular democracy and common ownership as two linked forms of sharing:

> The link between socialism and popular democracy is literally the key to our future. Without it, the practice of socialism can degenerate to bureaucratic state forms or to the political and

economic monopolies of command economies. Yet, if socialism is seriously to carry through the idea of sharing, it has to go beyond the limited forms of representative political democracy, which have been, historically, the liberal modifications of absolutist states, and which as such have been properly supported and where necessary, defended, by democratic socialists. To move on to real sharing, in all the decisions that affect our lives, not by some all-purpose mandate to others, but by direct participation and by accountable delegation, is the historic task of socialist democracy.

(Williams 1989c: 285)

The first book on Williams to appear after his death was Jan Gorak's *The Alien Mind of Raymond Williams* (1988). The theme is suggested in the title. In *Keywords* Williams had written that alienation was one of the most difficult words in the language (culture, incidentally, he described as one of the two or three most complicated words). After working through the history and various meanings of the word he concludes that 'in its evidence of extensive feeling of a division between *man* and *society*, it is a crucial element in a very general structure of meanings' (Williams 1976: 32). According to Gorak, Williams does not confront the idea of alienation, yet it is the clue to understanding his own life and work:

As a Welshman he belonged to an ethnic minority in England, while his working class status in an emphatically middle-class university marginalised him still further. But for all his silence on the issue, alienation is constantly at the margins of his work, gathering momentum over the course of his career, and in effect becoming the hidden theme behind his prolonged interrogation of English culture. As the following pages will suggest, the concept of alienation helps to locate the buried matter of Williams' work and also explains his peculiarities of manner. Constantly drawn by the desire to revisit old obsessions, to work through his own estrangements by an interpretation of an alien culture's monuments, beset by a compulsion to test the authenticity of his own responses, forever seeking to identify 'the real' shape of a situation or problem, Williams offers a case study in the psychology and methods of the alienated intellectual.

(Gorak 1988: 10)

What were the marks of this alienated self? Gorak underlines Williams' personal isolation as a writer. This, after all, is dealt with quite explicitly in *Politics and Letters*. After early enthusiasm there was disillusion with the first post-war Labour government. He cited the British acceptance of the American loan, and later the Marshall plan, as one reason since it put the Labour government in a dependency relationship to the USA and implied policy adaptations to American world views.

On domestic policies Williams disagreed with the government's handling of the fuel crisis of 1946–7 since it revolved around exhortations to the working class to increase productivity in the national interest without emphasizing the value of common sharing at a time of hardship. The experience of nationalization was also negative. Its over-bureaucratic character led to more, not less, control and discipline from above – and here he drew upon the direct experience of his father in the railway industry. In the cultural sphere, his attempt (with Paul Rotha) to get public money for a documentary film on the agricultural and industrial revolutions was blocked by the Central Office of Information.

At this time and in this context (1947–8) Williams, with Wolf Mankowitz and Clifford Collins, set up and was co-editor of the cultural journal, *Politics and Letters* (which incorporated an earlier venture, *The Critic*). He describes his own writing as being more combative at that time and cites Cyril Connolly, Noel Coward, Rebecca West and John Lewis as specific targets. Connolly was editor of *Horizon*, a cultural journal for which he sought and obtained American funding. This was the predecessor of *Encounter*, which was famously discovered to be in receipt of CIA funding. But Williams' attack on Lewis was because of his concern about the repression of writers in Russia. However, *Politics and Letters* – which while occupying a position on the left of the political spectrum and acknowledging a debt to the cultural radicalism of F.R. Leavis, wanted to avoid the different dogmatisms of *Scrutiny* and the Communist Party – foundered. There were financial problems and personal differences between the editors which proved fatal. In reflecting on all this Williams makes a poignant comment:

> The collapse of the periodical was a personal crisis for me. So many other initiatives, like the film, had also been blocked or failed. The experience confirmed the pattern of feeling I had found in Ibsen. For a period I was in such a state of fatigue and

withdrawal that I stopped reading papers or listening to the news. At that point, apart from going on with the actual adult education teaching, I felt I could only write myself out of this in a non-collaborative way. I pulled back to do my own work. For the next ten years I wrote in nearly complete isolation.

(Williams 1981a: 77)

What were the effects of this isolation? In what could be taken as an acid comment Gorak states: 'Williams' greatest source of intellectual development was probably Williams' (Gorak 1988: 11). He has at least two things in mind here. First, there is the neglect of relevant work in fields to which Williams applies himself. Thus *Drama from Ibsen to Eliot* (1952) ignored Eric Bentley's *The Modern Theatre* (1946) even though it covered similar ground with similar convictions. The author of *Culture and Society* (1958) was not aware of the parallel activities of Richard Hoggart and E.P. Thompson which led to the publication of *The Uses of Literacy* (1957) and *The Making of the English Working Class* (1963). (Williams was, however, an indefatigable reviewer and both these books were in due course reviewed by him.) The development of media studies in Europe and the USA was not addressed when he was working on *The Long Revolution* (1961) and *Communications* (1962). To some extent his own writing fed upon itself. The discussions of Austen, George Eliot, Dickens, Hardy and Lawrence in *The English Novel from Dickens to Lawrence* (1970) reappear, often word for word, in *The Country and the City* (1973), and Chapter 2 of *Towards 2000* (1983) is a reprint of Part Three of *The Long Revolution* (1961) – which, we should make clear, is plainly identified in the text. Secondly, there is an obsession (the word is Gorak's) with the contrasting meanings of the terms 'neighbour' and 'exile'. The Williams who, as a young man, had objected to L.C. Knight's statement in a lecture that in a corrupt, mechanical civilization there are no neighbours, was still wrestling with this in *The Country and the City* and *Towards 2000*. And the Williams who wrote on James Joyce's *Exiles* as early as 1948 in *Politics and Letters* explores it in his fictional and non-fiction work.

Williams, the man who knew the reality of neighbourliness from his upbringing in Wales, was the Williams who through geographical and social mobility engendered by his education (and of course the special circumstances of war) knew what it was to be an exile from his class and from his country. He is portrayed by Gorak as an internal migrant, alienated but indebted to the culture that reared him. At the end of a book which bristles with reservations about Williams' achievements he nonetheless identifies *Towards 2000* as

> the last in the line of imaginatively organised cultural diagnoses [and] points to his status as critic, radical socialist, and passionate utopian . . . . Williams' most significant contribution to the socialist tradition in *Towards 2000* lies in his unusual combination of progressive analysis and sympathetic human understanding. The work impressively combines a sustained opposition to existing society with some imaginative sketches of a more compassionate alternative.
>
> (Gorak 1988: 117–18)

Even here he wants to enter caveats about the limitations of the book, in particular what he regarded as 'the uniform solemnity of the prose that seems to raise agents, relationships and events to its own imperious level of abstraction' (ibid.: 120). This in itself tended to invest capitalism with a totemic force rather than more specifically identifying the controllers: 'In its unwillingness to pinpoint its targets or even to allow them the benefit of quotation, his style carries off the unlikely coup of making the apocalyptic sound soothing' (ibid.: 121). Yet, after all this, Gorak concludes that Williams is a cultural critic whose achievements will be difficult to surpass.

Shortly after Gorak's book came Alan O'Connor's *Raymond Williams: Writing, Culture and Politics* (1989). This is a relatively brief overview of Williams' life and work. O'Connor does not pursue the alienation theme although he does describe Williams' writing in the post-war period as having the kind of existential motif of blocked individual liberation. He has more to say about Williams' political activities and involvements, including his professional writing with the Communist Party. These were unsigned pamphlets whose topics were chosen by the party, such as the one he wrote with Eric Hobsbawm in 1940 justifying the Russian invasion of Finland. The chapter on politics takes us through the period of the New Left and the Campaign for Nuclear Disarmament, through Williams' relationship to the Labour Party and his role in the *May Day Manifesto 1968*, and through his work for the Workers' Educational Association and in adult education more generally. O'Connor manages to bring some human detail into this. We learn, for example, that Joy Williams was knocked down by supporters of the Smith regime in Rhodesia when she was taking part in a demonstration against the Rhodesian Unilateral Declaration of Independence. And he recalls that in 1971 the West German student leader, Rudi Dutschke, who had been shot in a demonstration, had come to England where he was interviewed by Williams at Cambridge and admitted for a research degree to work on Lukács.

> He was admitted to England by the Conservative Government of Edward Heath on condition that he should not engage in political activity. Following secret police surveillance which included the tapping of telephones, Dutschke was expelled from the country by a secret tribunal because he had communicated with political activists. The evidence adduced by the tribunal, said Williams, as a threat to national security was 'all of a kind which could be adduced against many of us: in work and contacts inside the university, to say nothing of any more general public life'. It was an issue of civil liberties.
>
> (O'Connor 1989b: 27)

Although O'Connor's book was not written as a direct response to Gorak, a rather different picture emerges. Williams' writing, his central life project, does involve isolation, but his political, educational and administrative commitments and duties took up a good deal of time, certainly in the 1960s and 1970s. O'Connor takes up three major themes of Williams' work – the ways in which keywords operate through their semantic instability; the concept of the knowable community in the novel; and what he terms 'complex seeing' in drama. This last, which extends in O'Connor's account to film and television as well as the theatre, seeks to draw our attention to the differing and changing experiences of audiences, the ways in which structures of feeling in the world and theatrical and televisual production may generate differing interpretations of what is seen and heard. It is, we may surmise, an attempt to come to terms with the realities of change in the world as well as the development of different forms and conventions within the theatre, some of which cross over to film and television; and with new forms of technology which themselves create new possibilities in audio-visual media.

O'Connor takes, as a working example from Williams, the use of complex seeing in Brecht's historical plays. Thus, it is argued, in *Mother Courage* there is a complexity of action as we see a woman live and move through a war with great physical determination, which at the same time destroys her family. In *Galileo* there is complexity of consciousness. We see Galileo separated from those he taught, his scientific community, while he continues in isolation his own scientific work. O'Connor suggests that

> The one play creates a complex action; the other dramatises a complex consciousness. Williams argues, however, that Brecht retains the structure of feeling of expressionist drama: an isolated individual in the face of a total world. What Brecht does is to change the values: the isolated individual is only a symptom and not the centre; the total world is now the source of values and explanation. The intermediate connections of any knowable community are simply absent. In this extension of an expressionist structure of feeling, there is a separation between a complexly seen action and a completely seen consciousness. This separation between action and consciousness is the actual history that Brecht lives out.
>
> (O'Connor 1989b: 89)

We can supplement this by referring to Williams' Cambridge 1974 inaugural lecture, 'Drama in a Dramatised Society' (reprinted in O'Connor 1989a). Towards the end of the lecture he tells us:

> I learned something from analysing drama which seemed to me to be effective not only as a way of seeing certain aspects of society but as a way of getting through to some of the fundamental conventions which we group as society itself. These, in their turn, made some of the problems of drama quite newly active.
>
> (in O'Connor 1989a: 11)

Williams wants to establish the point that we can learn to look both ways – at the stage and the text, and at society active and enacted within them. The seeing is complex because changes are taking place within and between 'drama' and 'society'. Hence he reminds us that at the turn of the twentieth century, Strindberg was experimenting with a new drama of moving images

> a wall papered with faces; aspects of character; and appearance dissolving, fragmenting, fusing, haunting, objects changing literally as you look at them; while Strindberg was writing this, beyond the capacity of the theatre of his time, other men, in quite different ways, were discovering ways of making images move; finding the technical basis for the motion picture: the new mobility and with it the fade, the dissolve, the cut, the flashback,

the voice-over, the montage, that are technical forms but also, in new ways, modes of perceiving, of relating, of composing and of finding our way.

(Williams in O'Connor 1989a: 12)

In this way we are strongly reminded of Williams' commitment to the study of drama. As he makes clear in his Foreword to John McGrath's *A Good Night Out: Popular Theatre: Audience, Class and Form* (1981), it is all too easy in an academic context to think of plays as ready-made for the study. For him it was always important to reconnect the text with those who made and performed it, whether in the theatre, the film or television. Recently, *Drama in Performance*, first published in 1954, has been reissued with a new introduction by Graham Holderness (1991). As Holderness fairly points out, it is common to trace Williams' intellectual history from *Culture and Society*, with its literary preoccupations, through to more extended concerns with communications in the media of print, television and film. Yet by 1954 he had written three books on drama and film. The theoretical analysis of drama in performance was, indeed, an early and continuing source of fascination. Holderness surmises that

> it may even begin to seem more appropriate to regard the later work on the media as flowing initially from the earlier studies in drama, rather than following as a logical progression from the move towards 'cultural studies' (though the later work would admittedly not have been possible without the prior development of a cultural theory and a literary sociological method).

(Williams 1991a: 1)

Certainly Williams' preoccupation with text as performance can be seen as a precursor of what he was to later elaborate as a cultural materialist perspective. What is also evident is the range of Williams' interests: Sophocles, English medieval drama, Shakespeare, Ibsen, Chekhov, Eliot, Brecht, Beckett and Bergman all figure. In Bergman's case, Williams is examining the film *Wild Strawberries* (1957). The continuities as well as the new possibilities that film opens up as a development of the dramatic tradition is a theme to which Williams returned many times.

In discussing the relations between text and performance Williams draws attention to a number of variable elements. There are, for example, the elements of speech, movement, design (including stage sets and lighting) and sound (music, sound effects and so on). Dramatic action itself may be differentiated in terms of acted speech, visual enactment, activity (the arrangement of events) and behaviour (where words and movement have no relation but are based on a conception of probable behaviour in the circumstances). The varying kinds of drama to which this can give rise all carry their own conventions, even those which in a new generation are at first seen as innovative. And limits may be placed in material terms to certain possibilities by the form of the text, the physical structure of the theatre; moreover, audiences have to learn to see and respond to the presentation of drama. Convention itself is not just a technical matter but 'embodies in itself those emphases, omissions, valuations, interests, indifferences, which compose a way of seeing life, and drama as part of life' (Williams 1991a: 165). So the very definition or understanding of reality will vary; it 'depends on a whole set of other interests, responses and assumptions; in fact on that selection of interests and values that we call a particular culture' (ibid.).

Film and television do show differences at the level of production and also in relation to audiences. While they clearly have innovative potential for dramatic method and performance, Williams noted the continuing uses of available conventions of different forms of theatre. What did cameras make possible?

> They could look into the room, with greater subtlety of detail in this face, this hand, this object, and they could solve technically, many of the problems of inset, extension, visual device. In a majority of cases, they have done no more; the essential conventions are still of the stage as a room, with some mechanically extended movements beyond it. Or, in a different convention, the camera could be, more powerfully than on the stages of expressionism, symbolism and the absurd, a watching, a shaping eye, which made a version of the world, and composed figures within it.
>
> (ibid.: 168)

When Williams was later to write *Television: Technology and Cultural Form* (1974; revised edition 1990), his work on drama was clearly a contributing element to his analysis. Television itself, he well understood, could be seen as a combination of a number of pre-existing forms of communication – the newspaper, the public meeting, the classroom, the sports stadium, the advertising columns and the billboards, radio broadcasting, as well as the theatre and the cinema. But so far as drama was concerned, its sheer availability to so many people is unprecedented in human history – soaps, serials, thrillers, westerns, detective and police drama, the classics of the theatre, the screening of films originally made for the cinema – these are now ingrained in our cultural and social life. Some writers chose to write mainly or only for television (such as Dennis Potter, David Mercer and John Hopkins). Some new developments did take place, notably the use of the drama-documentary, which Williams saw as a significant innovation. Although he recognized the dangers in such a form and made the point that we should be open about the conventions that were being employed, Williams argued that those who complained that it confused reality and fiction were naive or disingenuous. This was partly because he challenged the convention that factual reports simply showed in a neutral way what was happening, whereas there is always the mediation of directors, camera personnel and reporters involved in the selection and presentation of what is happening. Yet one of the strengths of television, as he saw it, was the possibility of entering into contemporary public and in some senses private experience more powerfully than any other form of communication technology. Clearly, although like any other technique it can be abused, it can form a basis for social critique, as in the still-quoted case of *Cathy Come Home* which led to the foundation of Shelter in 1967.

So there are continuities as well as innovation between television and earlier forms of communication, including drama in theatre and cinema. Moreover, the category of drama is not self-contained since it can move into other genres, such as news. However, there is something distinctive about broadcasting as a cultural form and as a technology, which Williams identifies with his concept of 'flow'. Whereas earlier forms of communication were essentially differentiated – a book or pamphlet to read, a meeting to attend, a play or film to go to – broadcasting makes available a variety of things – a comedy, a book programme, news, film and so on – as a programmed sequence. There are alternative programmes, so that we can enter in and out of sequences at the flick of a switch, and now, of course we have even more control with the advent of video recorders. It is the immediate availability of this flow and the organization of the flow itself, including, in what are now taken-for-granted ways, the commercials, the trailers and devices to hook our attention and smooth the path from one item to the next with scarcely any sense of interval, that is a central contemporary experience of communication. The analysis of flow itself can be conducted at different levels – an evening's viewing, the internal organization of a particular programme, the sequences of words and images. For the student of media culture they offer a way of identifying the meanings and values of a specific culture.

There is no doubt that Williams saw in the development of broadcasting in general and television in particular both dangers and opportunities. As he pointed out in a review of Himmelweit and Oppenheim's pioneering study, *Television and the Child* (1959):

> Can any simple value judgement on a technical medium of communication be adequate? Modern techniques are at worst neutral, and to ask whether television is a good or a bad thing is like asking whether injections are a good or bad thing. Still, to describe such a medium as one of 'mass-communication' is in fact a concealed value judgement, part of its meaning being communication 'to the mass', which in view of the derogatory meanings of 'mass' and 'masses' is already, in many minds, a condemnation of the medium, as well as being a description of the particular motives of some of those who use the medium. If we think of how a television audience actually watches, *mass communication* is especially inappropriate.
>
> (Williams 1959: 57)

The argument, for Williams, goes back to those who have control of the medium; he does not settle for market-based statements which assume that 'giving the public what it wants' justifies mediocrity. If one is to talk about irresponsibility it must be in relation to those with power and control; one must not castigate audiences as a nation of troglodytes. If we read his own television reviews in the light of this perspective, numerous examples will be encountered which illustrate his critical concerns.

There is, not surprisingly, an extended interest in television drama. The term he had coined for academic purposes emerges in these reviews in relation to a more general readership. 'In any work,' he tells us, 'the structure of feeling is decisive' and then proceeds to consider Tolstoy's *Resurrection* as one of the great transitional moments in modern feelings and relationships (Williams in O'Connor 1989a). In the adaptation of Elizabeth Gaskell's *North and South* the structure of feeling embodies an

> imaginative connection with a world in which relationships were articulate and settlements were arrived at. It is as if some part of the BBC, some part of England, turns with particular readiness to the years before 1900, as we shall see in *The Forsyte Saga*; but also with interest, with a connection to that history of the industrial revolution, the class wars, the struggle for democracy, which is so clearly unfinished but which can be looked at, carefully and seriously, if there is a bonnet or two about.
>
> (ibid.: 39)

In October 1969 we see a review of Alan Plater's *Close the Coalhouse Door* in which Williams expresses his preferences for realism in writing on working-class life 'because in a culture like this the hardest and most necessary task is to see people in their own terms, in a complex working and relating, rather than as symbolic or abstract figures for which the dominant consciousness is already prepared' (Williams in O'Connor 1989a: 78). A year earlier (7 November 1968), he had reviewed the documentary *Death of a Miner*, which has focused on Jack and Emma Elliott and their family. Williams liked the fact, unusual as it was on television, that here were working-class men and women talking about their own lives rather than being treated as objects in the coverage of a temporary dispute or a street interview. But he ponders the timing of the programme. It went out on a Sunday evening after the death of Jack Elliott. 'Yet, there was nothing detached in what the Elliotts had to say: this was the human reality of a continuing social experience which may be acceptable only on Sundays and about the past, but which is in fact weekday and contemporary: what is now happening to hundreds of thousands of men' (ibid.: 43).

Again and again Williams comes back to the issue of realism. In his novel *Second Generation* he had written a fictional account of television treatment of a car strike. In it he had conveyed the sense of news as a play with representative spokespeople in specific settings. But if it becomes a play then one can deploy the resources of dramatic criticism. This is what he did in a review of the way a strike of Ford car-workers was covered, particularly an interview with Robert Mackenzie, who was both academic and media pundit.

He wants to identify the way reality can break through in spite of the conventions:

> What I saw, in the Mackenzie interview, was not the isolable facts but the deciding relationship. Here was the calm academic, down to question the stewards, people who are calling wildcats. But the scene went wrong, with a master's touch. Not only were the stewards grave and wordy men, their academic questioner a clock watcher, a rusher, a very practitioner in loose ends. But also the bits of reality, to which the scene ironically referred came through and were neglected, as the stewards talked. Nineteen minutes (was it?) of 'Personal Relief Time' in an eight hour shift. It wasn't the ratio, it was the idea, that few dramatists could have conceived. Personal Relief Time: a mentality was coming through, a mentality profoundly inhumane and mechanical. Personal Relief Time: against a background quickly sketched and offered (but only to be ignored) of the speed of the assembly lines, the heat of the foundry. Steady, patient, informative talk, against scraps of ideology, debating points, hammers of public opinion polls. The dramatic situation could hardly have been clearer: the roles going wrong, the reality appearing involuntarily. Personal Relief Time: all the euphemism, the meanness, the subordination of men to a system; all the actual causes, behind the routine talk about constitutions and exports; human politics appearing, unlooked-for, past the edgy, dominative manner of the public interview.
>
> (ibid.: 57)

There is, then the reality of the experience of work, but there is also a reality constructed in and through the media. So, and recall that this was in 1969, Williams is reminding us of the social frameworks that impinge upon broadcasting – not the military intervention of Czechoslovakia, nor the authoritarian political intervention of France but

> the invading forces, we might say, are accountants (only, like soldiers, doing the job they have been asked to do). Accountants' reality, like soldiers' reality, has a limited but powerful reference to the reality of communications. . . . When 'reality' is defined by financial and administrative convenience, instead of by the only practical need, which is creation and communication, we get streamlined accounting and managerial systems but, in the

end, bad programmes. It is a more subtle invasion, and we have not learned our reactions to it; but it is now happening everywhere and there has never been more need to fight.

(ibid.: 60)

When, some twenty years later, an accountant became Director-General of the BBC and the language of efficiency, performance indicators and value for money was routinely spoken, we can see who won and who lost the fight.

These are ways of speaking about power and control in the media. And if we return to the concept of 'flow' we will, in following Williams' analysis, come to realize that it is neither neutral nor innocent. What he finds especially diminishing is the way in which techniques, which once sought to give new understandings of relationships and meanings, have themselves become incorporated into dominant political and commercial practices. He is angry to see the way the adaptation of Dostoevsky's *The Possessed* was given a trailer with footage of a demonstration outside Grosvenor Square, a loose and misleading association. He extends the point in the ensuing comment:

> For where reason, fact and discrimination are now urgently necessary, we are sodden with montage. What was originally a creative technique to express newly perceived relationships has become a manipulative evasion of all substantial connections. Nothing flows, nowadays, so well, as an Oxo commercial, a genteel art film, an elderly commentator's reminiscences of history. In this kind of work, where form is everything, we see dissolves of sunlit woods and revolutionary crowds and waves breaking and mouths opening and rockets and streaming hair. At any time in a generation in which so much art or pseudo-art is produced, the production habits of a majority of professionals compose a structure of associations, images, tones, which set limits to actual insights and perceptions, yet ensures, in the programmes that follow each other so closely, a certain confidence of address. The sheer bloody nerve of that trailer for *The Possessed* was not, as the people concerned might like to think, intellectual or creatively daring. It was a busy producer's unsurpassable confidence in the currently available clichés.

(ibid.: 53)

If we ask the questions about communication – who is addressing whom, to what purpose, in what voice and to what effect? – we can, one hopes, now come to appreciate that Williams gives us good guidance on this. He characteristically draws our attention to the complexity of analysis that is needed and to the struggle that any change would require in the existing structure of control. But the direction he points in is clear enough – to a more representative, more accessible system, which allows for a greater range of voices, more diversity and pluralism in production. This in its turn is part of a struggle for a more democratic culture in which we are able to speak to each other.

Tony Pinkney's *Raymond Williams* (1991) has a different point of entry. It consists, almost exclusively, of an analysis of Williams' fiction and especially the novels. Pinkney has a specific thesis to advance, namely that Williams can be seen as a postmodern novelist. Not realist, which in a specific sense, is the position taken in our study; not modernist, which again in a specific sense Pinkney had earlier argued (in Eagleton 1989 and Williams 1989d); but postmodernist. Indeed, although he has yet to complete his project, this is a more general argument about Williams, beyond the novels, that Pinkney intends to pursue:

> For if Williams is inseparably local and internationalist at once, so too – and no less paradoxically – is he simultaneously modernist and anti-modernist. But over the last two decades, we have come to term such ambivalences as '*post* modernist', and this, I believe, is the term we should now apply to the life and work of Raymond Williams and which makes him still, in these years after his death, our immediate contemporary.
>
> (Pinkney 1991: 16)

Of course, Pinkney knows full well that postmodernism is a contested concept. However, he also very well understands Williams' commitment to realism and how he was looking for a new realism, which he was later to claim was close to Lukács' position on the realist novel. We will discuss further Williams' treatment of realism in our exposition of *The Long Revolution* (see Chapter 4). But the reference to Lukács bears further comment here. In particular, we would draw attention to Williams' notable essay 'Crisis in English studies' (Williams 1991b). Among other things, he addresses the relation of Marxism to literary criticism, pointing out that a general claim in Marxism is to offer insights

into or understanding of the nature of social reality. But if, following
Marx, what appears to common sense to be reality may be illusory,
what implication does this have for the advocacy of realism in the
novel? The novel has, as it were, to uncover underlying social
movements. Lukács, Williams suggests, works from this position.
For this reason naturalism is attacked precisely because it only seeks
to reflect that which is on the surface, the immediately accessible.
Realism, properly understood, should be dynamic because it should
go beneath the surface to give an insight into underlying social
movements. Yet, Williams suggests, when writing of the kind that
Lukács was calling for in theoretical terms appeared in practice,
in Brecht for example, he attacked it. Williams contends that Lukács
'tended to remain deeply attached to that older version of realism
as reflecting and illuminating a general, and generally knowable,
reality' (Williams 1991b: 199).

But even if Lukács' inconsistency is duly registered there is the
wider question of Marxism and realism, which, as Williams well
knew, could slip into the authoritarianism of socialist realism based
on claims to privileged knowledge of realist and consequent aesthetic
(and political) judgements as to what constituted good and bad
literary work. In varying ways and in many places Williams was
to struggle with this issue, from his anti-Marxist stance in *Culture
and Society* to a specific kind of Marxism in *The Country and the City*
and a distinctive methodology identified as cultural materialism.
His position and his problem was that 'no Marxist, however he/she
refines the terms of this general proposition of social determination,
can wholly give it up without abandoning the Marxist tradition'
(Williams 1991b: 197).

The theoretical approach embodied in cultural materialism is
concerned with the analysis of all forms of signification within the
actual means and conditions of their production. This is illustrated
and elaborated in *Problems in Materialism and Culture* (1980) and
Marxism and Literature (1977). Much of this analysis hinges on
Williams' treatment of the base–superstructure problem in Marxist
theory. So he argues that 'contrary to a development in Marxism,
it is not "the base" and "the superstructure" that need to be studied,
but specific and indissoluble real processes, within which the decisive
relationship, from a Marxist point of view, is that expressed by
the complex idea of determination' (Williams 1977: 82). Determination is itself seen as a matter of setting limits and exerting pressures.
How then are we to understand social reality and therefore the

relationship between the individual and society? Williams tells us that 'society' is never only the 'dead husk' which limits social and individual fulfilment:

> It is always also a constitutive process with very powerful pressures which are both expressed in political economic and cultural formations and, to take the full weight of 'constitutive', are internalised and become 'individual wills'. Determination of this whole kind – a complex and interrelated process of limits and pressures – is in the whole social process itself and nowhere else; not in an abstracted 'mode of production' or in an abstracted psychology'. Any abstraction of determinism, based on the isolation of autonomous categories, which are seen as controlling or which can be used for prediction, is then a mystification of the specific and always related determinants which are the real social process – an active and conscious as well as, by default, a passive and objectified historical existence.
>
> (ibid.: 87–8)

In order to arrive at his position of cultural materialism, Williams finds it necessary to challenge, reject or modify terms which have characterized many variants of Marxist discourse: totality, mediation, reflection, mode of production, hegemony. For him, the mistake has been to separate the categories of 'material social process' and 'language': 'The problem is different, from the beginning, if we see language and signification as indissoluble elements of the material social process itself, involved all the time both in production and reproduction' (ibid.: 99). This does not diminish, for Williams, a sense of the importance of classes in society, but rather offers a point of entry for a more effective analysis of those relations in different times and places; in terms, for example, of what he termed structures of feelings and dominant, residual and emergent cultures.

The point of this brief theoretical detour is in part to remind ourselves that Williams took the question of how we understand the ensemble of real relations as seriously as Marx had done, and questions of class relations remained for him a manifest concern. We have yet to return to the novels but it is appropriate to observe that his thinking on modernism and postmodernism was consistently related to this problematic. Let us take, for example, Williams' lecture, 'When was Modernism?', which was given in 1987 and reprinted in *The Politics of Modernism* (Williams 1989d). His awareness of the selective tradition, which he had identified in his early work, notably *The Long Revolution*, is here turned on this topic. Why, he asks us, should not the extraordinary innovations in social realism as represented in Gogol, Flaubert and Dickens, not take precedence over the conventionally modernist names of Proust, Kafka and Joyce? 'But in excluding the great realists, this version of Modernism refuses to see how they devised and organised a whole vocabulary and its structures of figures of speech with which to grasp the unprecedented social forms of the industrial city' (Williams 1989d: 32).

What Williams wishes to underline is the selective way in which particular versions of modernity were foregrounded as if they were the whole of modernity. This is itself a form of ideological work which, paradoxically, has its parallels in the identification of a literary canon in literary criticism. Yet, this is not the only paradox. In the later nineteenth century there was a great range of new movements with visions of the new and of the future. Others were to follow. Their advocates and adherents disagreed, sometimes passionately and violently, with one another. Groups split and new ones formed as orthodoxies were continually challenged. Alongside this, great changes were taking place in the media of cultural production: photography, cinema, the gramophone and, later, radio and television. There was a complicated relationship between these new forms of cultural production and the technologies they entailed and the new artistic groups, whether in art, literature, drama or music. The cities – Paris, Berlin, Vienna, New York and London – were the international sites of finance capital, and of the new technologies of communication; they were also the gathering places of *émigré* and exiled writers and artists. Their relationship to bourgeois capitalism in this shared space was not straightforward. One could find those like Picasso and Brecht who supported communism, others like Wyndham Lewis and Ezra Pound who supported fascism. What it meant to be anti-bourgeois could vary politically. But what has happened in any event, according to Williams, is that modernism in practice lost its anti-bourgeois stance and was comfortably integrated into the new international capitalism.

Its attempt at a universal market, transfrontier and transclass, turned out to be spurious. Its forms lent themselves to cultural competition and the commercial interplay of obsolescence, with its shifts of schools, styles and fashion so essential to the market.

The painfully acquired techniques of significant *dis*connection are relocated, with the help of the special insensitivity of the trained and assured technicists, as the merely technical modes of advertising and the commercial cinema. The isolated, estranged images of alienation and loss, the narrative discontinuities, have become the easy iconography of the commercials and the lonely, bitter, sardonic and sceptical hero takes his ready-made place as the star of the thriller.

(Williams 1989d: 35)

The question which preoccupies Williams is this: how can we consider changes that have taken place in society and in the arts – which in terms of culture, technology, economics and politics are real enough – in such a way that we can conceive of a modern future in which community may be imagined again? Modernism, as he sees it, has ironically become fixed in the past by ideological fiat. Its historical fixity implies that what comes after it is postmodern. Yet the same question can be put to both modernism and postmodernism – how do they relate to capitalism: in an accommodating or oppositional way? That is why, in his essay on 'The Politics of the Avant-Garde' in the same volume, he points out that the politics of the New Right with its emphasis on the sovereignty of the individual can be traced back to bourgeois dissidents. But now, although we live in a world of concentrated economic and military power, the individual is depicted as free in a market-oriented society. Yet this lauded 'open' society in reality is leading to the dissolution of the social and cultural formations that are the prerequisite for community. At the same time the reality of corporate international capital has emasculated and taken over techniques that were once experimental for its own commercial purposes. Instead of revolt there is the planned trading of spectacle.

It is beyond the scope of this book to enter into the vast literature on modernism and postmodernism. Our purpose is rather to identify Williams' general orientation. It is worth pointing out, however, that Fredric Jameson's *Postmodernism, or the Cultural Logic of Late Capitalism* (1992) shares the sense of the significance of the inter-relation of the cultural and the economic. In the period of late capitalism it is such a developed kind of interrelation that it is difficult to prise them apart. Yet the very concept of postmodernism has for Jameson an ideological function – that of co-ordinating new forms of social practice and mental habits with the global division of labour of late capitalism. The rhetoric of the market has come to dominate everyday discourse, finding its political focus and energy in the New Right, and undermining and penetrating the discourse of the left. Writing from a left standpoint, Jameson argues that a statement claiming the market is in human nature cannot be allowed to pass unchallenged. He identifies it as 'the most crucial terrain of ideological struggle in our time' (Jameson 1992: 263–4). What he especially draws to our attention is the disappearance of the marketplace as a physical entity. This requires new forms of advertising and circulation of commodities. The relations between markets and media then become highly interwoven and symbiotic, so that the very boundaries between the two are abolished and

> an indifferentiation of levels gradually takes the place of an older separation between thing and concept (or, indeed, economics and culture, base and superstructure). For one thing, the products sold on the market become the very content of the media image, so that, as it were, the same referent seems to maintain in both domains. This is very different from a more primitive situation in which to a series of informational signals (new reports, feuilletons, articles) a rider is appended touting an unrelated commercial product. Today the products are, as it were, diffused throughout the space and time of the entertainment (or even news) segments, as part of that content, so that in a few well publicised cases (most notably in the series *Dynasty*) it is sometimes not clear when the narrative segment has ended and the commercial has begun (since the same actors appear in the commercial segment as well).
>
> (Jameson 1992: 275)

As we have seen in the UK, deregulation has become a crucial part of the rhetoric of the market and the media and in the light of the above we should not be surprised. The welfare state itself has been a subject for deregulation in the name of the market and the sovereign individual. The more general process in the West and Eastern Europe, 'the transition from socialism to capitalism', is something that Jameson wants to examine in historical terms and to do so it is a necessary part of his strategy to outflank the very claims of postmodernism to be ahistorical. Capitalism, for all its strength and durability, does not have to be the last word and socialism is not extinct but it will continue to take great tenacity to challenge these versions of the end of ideology, the end of history and to continue to imagine alternatives. But space for critique is the prerequisite of this possibility.

The affinities with Williams' position here are, we think, very close. His notable essay, 'Advertising: The magic system' (reprinted in Williams 1980) was originally intended to be part of *The Long Revolution*, so the position outlined is one he reached in the earlier part of his work. He points out that in the early stages of the factory system most products were sold without extensive advertising. The modern development he traces to the period 1880 to 1930 and connects it specifically with the development of modern distributive systems of large-scale capitalism. Advertising develops further in a society in which selling becomes central. Public relations become more professionalized: it is not only goods that are sold in a particular kind of economy but people who are 'sold' in a particular kind of culture. But why a magic system? Because he sees it as a highly organized, professional system of magical inducements and satisfactions functionally similar to the role of magic in simpler societies. Advertising is seen as a social and cultural form that responds to the gap between expectation and control by an organized fantasy:

> It is impossible to look at modern advertising without realising that the material object being sold is never enough; this indeed is the crucial cultural quality of its modern forms. If we were sensibly materialist, in that part of our living in which we use things, we should find most advertising to be of an insane irrelevance. Beer would be enough for us, without the additional promise that in drinking it we show ourselves to be manly, young in heart, or neighbourly. A washing machine would be a useful machine to wash clothes, rather than an indication that we are forward-looking or an object of envy for our neighbours. But if these associations sell beer and washing machines, as some of the evidence suggests, it is clear that we have a cultural pattern in which the objects are not enough but must be validated, if only in fantasy, by association with social and personal meanings which in a different cultural pattern might be more directly available.
>
> (Williams 1980: 185)

The system of magic, the system of fantasy, the system of modern advertising is, in short, the system of capitalism. For Williams it also represents a failure to find new forms of information and decision grounded in use and need rather than illusion. The consequences for the media, as he sees it, will be the domination of commercial interests. It is this which affects the viability of a newspaper, which can be closed as uneconomic even though it is still selling in millions; it is this which shapes the content and the form of broadcasting, even that which is called public service. Advertising revenue is at the root of it. The media not only serve as channels for other people's markets, they become a market themselves. The communications society and the consumer society chase one another, as public space itself becomes ever more privatized. Perhaps the most impressive recent exposition of this theme is to be found in Armand Mattelart's *Advertising International* (1991). When the theme is applied to television, as we have already seen, Williams developed the concept of flow. Pinkney points out that this has been invoked by later theorists of postmodernity. Be that as it may, Williams' use of the term is in part descriptive, but it is also analytical and critical, since flow is embedded in economic and commercial considerations. In permeating the cultural formation they can also have an effect on our capacity for reason and critique within this system of communications. This is what we have already seen in Williams' work as a television reviewer. It does not make him a postmodernist.

Central to Williams' critical concerns, and consistently so, is the effort to show the significance of the development of capitalism, especially late capitalism, on cultural formations. His critiques of modernism and postmodernism have to do with the ways in which potentially oppositional tendencies have been incorporated into these economic formations. Thus, when he writes of the two faces of modernism in *Towards 2000* (and elsewhere) it is to refer to the irony of this kind of incorporation:

> The originally precarious and often desperate images – typically of fragmentation, loss of identity, loss of the very grounds of human communication – have been transferred from the dynamic compositions of artists who had been, in the majority, literally exiles, having little or no common ground with the societies in which they were stranded, to become an effective surface, a 'modernist' or 'postmodernist' establishment. This, near the centres of corporate power, takes human inadequacy, self-deception, role-playing, the confusion and substitution of

individuals in temporary relationships, and even the lying paradox of the communication of the fact of non-communication, as self-evident routine data.

(Williams 1856: 141)

We can sense his anger at this establishment and he goes on to write of the ways in which these new forms become the routine diversions and confirmations of the international commodity exchange. Indeed, he points to the ways in which notions of the insignificance of this, the fictionality of all actions, the arbitrariness of language, can be used in such a way that they make it more difficult for us to understand what is going on – what is *really* going on. It is the difficulty of thinking through and beyond this that Williams identified, and the normality of it all is its strength. This is why he sees and opposes the conjunction of technological determinism (these technologies must produce these contents and effects) and cultural pessimism (there is nothing to be done about it):

> The climax of the pretensions by which this situation was hidden was the widely accepted proposition of the 'global village'. What was being addressed was a real development of universal distribution and of unprecedented opportunities for genuine and diverse cultural exchange. What was ideologically inserted was a model of homogenised humanity consciously served from two or three centres, the monopolising corporations and the elite metropolitan intellectuals. One practised the homogenisation, the other theorised it. Each found its false grounds in the technologies which had 'changed and opened up the world and brought it together'. But nothing in the technologies led to this theory or practice. The real forces which produced both, not only in culture but in the widest areas of social, economic and political life, belonged to the dominant capitalist order in its paranational phase. But this was the enemy which could not be named because its money was being taken.

(ibid.: 143)

Where then, to return to Pinkney, is Williams the postmodern novelist? Pinkney displays a detailed knowledge of Williams' fiction and there are many sharp observations to be found in his book. He is fascinated with the treatment of space and place, with mapping and what he calls the social spatial dialectic in the novels. He chooses to term Williams' last (unfinished) novel *People of the*

Black Mountains as a 'historico-geographic metafiction'. He is interested in the relation between the local and the international as it is treated in *The Fight for Manod*. Williams' use of the detective form for *The Volunteers*, is, for Pinkney, a postmodern move, 'as an instance of that aesthetic populism which seeks to break down the old dichotomy of high art/mass culture' (Pinkney 1991: 101). Here, as elsewhere, the important question for Pinkney is an ontological one: what kind of world or worlds are we in? As he sees it, Williams works through in his fiction the issue of what happens when different social worlds confront each other, as in *Loyalties*, or when boundaries between worlds are crossed (as in *Border Country* or *Second Generation*).

Now since we share the sense of postmodernism as a contested concept we may simply have to leave this as a matter of agreeing to disagree. In this area of discourse, above all, it is easy to talk past one another. So Pinkney sees Williams as a postmodernist Marxist – a free-thinking Marxist whose interests in later years converge with those of other Marxists writing about the city, such as Henri Lefebvre, Manuel Castells and David Harvey. Our point of disagreement would be this: it is one thing to write of situations and address issues that engage with the condition of modernity or postmodernity; it is quite another to be explicitly and avowedly a postmodernist. However elusive and uncertain the relations between one space and another, one world and another, between the self and society, there are still connections to be made under the surface, with all its surface illusions and taken-for-granted common sense. There are the connections, of money, power, the insatiable restless movement of capitalism. To make sense of these connections, whether in fiction or in cultural analysis, called for a new realism, which could understand and interpret, without resort to mechanistic dogma, these new times.

Keywords was first published in 1976 and reissued in 1983 with amendments and additions. In his introduction Williams refers to continual encounters between groups where value conflicts at different levels of explicitness and consciousness are indicated in struggles over the meaning of words. In the development of a language 'certain words, tones and rhythms, meanings are offered, felt for, tested, confirmed, qualified, changed' (Williams 1983a: 10). These are sometimes long and slow processes and sometimes, as in periods of war, quick and conscious.

Williams was heavily preoccupied with the term 'culture'. Indeed, there is a sense in which the other keywords in the list grow out of that concern. Typically, Williams identifies, out of his own experience, his experience of the changing usage of the term culture between the immediate pre-war and post-war periods – the 1930s compared to the late 1940s. To the two meanings of culture as a way of describing and claiming social superiority and as a word which encapsulated the activities of painting, writing, film-making, theatre and such-like, two others were identified. Culture can be defined as a way of referring to some critical formation of values (as in the study of literature) and it can also be used in the anthropological sense of a 'way of life' (which is close to some concepts of society). This, at the time, was a puzzle for Williams and was to engage his critical powers. In important ways it was to stimulate his life's work.

The reaching out to look not only at keywords but at their interconnectedness is clearly stated in his reference to T.S. Eliot's *Notes towards a Definition of Culture* (1948). He tells us: 'The words I linked it with (i.e. culture) because of the problems its uses raised in my mind, were *class* and *art* and then *industry* and *democracy*. I could feel these five words as a kind of structure. The relations between them became the more complex the more I considered them' (Williams 1983a: 13). What Williams came to recognize was that this was not some abstract intellectual matter but required attention to history. In order to understand something about the problem of the contemporary world consideration had to be given to how the past was interpreted and, indeed, how it could be reinterpreted. The articulation of connections, the changing social relations which both link and distinguish the past from the present, became for Williams a crucial task. This kind of work could not be confined to any one disciplinary category, although Williams himself starts from the standpoint of literature. This he came to think was why *Culture and Society* was responded to by people from a range of disciplines and interests:

> I found that the connections I was making, and the area of concern I was attempting to describe, were in practice exper-ienced and shared by many other people, to whom the particular study spoke. One central feature of this area of interest was its vocabulary, which is significantly not the specialised vocabulary of a specialised discipline, though it often overlaps with several

of these, but a general vocabulary ranging from strong, difficult and persuasive words in everyday usage to words which, beginning in particular specialised contexts, have become quite common in descriptions of wider areas of thought and experience. This, significantly, is the vocabulary we share with others, often imperfectly, when we wish to discuss many of the central processes of our common life. *Culture*, the original difficult word, is an exact example.

(Williams 1983a: 14)

Making connections in the course of this activity actually meant several things:

1 identifying relations between words and their changing usage;
2 connecting usage with context;
3 connecting past usage and variations with recent usages;
4 making intellectual connections across disciplines since it was the problem not the discipline which mattered
5 making analytical connections between discrete parts of social life through reflection on common vocabulary.
6 recognizing the connection between specialist vocabularies and the general language of discourse.

So Williams writes:

Every word which I have included has at some time, in the course of some argument, virtually forced itself upon my attention because the problem of its meanings seemed to me inextricably bound up with the problems it was being used to discuss. . . . I began to see this experience as a problem of *vocabulary*, in two senses: the available and developing meanings of known words, which needed to be set down; and the explicit but as often implicit connections which people were making, in what seemed to me, again and again, particular formations of meaning – ways not only of discussing but of seeing many of our central experiences.

(Williams 1983a: 15)

What makes some words keywords for Williams? They are so, he writes,

in two connected senses: they are significant, binding words in certain activities and their interpretation; they are significant, indicative words in certain forms of thought. Certain usages bound together certain ways of seeing culture and society, not least in these two most general words. Certain other uses seemed to me to open up issues and problems, in the same general area, of which we all needed to be very much more conscious.

(ibid.)

So the reflections on keywords are not only ways of making connections where no connection was explicit before but also ways of drawing attention to different social perspectives – different ways of seeing the world. Concepts, after all, in their relation to other concepts, are ways of seeing the world but they are also ways of not seeing the world. To show what is present and what is absent in our seeing and in our understanding eventually has political implications. Moreover, differing or changing meanings of words can draw attention to struggles between different groups in society. Through careful scrutiny of words and their usage we can get clues both to the locus of power in a society and to the sources of resistance to it.

To be reflexive about this we should recognize that Williams himself has a way of seeing his project. Although he does not elaborate on it in the introduction to *Keywords* he is clear enough about what he is and is not doing in a theoretical sense. He locates his task within the field of historical semantics:

This recognises, as any study of language must, that there is indeed a community between past and present, but also that *community* – that difficult word – is not the only possible description of these relations between past and present; that there are also radical changes, discontinuity, and conflict, and that all these are still at issue and are indeed still occurring. The vocabulary I have selected is that which seems to me to contain the key words in which both continuity and discontinuity, and also deep conflicts of value and belief, are in this area engaged.

(ibid.: 23)

Williams' own project embodies a particular kind of commitment and is rooted in a view of human agency. He does not suppose that conflicts over terminology will be resolved by some independent arbiter or linguistic philosopher who will determine correct usage. Conflicts are built in because they relate to different experiences and readings of experiences. What then does he hope to accomplish?

What can really be contributed is not resolution but perhaps, at times, just that extra edge of consciousness. In a social history in which many crucial meanings have been shaped by a dominant class, and by particular professions operating to a large extent within its terms, the sense of edge is accurate. This is not a neutral review of meanings. It is an exploration of the vocabulary of a crucial area of social and cultural discussion, which has been inherited within precise historical and social conditions and which has to be made at once conscious and critical – subject to change as well as to continuity – if the millions of people in whom it is active are to see it as active: not a *tradition* to be learned, nor a *consensus* to be accepted, nor a set of meanings which, because it is 'our language', has a natural authority; but as a shaping and reshaping in real circumstances and from profoundly different and important points of view; a vocabulary to use, to find our own ways in, to change as we find it necessary to change it, as we go on making our own language and history.

(ibid.: 24–5)

In a study of Williams' work, this surely stands as a good point of departure.

Chapter 3

Culture – and society

The organising principle of this book is the discovery that the idea of culture and the word itself in its general modern uses, came into English thinking in the period which we commonly describe as that of the Industrial Revolution.

(Williams 1961: 11)

In the Foreword to *Culture and Society* Williams looks to the possibility of developing a new general theory of culture, by which he means a theory of relations between elements in a whole way of life. This, he maintains, would have to take on the idea of an expanding culture, its nature and content, as well as the social and economic problems of expansion. From the outset, therefore, his work is ambitious in scope and aspiration.

The Introduction to *Culture and Society* immediately introduces his five keywords – industry, democracy, class, art and culture:

The changes in their use, at this critical period, bear witness to a general change in our characteristic ways of thinking about our common life; about our social, political and economic institutions; about the purposes which these institutions are designed to embody; and about the relations to these institutions and purposes of our activities in learning, education and the arts.

(Williams 1961: 13)

Language, and these key words in particular, is seen as a way into the understanding of social change over the period 1780–1950. This takes us almost to the time when Williams began writing the book. Industry comes to signify not just human attributes such as skill or diligence, but a new system, a body of activities, sometimes called industrialism. The industrial revolution is a term used as analogous with the French Revolution, from which the term democracy had become an essential part of the political vocabulary, entering ordinary speech in England. Democracy becomes a practical matter relating to struggles for representation rather than a term which, in an academic context, could be traced back to the Greeks.

Class, according to Williams, in its modern usage dates back to 1740, with varying permutations as time goes on – lower classes, upper classes, upper middle classes, the lower middle classes. Class is an elastic word more indefinite than rank and points to a changing social structure and changed social feelings.

Art, like industry, changes from individual skill to sets of activities – literature, music, painting, sculpture, theatre. But culture is for Williams *the* keyword so far as his project is concerned. From a term which had once referred to the tending of natural growth – as in agriculture – Williams indicates four meanings which developed through the eighteenth and nineteenth centuries: 1) A general state or habit of mind connected with the idea of human perfection; 2) the general state of intellectual development in a society as a whole; 3) the general body of arts; and 4) a whole way of life; material, intellectual and spiritual. The centrality and significance of the word culture for the task he has set himself is clearly stated:

> The development of *culture* is perhaps the most striking among all the words named. It might be said, indeed, that the questions now concentrated in the meanings of the word *culture* are questions directly raised by the great historical changes which the changes in *industry*, *democracy* and *class* in their own way represent, and to which changes in *art* are a closely related response. The development of the word *culture* is a record of a number of important and continuing reactions to these changes in our social, economic and political life, and may be seen, in itself, as a special kind of usage by means of which the nature of the changes can be explored.
>
> (Williams 1961: 16)

The changes referred to (and Williams points to other words that enter English vocabulary during this period) are changes in structure, in situation and in feeling. It is a way of approaching the topic of modernity. Williams' method is to study the language of individual thinkers rather than to deal with a number of abstracted problems. This is a clearly stated preference: 'I feel myself committed to the study of the actual language: that is to say, to the words and sequences of words which particular men and women have used in trying to give meaning to their experience' (ibid.: 18). This is why *Culture and Society* is in large part a commentary on the writings of a range of people: political thinkers, polemicists, novelists and so on. The book itself is divided into three sections: A Nineteenth Century Tradition, Interregnum and Twentieth Century Opinion. We will comment on each.

In Part I Williams begins with two contrasts: between Edmund Burke and William Cobbett and between Robert Southey and Robert Owen. What is the intention? Burke, well known for his scepticism about the benefits of the French Revolution (Burke 1950), is seen as the one who exemplifies the virtue of prudence in civil government. This means taking into account the sheer difficulty of government. Hence: 'It is the want of nerves of understanding for such a task, it is in the degenerate fondness for tricky short cuts, and little fallacious facilities, that has in so many parts of the world created governments with arbitrary powers' (Burke cited in Williams 1961: 2, 5–6). Prudence, circumspection and caution are ways of talking about the importance of experience – the readiness to subject plans to discussion and argument and the practical reconciling of differences. For Burke, it followed that democracy tended to tyranny and destroyed the humanity of the people and the historical communities they had created. On this view democracy can be seen as the enemy of civil society. For Burke, the concern for social stability was connected with the idea of 'organic society' with a stress on the interrelation and continuity of human activities. Yet it was this 'organic society' which new economic forces were breaking up.

Cobbett was a robust social critic who was aware of the changes taking place in rural England: a concentration of property in fewer hands, small farmers ruined and labourers reduced to poverty and starvation. And not only in rural areas did such contrasts exist. In Coventry there were, said Cobbett, 8,000 paupers in a population of 20,000. What was the root of it? 'England has long groaned under a *commercial system*, which is the most oppressive of all possible systems; and it is too, a quiet, silent, smothering oppression, which is more hateful than all others' (cited ibid.: 33). This, he claimed, had produced a new system of social relations, relations of dependency, where men were reduced to 'hands'. It was *unnatural*. For this reason he supported the labouring poor in their struggles and condemned the Combination Acts, which sought to prevent trade unionism. And he clearly saw the emergence of class conflict in the relations between masters and men.

Burke and Cobbett, who in many respects represented opposed political positions, both offer criticisms of the emerging industrial society. Both were making efforts to comprehend the great changes – political and economic – and to learn in and from new experiences. The contrast between Southey and Owen also turns out to contain an overlap. Southey sees the development of manufacturing industry as producing a physical and moral evil in proportion to the wealth it created. Indeed, although Williams does not say so, Southey in his comment on men and machines gives a version of the Weber thesis:

> He who at the beginning of his career uses his fellow creatures as bodily machines for producing wealth, ends not infrequently in becoming an intellectual one himself, employed in continually increasing what it is impossible for him to enjoy.
>
> (cited ibid.: 41)

Against the *laissez-faire* views of the economists Southey argued for the role of active and responsible government to promote the health of society: the moral culture of the species must keep pace with the increase of its material powers. Both Southey, the Tory reformer, and Owen, the socialist, saw the causes of moral difficulties not in some fixed human nature but in the constitution of society, which is why Owen developed the community at New Lanark in which the education of children was a crucial feature explicitly set against the punitive practices of the time. Again, Williams highlights the role of experience: 'Always it is Owen's experience that is impressive – the lived quality of his new view of society' (ibid. 46). The significance of Owen for Williams is that, for him, human nature itself is the product of a 'whole way of life', of a 'culture'.

From these contrasts, which for all their differences represent a critique of industrialism (albeit with varying emphases on the economic and political dimension) Williams moves on to consider the Romantic protest, drawing on Blake, Wordsworth, Shelley and Keats, all of whom were intensely involved in social criticism. They were, after all, living in a society where art and literature were coming to be regarded as market commodities. So Blake wrote of 'the interest of the Monopolising Trader to Manufacture Art by the Hands of Ignorant Journeymen till ... he is Created the Greatest Genius who can sell a Good-for-Nothing Commodity for a Great Price' (cited ibid.: 55). This kind of society and its quality of life, where market values reigned, was seen as antithetical to the creative imagination and its search for human perfection, which, as we have seen, constitutes one idea of culture.

Williams writes:

> The emphasis on a general common humanity was evidently necessary in a period in which a new kind of society was coming to think of men as merely a specialised instrument of production. The emphasis on love and relationship was necessary not only within the immediate suffering but against the aggressive individualism and primarily economic relationships which the new society embodied. Emphasis on the creative imagination, similarly, may be seen as an alternative construction of human motive and energy, in contrast with the assumptions of the prevailing political economy.
>
> (ibid.: 59)

But if the anti-industrialism of the Romantics was against the market, its idealism also contrasted with the utilitarian tradition of Bentham. This, no doubt, is one reason why Williams moves on to consider Mill's essays on Bentham and Coleridge (1838 and 1840). Yet, here again, the contrasts are not total. Whereas Bentham was looking for the extinction of former institutions and creeds, Coleridge was looking for ways of making them a reality. Yet, according to Mill,

> We hold that these two sorts of men, who seem to be, and believe themselves to be, enemies, are in reality allies. The powers they wield are opposite poles of one great form of progression. What was really hateful and contemptible was the state which preceded them, and which each, in its way, has been striving now for many years to improve.
>
> (ibid.: 75)

For Coleridge, the idea of Cultivation or Culture was something that had to be socially constructed, hence his advocacy of a clerisy whose task was one of general cultivation, set against a society whose relationships were ever more based on the cash nexus. Only in this way could the development of humanity take place. For his own purposes Mill tried to synthesize and modify Bentham and

Coleridge. As Williams points out: 'Mills' later work is dominated by two factors: his extension of methods and claims of Utilitarian reform to the interests of the rising working class; and his effort to reconcile democratic control with individual liberty' (ibid.: 74). This was to have its influence on Fabian socialism and much modern legislation.

The awareness of what is happening to a society whose commercial and industrial systems are changing so rapidly and the close association of machine production, the cash nexus and *laissez-faire* economics forms the basis of critique. For some there is the looking back for pre-industrial stability; for others the stress is on political reform; and for others still, the concern is for culture or cultivation which can both set standards for living that are not dominated by economic considerations and can set free the creative capacities of individuals.

Williams gives further instances of these kinds of critique from the works of Thomas Carlyle, John Henry Newman and Matthew Arnold. Carlyle, for example, in his 1829 essay 'Signs of the Times', referred to the age of Machinery in which people now lived. Changes in the method of production were changing social relations and increasing the gap between rich and poor, he argued. Not only so but: 'Men have grown mechanical in hand and in heart as well as in hand.' Modes of thought and feeling have thus been transformed and even religion has come to be a matter of calculation and profit. Yet possibilities remain:

> This age also is advancing. Its very unrest, its ceaseless activity, its discontent contains matter of promise. Knowledge, education are opening the eyes of the humblest: we are increasing the number of thinking minds without limit. This is as it should be, for not in turning back, not in resisting, but only in resolute struggling forward, does our life consist. ... There is a deep-lying struggle in the whole fabric of society; a boundless, grinding collision of the New with the Old.
>
> (cited ibid.: 88)

While Carlyle's later writings were to become preoccupied with the theme of heroic leadership and reverent obedience, Williams points out that in other places – notably his 1839 essay on Chartism where he accepts that the working classes have good reason to be discontented and bitter – Carlyle argues for state-promoted education: 'To impart the gift of thinking to those who cannot think, and yet who could in that case think: this, one would imagine, was the first function a government had to set about discharging' (cited ibid. 94). Thus is the gauntlet thrown down against the *laissez-faire* thinking and also against the notion that social change is simply to be thought of as a change in political institutions. It is a change in culture – a whole way of living – and without which democracy itself would only be another expression of *laissez-faire*.

Central to the discussion of the nineteenth-century tradition is Matthew Arnold, who already had the work of Coleridge, Burke, Newman and Carlyle to draw upon. Education, if it was to be the agency of culture – 'the harmonious development of those qualities and faculties that characterise our humanity' – would be the enemy of utilitarianism which saw in education the usefulness of training people to carry out specific tasks in an industrial society. For Williams, it is Arnold's definition of culture in *Culture and Anarchy* (1869) that gives the tradition a single watchword. It is in Arnold both a study and a pursuit, which goes beyond the idea of a literary culture and applies to society itself, not simply to individuals. As a critical activity culture was not only a matter of acquiring knowledge but of using it to examine stock notions and habits instead of following them mechanically. As Williams points out, Arnold not only argued for state education but served as an inspector of schools and devoted much of his life to the detailed application of his general position.

There was indeed a problem which Arnold recognized. Those involved in the administration of the state and of education somehow had to transcend class interest. They must be people 'who are mainly led, not by their class spirit, but by a general humane spirit' (cited ibid.: 130). Yet such a state did not exist in reality. Moreover, the working class is seen as a threat to order: its claims, threats and assertions are tending to anarchy. This the state must resist, 'because without order there can be no society, and without society there can be no human perfection' (ibid.: 132). Williams concludes that, for Arnold,

> culture was a process, but he could not find a material for that process, either, with any confidence, in the society of is own day or, fully, in a recognition of an order that transcended human society. The result seems to be that, more and more, against his formal intention, the process becomes an abstraction. Moreover, while appearing to resemble an absolute it has no absolute ground.
>
> (ibid.: 135)

Williams was never to deny his respect for Arnold as one who had a genuine and practical commitment to the extension of popular education, taking knowledge beyond what he had called 'the clique of the cultivated and the learned'. But in a later lecture, 'A hundred years of culture and anarchy' (reprinted in Williams 1980) he was to recall that the first chapter of *Culture and Anarchy* was entitled 'Culture and its Enemies', and in this Arnold reflects on the 1866 demonstration in Hyde Park, called by the Reform League after the Liberal government fell and with it the first attempt to extend the franchise to working-class men in the towns. The gates of Hyde Park were locked against the demonstrators and railings were displaced by some of them. It was one thing for the gentry to ride their horses in Rotten Row in the park; it was another to demonstrate for the extension of voting rights, according to the authorities. While John Stuart Mill, among others, challenged this in Parliament, Arnold at the time supported the authorities:

> For us, who believe in right reason, in the duty and possibility of extricating our best self, in the progress of humanity towards perfection, for us the framework of society, that theatre on which this august frame has to unroll itself, is sacred; and whoever administers it, and however we may seek to remove them from their tenure of administration, yet, while they administer, we steadily and with undivided heart support them in repressing anarchy and disorder; because without order there can be no society; and without society there can be no human perfection.
>
> (cited in Williams 1980: 6)

The problem of this position, for Williams, is that it has as its starting point the response to repression, a government denying democratic rights to large numbers of its citizens. Writing in the late 1960s Williams sensed how the genuine reforming activities of Arnold could be forgotten and appeals could be made to him by members of the New Right, who saw demonstrations as forms of anarchy and chaos, to be opposed in the name of reason, culture and education. So he makes the point more sharply than in *Culture and Society*:

> The attachment to reason, to informed argument, to considered public decisions, and indeed, in Arnold's terms, to learning from all the best that has been said and thought in the world, requires something more than an easy rhetorical contrast with the

practice of demonstrations of direct action. For these in the eighteen-sixties as in the nineteen-sixties, were entered into at just those points where truth and reason and argument were systematically blocked, and where 'authorised' force was invoked not to clear the barriers but to erect and defend them.

(Williams 1980: 8)

Two other elements are used by Williams to exemplify the nineteenth-century tradition: the industrial novels and the discussion of art in Pugin, Ruskin and Morris.

The industrial novels, written in mid-century by authors such as Elizabeth Gaskell, Charles Dickens, Benjamin Disraeli, Charles Kingsley and George Eliot, are used by Williams for illustrative purposes, since they tell us something about what the new industrial society is like and also convey a *structure of feeling*. This last phrase, as we shall see, occurs in much of Williams' writing. We shall return to some of these writers since they are dealt with in a number of places in the Williams' corpus. For the moment we need only draw attention to Williams' conclusion:

> These novels, when read together, seem to illustrate clearly enough not only the common criticism of industrialism which the tradition was establishing, but also the general structure of feeling which was equally determining. Recognition of evil was balanced by fear of becoming involved. Sympathy was transformed, not into action, but into withdrawal. We can all observe the extent to which this structure of feeling has persisted, into both literature and the social thinking of our time.

(ibid.: 119)

What part do Pugin, Ruskin and Morris play in the general analysis? In their different ways they connect art with the society in which it is found. This might be a matter for celebration or critique of a particular society or period. Thus, Pugin, in *Contrasts*, compares the present unfavourably with the past:

> The erection of churches, like all that was produced by zeal or art in ancient days, has dwindled down into mere trade. . . . They are erected by men who ponder between a mortgage, a railroad, or a chapel, as the best investment in their money, and who, when they have resolved on relying on the persuasive eloquence of a cushion thumping popular preacher, erect four walls, with apertures for windows, cram the same full of seats, which they

readily let; and so greedy after profit are these chapel raisers, that they form deep and spacious vaults underneath, which are soon occupied at a good rent, by some wine and brandy merchant.

(cited ibid.: 138–9)

As for Ruskin, Williams sees him as a writer whose

social criticism would not have taken the same form if it had not arisen, as it did inevitably, from his kind of thinking about the purposes of art. . . . This absolute standard of perfection in works of art; the conditions of perfection in man; these are the common bases of the tradition.

(ibid.: 141–2)

Ruskin's critique of *laissez-faire* society was that it had destroyed the organic character of what had preceded it. The very division of labour was destructive:

We have much studied and much perfected, of late, the great civilised invention of the division of labour: only we have given it a false name. It is not, truly speaking, the labour that is divided; but the man: Divided into mere segments of men – broken into small fragments and crumbs of life.

(cited ibid.: 147)

The problem, as Ruskin defined it, was to have 'a right kind of understanding on the part of all classes, of what kinds of labour are good for men, raising them and making them happy' (ibid.: 147). This involved for him not the abolition of classes but their correspondence to proper function, both in design and social organization. For all his criticism, however, he had no realistic way of implementing proposals for change. For Williams, this is the crucial difference between Ruskin and William Morris: 'The significance of Morris in this tradition is that he sought to attach its general value to an actual and growing force; that of the organised working class' (ibid.: 153). Morris was not concerned with looking back, as in the medievalism of Pugin, or about the functional reform of the class system, as in Ruskin, but looked forward to the over-throw of the class system, and the establishment of socialism. Precisely because of his concern that art should be 'the cause of the people' and 'the pleasure of daily life', Morris looked beyond the machinery of socialism to a sense of values and spirit which should infuse socialism as lived experience.

The second part of *Culture and Society* deals with the years 1880–1914. This period, which Williams calls 'Interregnum', is very briefly dealt with. In the space of some thirty pages there are short discussions of W.R. Mallock, Oscar Wilde, Walter Pater, James Whistler, George Gissing, Bernard Shaw and the Fabians, Hilaire Belloc, G.D.H. Cole and the Guild Socialists and T.E. Hulme. The reason for this very compressed treatment is in essence because Williams took the position that by 1880 the tradition he is identifying had been formed, in terms of the analysis, descriptions and opinions it represented. From the standpoint of his thesis the interregnum had very little new to offer. 'Such work requires notice, but suggests brevity' (ibid.: 165). We will return to this.

The third part – Twentieth Century Opinions – is a very different matter. There we find discussions of D.H. Lawrence, R.H. Tawney, T.S. Eliot, I.A. Richards, F.R. Leavis and George Orwell. There is also a short chapter on 'Marxism and culture'.

Williams sees in Lawrence a writer who links with the nineteenth-century tradition in his condemnation of industrialism, who sees its acquisitiveness as debasing human purpose to 'sheer mechanical materialism'. Individuals become mechanical, disintegrated and amorphous, a condition of mind which contributes to the ugliness of industrial society. It is a product of human energy being forced into a competition of mere acquisition. What Lawrence termed 'the instinct of community' had, he claimed, been frustrated by industrialism. For Lawrence, 'the actual living quick itself is alone the creative reality', and 'the living self has one purpose only: to come to its own fulness [sic] of being' (cited ibid.: 207). This for him was the most difficult thing of all, although one could look to education as one agency. Yet this could only be possible on the basis of equality. By this Lawrence meant that the basic needs of all people for clothing, shelter, food, work and leisure had to be met. Industrial society is criticized because it destroys common sympathy between people as a result of competition for money and property. His treatment of sexual relationships has to be viewed in this context:

> If only our civilisation had taught us . . . how to keep the fire of sex clear and alive, flickering or glowing or blazing in all its varying degrees of strength and communication, we might, all of us, have lived our lives in love, which means we should be kindled and full of zest in all kinds of ways and all kinds of things.
> (cited ibid.: 213)

It is, then, to culture as community, communication and love that this points, moving as it does against the grain of an industrial civilization.

Richard Tawney, the social and economic historian, is presented primarily through two of his books *Equality* (1931) and *The Acquisitive Society* (1921). Again there is continuity with the nineteenth-century tradition, with its criticisms of the market philosophy and of industrialism (including some socialist versions of it). These critiques are seen as in the line coming from Arnold and Ruskin. Williams observes, however, that 'it is not only the lack of purpose in society which distorts effort, it is also the existence and approval of inequality' (ibid.: 217). The foundations of a common culture, therefore, are grounded in equality of condition. This is essentially a distributive matter and constitutes a full-scale attack on private property. The issue here is a crucial one: does a cultivated/cultural minority depend upon economic inequality and would its removal lead to a levelling down to mediocrity? Tawney's view was that culture could and should be extended beyond a minority class. Williams took the view that Tawney was advocating the humanizing of the modern system of society on its own best terms and saw this as a mark of Tawney's achievements and limitations.

To move from Tawney to T.S. Eliot is to shift from a Christian socialist to a Christian conservative perspective. It is the Eliot of *The Idea of a Christian Society* (1939) and *Notes towards a Definition of Culture* (1948) that Williams focuses on. The criticism of a society whose real values are unexamined but were grounded in the pursuit of money and profit are set against the idea of a Christian community 'in which the natural end of man – virtue and well being in community – is acknowledged for all, and the supernatural end – beatitude – for those who have eyes to see it' (cited ibid.: 225). Williams then cites a passage which anticipates a theme of the Green movement and makes quite clear what sort of conservatism Eliot embraces:

> We are being made aware that the organisation of society on the principle of private profit, as well as public destruction, is leading to the deformation of humanity by unregulated industrialism, and to the exhaustion of natural resources, and that a good deal of our material progress is a progress for which succeeding generations may have to pay dearly.
>
> (ibid.: 226)

There are continuities in Eliot stemming from Coleridge and Carlyle but this is extended into a critique of mass society. So it is argued that the standards of art and culture are depressed in a profit-oriented society with its advertising, propaganda and even its system of education (characteristically dubbed 'mass'). But the conservative element is located in the concept of hierarchy and of cultural elites for the maintenance of civilized values and the defence of the social order against the incipient mob. Hence the idea of culture is set against equalitarianism. In Eliot's perspective, in contrast with Tawney, they can scarcely coexist.

The style and tone of Williams in *Culture and Society* is one of critical sympathy towards the writers he is discussing, yet he does express some irritability with Eliot. After all, if the idea of culture is to be extended to a way of life, as Eliot allows, then a more equalitarian society will be a way of life. 'Culture' can only be set against it as a concept if a more specialized definition is adhered to – as in religion, the arts and learning – although the empirical status of the claim would still remain to be examined rather than assumed.

Williams contended that there is a contradiction at the heart of Eliot's position – a new conservatism which is actually inferior to that of Burke or Coleridge. Why?

a genuine theoretical objection to the principle and effects of an 'atomised', individualist society is combined, and has to be combined, with adherence to the principle of an economic system which is based on just this 'atomised', individualistic view. The 'free economy' which is the central tenet of contemporary conservatism not only contradicts the social principles which Eliot advances (if it were only this one could merely say that he is an unorthodox conservative), but also, and this is the real confusion, is the only method of ordering society to the maintenance of those interests and institutions on which Eliot believes his values to depend. Against the actual and powerful programme for the maintenance of social classes, and against the industrial capitalism which actually maintains the human division that he endorses, the occasional observation, however deeply felt, on the immorality of exploitation or usury seems, indeed, a feeble velleity. ... The triumphant liberalism of contemporary society, which the practice of conservatives now so notably sustains, will, as anyone who thinks about 'a whole way of life' must realise, colour every traditional value. . . . If Eliot, when read attentively, has the effect of checking the complacency of liberalism, he has also, when read critically, the effect of making complacent conservatism impossible. The next step, in thinking of these matters, must be in a different direction, for Eliot has closed almost all existing roads.

(ibid.: 238)

But what direction? If Eliot's emphasis on the role of tradition and faith in maintaining moral and cultural standards against the threats of a mass society only leaves us with unresolved contradictions, can we find more positive guidance in the work of influential literary critics? This leads Williams to consider the contributions of I.A. Richards and F.R. Leavis. Richards is considered primarily with reference to *Principles of Literary Criticism* (1924) and *Science and Poetry* (1926). There we find a discussion of the growth of mass society which emphasizes both the numerical growth of such societies and the growth of science. If the first provides a challenge to standards of morality the second cannot tell us how to live. Yet science has undermined the old keys of wisdom in philosophy and religion. So what safeguards are there against the encroachment of commercialism which controls majority taste? The answer has to be sought in the development of a new consciousness as a defence against anarchy, rather than a return to tradition. What this amounts to for Richards is that the experience of literature can become a training ground for general experience so that we will be more adequately equipped to respond to the changing modern world. For Williams, this will not do. First, it begets an attitude to servility to the literary establishment:

Richards' account of the inadequacy of ordinary response when compared with the adequacy of literary response is a cultural symptom rather than a diagnosis. Great literature is indeed enriching, liberating and refining, but man is always and everywhere more than a reader, has indeed to be a great deal else before he can even become an adequate reader; unless indeed he can persuade himself that literature, as an ideal sphere of heightened living, will under certain cultural circumstances operate as a substitute.

(ibid.: 245)

Williams is concerned with the essential passivity of this position. Secondly, in Williams' view, one does not get a developed sense of the social in Richards. It is not enough to write of the individual man and his environment, which is yet another version of Aesthetic Man, which Richards had set out to challenge. Rather one has to take account of the complexity of social action and interaction which constitutes the practice of living.

> Richards' account of the genesis of our problems is a selection of certain products, not only science as a product but even, in terms of the discussion, increased population as a product. His business, then, is to find another product that is redeeming. Yet this innocence of process, which follows naturally enough from an innocence of company, is disabling. We are faced not only with products but with the breath, the hand, that makes, maintains, changes or destroys.
>
> (ibid.: 246)

In 1930 F.R. Leavis published an influential pamphlet *Mass Civilisation and Minority Culture*. The minority culture referred to is literary tradition and the critical spirit that should accompany it. While the continuity with Coleridge and Arnold is remarked upon by Williams, the new situation in the twentieth century is also engaged. This involved developments in the press, advertising, popular fiction, films and broadcasting. Williams comments:

> The critics who first formulated the idea of culture were faced with industrialism and with its causes and consequences in thinking and feeling. Leavis, in 1930, faced not only these but certain ways of thinking and feeling embodied in immensely powerful institutions which threatened to overwhelm the ways that he and others valued.
>
> (ibid.: 250)

What Leavis' analysis rests upon, is a view of an organic pre-industrial, rural society with 'right' relationships in a natural environment, contrasted favourably with modern urban society – its meaningless work and commercialized, degraded values. Those involved in the contemporary minority culture are struggling against the tide and are continually having to formulate defensive positions. Yet, as Williams points out, this analysis rests upon a myth of the past. In a sentence which anticipates *The Country and the City* he observes: 'If there is one thing certain about "the organic community", it is that it has always gone' (ibid.: 255). Moreover, such dogmatic judgements and neglect of history do not pay attention to real social experience. Literary criticism could not stand in judgement on culture as a whole way of life. If culture is to be understood in this anthropological way then the very concepts of minority and majority culture become increasingly problematical. We have to find ways of understanding the variations of social experience in modern industrial societies and the causes of those variations, as a necessary prelude to critique. For all his energy and indeed his dislike of capitalism and its establishments, Leavis lapses into a mixture of mythology, conjecture and dogmatism.

As Williams addresses twentieth-century opinions we can see that there is a change of focus, a different kind of engagement with his project. These are contemporaries, or near contemporaries, about whom he writes and who are analysing a society of which he is a member. He notes both the differences between nineteenth- and twentieth-century experience and social structure and the repertoire of critical responses which the twentieth-century writers draw upon and develop. He is, at this point, not only bringing to light a critical tradition but also wanting to contribute to it on the grounds that a number of conceptual and analytical problems remain unsolved. But there are still two more matters to discuss before he is prepared to reveal his own hand: the question of Marxism and culture and the contribution of George Orwell. Both of these were to preoccupy him in later years and represented a continuing challenge to his own thinking and attempts to place himself.

The discussion on Marxism and culture is fairly brief, but, in its own way, revealing. Williams clearly indicates that he is not a Marxist and, for that reason, is not prepared to enter into the intra-Marxist quarrels about whether Christopher Caudwell's *Illusion and Reality* (1938) puts forward a Marxist or bourgeois theory of art. Again, he expresses surprise that E.P. Thompson in his study *William Morris* (1955) should criticize Morris for seeing economic and social development as the master process, with the arts passively dependent on social change. Williams writes:

> In one way or another, the situation will have to be clarified. Either the arts are passively dependent on social reality, a proposition which I take to be that of mechanical materialism, or a vulgar misinterpretation of Marx. Or the arts, as the creators

of consciousness, determine social reality, the proposition which the Romantic poets sometimes endorsed. Or, finally, the arts, while ultimately dependent with everything else, on the real economic structure, operate in part to reflect this structure and its consequent reality, and in part, by affecting attitudes towards reality, to help or hinder the constant business of changing it. I find Marxist theories of culture confused because they seem to me, on different occasions and in different writers, to make use of all these propositions as the need serves.

(ibid.: 266)

This is clearly a significant passage. Williams is distancing himself from this Marxist methodology because it is both confused and self-serving. Politically, this can lead to socialist realism as defined by the party ideologues. Theoretically, it raises but does not solve questions about the relation between base and superstructure. Williams returns to both these considerations many times in his writing. There is, of course, the question of what Marx and/or Engels actually said and with what degree of consistency. But there is, in any event, so far as Williams is concerned, the danger of reducing cultural analysis to a rigid methodology. Yet

even if the economic element is determining, it determines a whole way of life, and it is to this, rather than to the economic system alone, that the literature has to be related. The interpretative method which is determined, not by the social whole, but rather by the arbitrary correlation of the economic situation and the subject of study, leads very quickly to abstraction and unreality.

(ibid.: 272)

What about Orwell? He is treated with respect but reservation; Williams, as a non-Marxist socialist (at this time) might have expected to have found a way forward through Orwell's approach to the study of culture and society (even though they came from different class positions and nationalities). The problem for Williams, however, is that, while he admires Orwell's human concern and sympathy with the victims of society – the poor, the outcast, the exploited – he finds there a mood of disillusion, unredeemed by hope. Williams is sympathetic to the pressures – personal and social – to which Orwell was subjected. He was an exile, sometimes from his own country, typically from his class, without any settled way of living in which his own individuality could be confirmed. It was this distrust of society, caused by his own lack of grounding in community, that leads Orwell to portray society as inherently leading to totalitarianism. Orwell, for Williams, was a man who, while rejecting the consequences of an atomistic society, retained within himself its characteristic mode of consciousness. The pessimistic mood in Orwell's writing is seen as an outcome of the pressures and tensions he experienced. This is not an affirmative mood, it is a negative one; it is a mood of despair not hope. Yet it is resources of hope that Williams is seeking to recover and nourish in reviewing the critical tradition of opposition to capitalism. Some opposition was limited, some logically inconsistent, some fatalistic. Williams saw his task as moving beyond these disabling features to establish some basis for the hope that capitalism was not the last word. The conclusion of *Culture and Society* represents an early treatment of this theme.

It is in the conclusion that Williams shows his hand: 'The working out of the idea of culture is a slow reach again for control' (ibid.: 285). In a formal way, we can summarize the phases of change in Figure 3.1:

Phase 1 1790-1870	Rejection of machine production and social relations of the factory system	Threat to minority values	Independent value of art and its qualitative importance to the common life
Phase 2 1870-1914	Hostility to machinery	Community/organic society versus dominant individualist ethics and practice	Art as value in itself
Phase 3 1914-45	Acceptance of machine production but social relations in industrial system of production problematic	Twentieth-century version of Phase 1: concern with mass communication	Reintegration of art with common life - communication

Figure 3.1 Culture and Society: the sequence of change

This periodization is not meant to be abrupt but represents, for Williams, times when there were dominant modes of thinking in response to the development of a capitalist society in England. Yet things are still, as it were, out of control. What contribution can critical thinking about culture make in the second half of the twentieth century? Williams offers a set of interrelated reflections which hinge on the concepts of 'mass', 'communication', 'community' and, of course, 'culture'.

'Mass' is a word with different meanings attached to it. Williams seeks first to disentangle the meanings then to question the value of the term itself. So, for example, out of the phenomenon of urbanization with its concentrations of population comes the mass meeting; from the machine production of the factories comes mass production; and from the working class, the product of industrialism, comes mass action. The term 'mass' came to be used as a synonym for 'mob', when applied to people. This was then seen as a threat to 'culture', and by extension to the elite guardians of culture. But culture was also threatened in terms of the quality of its artefacts by mass production. When democracy itself is described as mass democracy we can begin to see some of the grounds on which it was resisted. The masses = mob = rule by majority = (mass) democracy = threat to culture. Mass then becomes a negative term and whatever is linked with it is negatively defined – mass education, mass prejudice, mass thinking, mass suggestion, mass communication. When the term is routinely used in this way it can be deployed to justify the idea of minority culture, to confirm elites and establishments and to capture the idea of culture so that it justifies exclusivity and systems of control over incipient mobs. For Williams, the power of this line of thinking needs first to be understood, named for what it is, and then to be challenged in order to argue that culture is not the enemy of democracy but can be enlarged by it for the common good. This is why Williams makes such a direct challenge to the validity of the concept of 'mass':

There are in fact no masses; there are only ways of seeing people as masses. In an urban industrial society there are many opportunities for such ways of seeing. The point is not to re-iterate the objective conditions but to consider, personally and collectively, what these have done to our thinking. The fact is, surely, that a way of seeing other people which has become characteristic of our kind of society, has been capitalised for the purpose of political or cultural exploitation. What we see, neutrally, is other people, many others, people unknown to us. In practice we mass them, and interpret them, according to some convenient formula. Within its terms the formula will hold. Yet it is the formula, not the mass, which it is our real business to examine. It may help to do this if we remember that we ourselves are all the time being massed by others. To the degree that we find the formula inadequate for ourselves, we can wish to extend to others the courtesy of acknowledging the unknown.

(ibid.: 289)

Here then is the direct statement of Williams' views on cultural and political exploitation which provided the underlying motivation for the writing of *Culture and Society*. Out of the cool analysis and reconsideration of the literary record and the historical witnesses is this sense of the many being robbed of their common culture by the few. The language itself is also captured, and yet it is in and through language that resistance must begin. The challenge to the use of 'mass' as a concept is, therefore, not some quirky pedantry, but a way of drawing attention to its ideological functions and control implications.

Where does this leave the concept of mass communication? It is one thing to recognize the growth in communications, both in terms of physical forms like roads, railways, ships and aeroplanes and in terms of books, newspapers, films, radio, television and so on, but we should not assume things about the nature of populations or audiences who are so linked. The fact of expansion and of growing diversity of communications is an important set of phenomena, but the nature of the relationships between those who send and those who receive messages contains a range of possibilities. Certainly the notion of masses is a convenient way of looking at audiences if the intention is to manipulate, as in the case of propaganda or advertising. Yet this can be contested in the name of democracy, even if we have to recognize the commercial base of much media activity, the concentration of ownership and the challengs to public service broadcasting even in its paternalist forms. At root, the way we look at the media and the decisions we make about control of it in our society are political questions. Definitions in this respect, in so far as they represent taken-for-granted assumptions or political judgements, are important. They have to be seen for what they are and what they enable specific groups to accomplish if we are to go beyond that and think of democratic alternatives.

The significance of this is emphasized when we think of the way in which concepts are interlinked and affect our ways of thinking, our maps of the world. So, for example, the way we think about communication will affect the way we think about community:

> any real theory of communication is a theory of community. . . . It is very difficult to think clearly about communication, because the pattern of our thinking about community is, normally, dominative. We tend, in consequence, if not to be attracted, at least to be pre-occupied by dominative techniques. Communication becomes a science of penetrating the mass mind and of registering an impact there. It is not easy to think along different lines.
>
> (ibid.: 301)

Yet this is precisely what needs to be done if we wish to develop the idea and experience of democracy. Mass communication theory carries with it the idea of the few controlling the many, and this is what has to be publicly contested. Whereas the dominative thinking will depict the masses in terms of mobs, rioters and strikers – that is, an incipient threat to order – or as apathetic and unresponsive to exhortations from above, democratic theory will rethink the questions of transmission and reception of messages, which will have implications for ownership, access, diversity of outlets and education – and will be grounded in the value of equality of being. This value is central to Williams' concept of a common culture – a concept which is both an ideal and something to struggle for.

Education and communication can be channels or blockages to the realization of common culture. This is, of course, both a critique of and an alternative possibility to bourgeois individualism. This is quite different from the notion of replacing bourgeois culture by working-class culture or minority culture by majority culture. It is more than an appeal to the middle-class reforming virtues of service or the working-class value of solidarity: 'The struggle for democracy is a struggle for the recognition of equality of being or it is nothing. Yet only in the acknowledgement of human individuality and variation can the reality of common government be comprised' (ibid.: 323).

The deep seriousness of *Culture and Society* is summed up in the concluding sentences, which make abundantly clear that this was not just a commentary or history of ideas but an intellectual engagement with the issues laid before contemporary society and a challenge to others to join in the cultural struggle:

The human crisis is always a crisis of understanding: what we genuinely understand we can do. I have written this book because I believe it records a major contribution to our common under-standing, and a major incentive to its necessary extension. There are ideas, and ways of thinking, with the seeds of life within them, and there are others, perhaps deep in our minds, with the seeds of a general death. Our measure of success in recognising these kinds, and in naming them making possible their common recognition, may literally be the measure of our future.

(ibid.: 324)

Here we see the idea of culture as a natural growth with its selection, nurturing and development, but also as a process which involves a struggle between contending powers. It is a cultural struggle about ways of life and between ways of life. To name the elements in, and the significance of, the struggle is a form of empowerment against those who, consciously or unconsciously, exploit and dominate the lives of others, whose 'ways of life' are actually 'ways of death'.

CRITIQUES AND CONTINUITIES

Almost twenty years after the publication of *Culture and Society* Williams was interviewed by three members of the *New Left Review* editorial board: Perry Anderson, Anthony Barnett and Francis Mulhearn. The result was published as *Raymond Williams: Politics and Letters* (1979). The conversations proved to be very searching and Williams was prepared to use the occasion to reflect upon his work in an open, non-defensive way. We will use this source as a point of departure in consideration of the issues and problems raised by *Culture and Society*.

Early in the interview Williams gives a good summary of his reasons for writing *Culture and Society*:

It was oppositional, to counter the appropriation of a long line of thinking about culture to what were by now decisively reactionary positions. There was a question for me whether I should write a critique of that ideology in a wholly negative way, or whether the right course was not to try to recover the true complexity of the tradition it had confiscated – so that the appropriation could be seen for what it was. In the end I settled for the second strategy. For it allowed me to refute the increasing contemporary use of the concept of culture against democracy, socialism, the working class or popular education in terms of the tradition itself.

(Williams 1981a: 97–8)

This clearly represents an aspiration to influence political and literary thinking. Yet as the interview proceeds we find Williams distancing himself from the book:

It is not a book I am greatly attached to now.

Well I respect *Culture and Society* but it is not a book I could conceive myself writing now. I don't much know the person who wrote it. I read this book as I might read a book by someone else. It is a work most distant from me.

(ibid.: 100, 107)

We can certainly sense this in the way Williams replies to some of the criticisms. Take, for example, the view that *Culture and Society* gives the impression of a single discourse about the relation between the industrial revolution and the shape of culture, and that politics is minimized even to the exclusion of the significance of the French Revolution. Williams agrees and puts it down to a mistaken strategy. To recover a tradition was to look for a coherent discourse under the surface, as it were. Yet to recognize an oppositional motif in writers who, in some respects, were reactionary was to draw attention to the fact that pigeon-holing writers as reactionary or progressive might be to miss the paradoxical character of their writing. But to do this was itself a process of exploration and his concession has to be seen in that light:

The fact is that I could not go, as you can normally if you are attempting this kind of study, to any academic authorities which, even if you disagreed with them, at least map out the area of the subject. There was no area. I had to discover for myself Carlyle's *Signs of the Times* essay, which was the single most exciting revelation for me because it contained all the terms of the argument forty years before they were supposed to have emerged. . . . The whole process of locating the writers who were relevant to my enquiry was a pretty amateur job of reading from one book to another . . . and finding always that I had to revise the formation with which I had originally started. But it is a curious effect of the style of the book that it reads like somebody selecting and redisposing of something which is already a common property. Whereas what the book was really doing was making one.

(ibid.: 99)

If we allow that this was a pioneering work then what is included and what is excluded becomes more understandable. Nevertheless it is important to note the absence of a developed historical dimension, since this does lead to a very muted treatment of poltics. Again, Williams acknowledges this. He points out, for example, that he was not in contact with Edward Thompson who, at that time, was writing *The Making of the English Working Class* (1963) 'so these crucial conjunctions were never made' (Williams 1981a: 108). Consequently, even while the point is made in a formal sense about the way concepts are understood through history in *Culture and Society*, and indeed this becomes a methodological principle in *Keywords*, there are important omissions in Williams' treatment. His very brief treatment of the period he labelled the Interregnum is a case in point. This had affected the whole structure of the book. Later, Williams admitted that to diminish the significance of the Interregnum on the grounds that it represented narrow specialisms in the arts on the one hand and a preoccupation with direct politics on the other was a wrong judgement (1981a: 102). Part of this he puts down to personal experiences at the time of starting *Culture and Society*: a tiredness and contempt for party politics in the late 1940s and early 1950s. This, we can see, is part of the distance he was later to feel from the book. This is very plainly stated:

> *Culture and Society* seems to me a book which is negatively marked by elements of disgusted withdrawal – let me use a word as strong as that – from all immediate forms of collaboration, combined – and this eventually made the difference – with an intense disappointment that they were not available; a disappointment that connects, directly, to the nature of the renewal of belief which is the conclusion; the renewal in those terms which is the book's innovation in its period. But on my way through this I could slip into tones which are in effect the self-defence of an intellectual who has retired from immediate politics and is now, hopefully, looking at deeper forces.
>
> (Williams 1981a: 106)

As Stuart Hall has wryly observed, it has become something of an intellectual game to identify what has been left out of *Culture and Society*, and this is a tribute to the influence of the book. To take the case of the lack of reference to the French Revolution:

> its absences as a precipitating intellectual force within the corpus of English ideas means that not only is there little indication of the radical character, the growth and challenge, of popular radicalism, and the quite striking non-intellectual culture that sustained it; but also the book lacks, as a dramatic episode, the sharp ruptures in the very liberal-intellectual climate of thought which Jacobinism provoked which *is* the centre of the book's concern.
>
> (Hall in Eagleton 1989: 60)

But Hall goes on to argue that an even more important omission is any developed discussion of the dominant intellectual formations of the time to which the 'culture and society' tradition was responding. If the ideas of Hobbes, Locke, Adam Smith and Bentham, for example (representative figures of English ideology and its 'common sense' tradition), had been given attention then 'this would have given us a better sense of the somewhat "exceptional" character of the literary-moral social critics, and placed them, as a formation, more appropriately, socially and historically' (ibid.).

It is difficult to deny the force of this criticism and it has to be seen as a limitation of the literary basis of the work, which, despite developing its own position, is an extension of the Leavisite perspective, although manifestly socialist in its values. There are also other absences. There is no treatment of Marx and the industrial revolution. It would, Williams concedes, have radically improved the book, though, as he rather ruefully comments, to take these and other suggestions on board would have led to a bigger book that he would still have been writing at the time of the interview. The omission appears to have been based on a rather specific treatment of the English tradition (although Carlyle, the Scot, was a crucial figure).

Again, there is very little reference to the growth of the British Empire despite the fact that it became the largest empire in the world between 1790 and 1920. This is linked with the absence of discussion of the concept of nation. This, again, is a matter of some magnitude since it affects the treatment of the concepts of community and state. In the rhetoric of politics, community can be connected with nation and mobilized by those in power to generate feelings of patriotism. Williams accepts this and makes the revealing comment that his idea of community was grounded in his memories of Wales. Yet that Welsh experience 'was also precisely one of subjection to English experience and assimilation historically. This is what ought to have most alerted me to the dangers of a persuasive type of definition of community, which is at once dominant and exclusive' (Williams 1981a: 118–19). How did he miss this? The clue is in an earlier part of the interview, where he explains that in writing about co-operation, community and solidarity he was generalizing from his knowledge and experience of Welsh social relations, yet 'at this time my distance from Wales was most complete' (ibid.: 113). There is then the personal position together with the emphasis on *English* writing (again noting the inclusion of Carlyle) which seems to account for this. By the same token, it was only later that Williams saw the idea of a national literature as supportive of a specific political and social ideology. Arising out of this, Williams indicates, is his uneasiness with the concept of community precisely because it can be the bearer of so many, and contradictory connotations. 'I would myself no longer use the word "community" in the way I did in *Culture and Society*' (ibid.: 120). While it could be contrasted with individualism, or refer to utopian communities, or, again, working-class communities, it could also be used in terms of specific interests. So one may speak of the interests of the community being opposed by the activity of strikers. The rhetoric of community could stretch across the political spectrum: 'It was when I suddenly realised that no-one ever used the term "community" in a hostile sense that I saw how dangerous it was' (ibid.: 119).

If community and nation could be used synonymously, or conjoined, so too could nation and state. Here Williams touches on an important issue so far as socialism is concerned. He properly points out that the very term 'nationalization' carries with it the assumption that the state is an unproblematic entity. This was certainly how things stood in the immediate post-war period in Britain. It has since necessitated a good deal of thinking on the left, to which Williams himself has contributed (see, for example, *Towards 2000*). In a sentence the point to be made is that socialist advances are not to be equated with advances of the state. This awareness helps us to understand Williams' growing interest in questions of region and decentralization.

Williams' interlocutors make a strong point when they note that in *Culture and Society* there is a marked absence of attention to religion, even though many of the writers he covered were themselves centrally interested in religion, with varying commitments. This, after all, is very much a matter of 'ways of life'. In the English context different kinds of Christianity, not simply Protestant and Catholic, but evangelical, high church and dissenting strands, argued with one another. Newman's *Apologia*, for example, was a reply to Charles Kingsley's polemic. And, of course, there was the growing problem of science and religion, represented especially in Darwin's theory of evolution. This was part of the more general process of secularization. Williams admits the absence and puts it down to tone-deafness as far as religion is concerned. Given the role of religion in Welsh community life, with which he was directly familiar, this is a little surprising. More specifically, he acknowledges that he had not taken into account sufficiently Christopher Hill's point that it is inappropriate to transpose religious discourse into social discourse. That is to say, for certain purposes religion as a set of beliefs and practices has to be considered in its own terms and with its own connotations. Clearly, religion can sometimes be seen as a mechanism for social control, as E.P. Thompson notably showed in *The Making of the English Working Class* (1963), but in some manifestations it can also constitute a critical response to the advent of industrial capitalism. This may be the reason why possible continuities between the Puritan and radical pamphleteers and the nineteenth-century radical pamphleteers were not discussed even though the nineteenth-century radicals are considered in *The Long Revolution*.

There is one other crucial consideration raised in *Politics and Letters*: the absence of a European dimension and, connected with this, the lack of reference to the sociological tradition. Yet, in their varying ways, Comte, Saint-Simon, Durkheim, de Tocqueville, Weber and Tonnies were all seeking to understand the transformations in economy, polity and society in this modern period. For them, issues of the growth of the market and the nature of democracy were central concerns.

Durkheim stands as an instructive example. His interest in social reconstruction stemmed from an awareness of the large-scale economic changes which industrialism entailed. How could a moral order develop when the old religious faith had lost its commanding position, whilst the economic sphere, with its practice of ever-intensifying competition, was devoid of any values other than profit and greed? Interestingly, Durkheim inverts the organic metaphor. He sees early societies as bound together by mechanical solidarity – the solidarity of resemblance. It was the industrializing societies which had the opportunity to develop into organic societies. The social reality, for Durkheim, was that industrial societies were out of joint – in a state of normlessness and no settled values – the condition he called anomie. The solution he envisaged to engender movement towards the potential organic character of industrial societies involved a radical critique of property and inheritance. Education, too, was crucial for the development and transmission of values appropriate for the organic society (see Eldridge 1971).

A different, but also important, example is Weber's well-known *Protestant Ethic and the Spirit of Capitalism* (1930). This takes us back to the issue of religion again. It is a study of the ways in which religious values became, in unintended ways, a seed-bed for the growth of capitalism in the West, and of the growth of secularization, to which this process contributed. The significance of this for some of the problems addressed by Williams in *Culture and Society*, not least the base-superstructure question, is clear, if we recall Weber's methodological position:

> We only wish to ascertain whether and to what extent religious forces have taken part in the qualitative formation and quantitative expression of that [capitalist] spirit over the world. Furthermore, what concrete aspects of our capitalistic culture can be traced to them. In view of the tremendous confusion of interdependent influences between the material basis, the forms of social and political organisation, and the ideas current in the time of the Reformation, we can only proceed by investigating whether and at what points certain correlations between forms of religious belief and practical ethics can be worked out. At the same time, we shall as far as possible clarify the manner and general *direction* in which, by virtue of those relationships, the religious movements have influenced the development of material culture.

(Weber 1930: 91–2)

Hall had suggested that the absence of a sociological input in *Culture and Society* is not so surprising given the dominance of the American structural functionalism of the social anthropologist

Ruth Benedict in *The Long Revolution*. More importantly, there was no reason to see sociology in these terms even then. Not only was the European tradition available then, as we have indicated, but there was also a considerable body of community studies in existence. There were the famous Middletown studies of the Lynds (1929, 1937); and the Lloyd Warner Yankee City series (1941, 1942, 1947, for example) in the USA. These and other studies have been fruitfully examined by Stein in *The Eclipse of Community* (1960). In the British context there were also a number of studies. By way of example we may cite Brennan, Cooney and Collins *Social Change in South West Wales* (1954); Willmott and Young *Family and Kinship in East London* (1957); Williams *The Sociology of an English Village* (1956) and Rees *Social Life in the Welsh Countryside* (1950). For someone so interested in the concept of community these absences are surprising.

Still, if Williams neglected some relevant sociology, sociologists did not always neglect him. A very explicit example is Robert Nisbet's *The Sociological Tradition* (1966). This is a book which precisely roots the fundamental ideas of European sociology in terms of responses to the problem of order created by the advent of industrialism and political democracy. Nisbet cites Williams' work, and in a way which parallels the Williams project he writes:

> I have chosen five ideas as the constitutive elements of sociology: *community, authority, status, the sacred,* and *alienation.* These, I believe, are the ideas which in their functional relation to one another, form the nucleus of the sociological tradition ... giving it the continuity and coherence it has had for more than a century.
>
> (Nisbet 1966: vii)

In fact Nisbet juxtaposes against each of these ideas a contrasting concept: *society, power, class, secular, progress,* and then observes:

> Considered as a linked antithesis, they form the very warp of the sociological tradition. Quite apart from their conceptual significance in sociology, they may be regarded as epitomisations of the conflict between tradition and modernism, between the old order, made moribund by the industrial and democratic revolutions, and the new order, its outcomes still unclear and as often the cause of anxiety as of elation and hope.
>
> (ibid.: 7)

There is considerable overlap between the keywords deployed by Nisbet and those used by Williams, particularly if we include *The Long Revolution*, to which we turn next. If Nisbet is concerned to trace the emergence of democratic societies, in sociological terms, Williams wants to consider the barriers and hindrances as well as the opportunities for expanding a democratic culture. Despite criticisms, we should not lose sight of the pioneering character of this work. It was for Williams an exploratory and sometimes surprising journey.

One important marker, however, which does clarify his general orientation, is his 1958 essay, 'Culture is ordinary' (reprinted in Williams 1989c). If we take that alongside his 1968 essay, 'The idea of a common culture' (also in Williams 1989c) it is possible to identify in a succinct way what is embedded in Williams' treatment of the relationship between culture and society. If we enumerate this position in a number of short statements this will, we hope, illuminate the nature of his concern for a common culture, which, it should almost go without saying, is the very opposite of a homogenized, uniform one. Much of his work – especially *Culture and Society*, *The Long Revolution* and *Towards 2000* – can be matched against this template:

1 Culture can refer to (a) a whole way of life and its common meanings and (b) the arts and learning.
2 We should recognize that these are interconnected and not mutually exclusive and proceed accordingly with our 'cultural analysis'.
3 It is wrong to speak of a dying culture or of the ignorant masses as some Marxists do.
4 It is wrong to prescribe what is and is not acceptable in cultural acivity from a political party standpoint.
5 Labour-saving devices and material improvements are real gains and a real service to life. Thus: 'An account of our culture which explicitly or implicitly denies the value of an industrial society is really irrelevant; not in a million years would you make us give up this power' (Williams 1989c: 10).
6 The central problem of our society is to make a good common culture through appropriate uses of new resources.
7 Popular education did not cause commercial culture; the latter was the product of industrialism.
8 We cannot infer the state of mind, feeling or quality of life of the consumers of popular culture from the character of the product.

9   Education is a society's confirmation of its common meanings
    and of the human skills for their amendment.
10 To think of our culture as divided into a sophisticated elite and
    a doped mass is both incorrect and anti-democratic.
11 To advocate a common culture is a way of criticizing an existing
    divided or fragmented culture; specifically of a class society.
12 A socialist society – with a common culture – would be an
    educated and participatory democracy.
13 Questions of culture are questions of value and hence questions
    of politics.
14 A common culture is not a consenting, conformist society; it
    is a free, contributive and common process of participation in
    the creation of meanings and values.

The task Williams was engaged in was fundamentally oppositional. He opposed those who regarded themselves as the custodians
of the higher values; those who thought of culture as a finished static
product. He fought against received 'official' definitions of English
culture. There is, consequently, a mix of the analytical, normative
and political work which springs from this perspective. At the end
of 'Culture is ordinary' this is stated plainly:

> the business of the socialist intellectual is what it always was:
> to attack the clamps on energy – in industrial relations, public
> administration, education for a start; and to work in his own
> field on ways in which that energy, as released, can be con-
> centrated and fertile. The technical means are difficult enough,
> but the biggest difficulty is in accepting, deep in our minds, the
> values on which they depend: that ordinary people should govern;
> that culture and education are ordinary; that there are no masses
> to save, to capture, or to direct, but rather this crowded people
> in the course of an extraordinary, rapid and confusing expansion
> of their lives.
>
> (Williams 1989c: 18)

This statement, and the commitment it embodies, is at the very
centre of what Williams called 'the work'. Necessarily it involved
him in controversy: in the culture of politics and the politics of
culture.

Chapter 4

The Long Revolution

The book was an attempt to think through the idea of revolution in a society with substantial levels of cultural development and of democratic practices – in other words, a capitalist democracy as distinct from an absolutist state or from societies marked by more absolute forms of material deprivation and poverty. The received images of revolution related to social orders where the majority of the oppressed were largely cut out from the cultural or political spheres. To stress the processes of cultural development, with all their contradictions – in the popular press, in the educational system, in the newer means of communication – and the political complications that follow from them seemed to me a pre-condition for re-thinking the notion of revolution in a society like Britain.

(Williams 1981a: 111–12)

The Long Revolution is explicitly a continuation of the work begun in *Culture and Society*. Williams has in mind three interrelated processes: the democratic revolution, the industrial revolution and the cultural revolution. The third of these and what would for most readers be the least familiar refers to 'the aspiration to extend the active process of learning, with the skills of literary and other advanced communication, to all people rather than to limited groups' (Williams 1965: 2). It is comparable in importance to the other two revolutions.

Williams writes:

Our whole way of life from the shape of our communities to the organisation and control of education, and from the structure of the family to the status of art and entertainment, is being profoundly affected by the progress and interaction of democracy and industry, and by the extension of communications. This deeper cultural revolution is a large part of our most significant living experience, and is being interpreted and indeed fought out, in very complex ways, in the world of art and ideas. It is when we try to correlate change of this kind with the changes covered by the disciplines of politics, economics and communications that we discover some of the most difficult but also some of the most human questions.

(ibid.: 12)

The distinction between cultural revolution as part of a trilogy (political, industrial and cultural) and the *deeper* cultural revolution, constituting the interrelation of all three in terms of 'way of life', can be confusing. But the idea of *process* is central. There is nothing inevitable about outcomes since changes are contested – 'fought out in very complex ways'. Complex is a recurring word in the Williams corpus. He wants to affirm the process of democratization in society and to write from the standpoint of one concerned with the relationship between theory and practice: 'My own view is that we must keep trying to grasp the process as a whole, to see in it new ways as a long revolution, if we are to understand either the theoretical crisis, or our actual history, or the reality of our immediate condition and terms of change' (Williams 1965: 13).

Part of this task of understanding is to work through the significance of the distinction between culture as creative activity and culture as a way of life since this counterposes the issues of change and continuity. Early on in the *Long Revolution* a close linkage is expressed between culture, communication and community:

Since our way of seeing things is literally our way of living, the process of communication is in fact the process of community: the sharing of common meanings and their common activities and purposes; the offering, reception and comparison of new meanings, leading to the tensions and achievements of growth and change.

(ibid.: 55)

Williams was later to put his own question mark against the concept of community but the emphasis here is on social reality as a process which involves us in continual negotiating and renegotiating with others. That process is a communicative task. Communication, therefore, is intrinsic to culture as a way of life and not just a means for commenting upon it.

What does it mean to analyse culture? This is dealt with at length in the second chapter of *The Long Revolution* and is pivotal to Williams' project and indeed to subsequent developments of his work. There is a threefold answer:

Definition of culture	Type of analysis
1 The 'ideal' state or process of human perfection	Discovery and description of 'timeless' values that refer to the universal human condition
2 'Documentary' - intellectual and imaginative work reworking human thought and experience	Activity of criticism
3 'Social' - culture as a way of life	Clarification of meanings and values in art, learning and institutional life, and in everyday behaviour

The third of these meanings is primarily descriptive, though with the need for explanation built in if we are to understand the complexity between different 'parts' of the way of life. The first and second have to do with values and judgements relating to them. The first exemplifies the notion of values that are put before us as ideals. Williams draws back somewhat from the notion of absolute values applicable to all humanity. It is partly a matter of specific societies endorsing values that in practice can enrich lives and control the environment; but some of these possibilities transcend particular societies, as in the growth of medicine or communications. Williams characteristically urges the inter-connectedness of the three definitions, rather than treating them as mutually exclusive. The variations in meaning and reference represent a genuine complexity corresponding to real elements in experience:

> There is a significant reference in each of the three main kinds of definition, and, if this is so, it is the relations between them that should claim our attention. It seems to me that any adequate theory of culture must include the three areas of fact to which the definitions point, and conversely that any particular defini-tion, within any one of the categories, which would exclude reference from the other is inadequate.
>
> (Williams 1965: 59)

The task is both descriptive and explanatory, moral and critical, if we are to have an adequate theory of culture. To attempt this is to be involved in a cross-disciplinary project. Sociology, social anthropology, social psychology, moral philosophy, history, literary and art criticism all have their relevance. At the same time, the approach tries not to privilege certain terms as though they were 'outside' of society, as in a phrase like 'art and society'. The emphasis is on discovering *patterns* of interrelations. The influence of Ruth Benedict's *Patterns of Culture* (1935) was seminal. The programmatic passage is worth quoting in some length:

> Cultural history must be more than the sum of particular histories, for it is with the relations between them the particular forms of the whole organisation, that it is especially concerned. I would then define the theory of culture as the study of relationships between characters in a whole way of life. The analysis of culture is the attempt to discover the nature of the organisation which is the complex of these relationships. Analysis of particular works or institutions is, in this context, analysis of their essential kind of organisation, the relationships which works or institutions embody as parts of the organisation as a whole. A keyword, in such analysis, is pattern: it is with the discovery of patterns of a characteristic kind that any useful cultural analysis begins, and it is with the relationships between these patterns, which sometimes reveal unexpected identities and correspondences in hitherto separately considered activities, sometimes again reveal discontinuities of an unexpected kind, that general cultural analysis is concerned.
>
> (Williams 1965: 63)

But how is this to be done? It will always be a demanding and unfinished task, especially trying to understand historical periods and situations where we were not present. The way into this for Williams, as in so much of his work, was through his concept of 'the structure of feeling'. If we try to understand past 'ways of life' then we are dependent on documentary material to give us clues to what the lived experience of the period was like. This, after all, is what we have left when the living witnesses are silent. In more recent times documentation includes the archive footage of films, radio and television. The centrality of the concept can be appreciated from the following comment:

I do not mean that structure of feeling, any more than social
character, is possessed in the same way by the many individuals
in the community. But I think that it is a very deep and very
wide possession, in all actual communities, precisely because it
is upon it that communication depends.

(Williams 1965: 65)

How are lived cultures connected with past cultures? Through
selective tradition. This process of selection, with its accompanying
interpretations of the past, is interwoven into contemporary culture
and will be shaped by special interests including, Williams maintains, class interests. Selectivity of one sort or another is inevitable,
but if we can show how particular forms of selectivity operate –
the real relations on which they are based – then a critical task will
be accomplished: 'What analysis can do ... [is] to make the
interpretation conscious, by showing historical alternatives; to relate
the interpretation to the particular contemporary values on which
it rests; and, by exploring the real patterns of the work, confront
us with the real nature of the choices we are making' (ibid.: 69).

We must remark upon the repetition of the term 'real'. There
is something to be uncovered in both past and present culture as
well as in the links between them. In digging below the surface
we can, the argument suggests, make visible the ensemble of real
relations. In doing so we make connections between past and present
– but we also, through critique, recover opportunities for making
different connections that allow for greater possibilities of human
development and growth.

In order to develop his position Williams feels the need to
illustrate it with a specific case study and, through this, to elaborate
further his conceptual distinctions. The case study focuses on the
England of the 1840s. He has two main analytical tools: structure
of feeling and social character. The second is found in the work
of Erich Fromm (e.g. Fromm 1942) and refers to the value systems
of behaviour and attitudes taught formally and informally. The
strategy is to outline in ideal-type terms three social characters based
on class – aristocratic, middle and working – each with its own
values attributed to it. Of these three, the middle class, with its
values of work, effort, thrift, sobriety, piety and success, is treated
as the dominant one. However, all three social characters have to
be studied in relation to one another if we are to get some understanding of the whole way of life of the period. So it is that the

structure of feeling has the dominant social character as its principal reference point, but is more precisely seen as emerging out of the interrelation of the three social characters and the tensions and pressures that are generated. So, in general terms, a middle-class view of a society based on the value of rewards for individual success can be contrasted with an aristocratic ideal of hierarchy grounded in birth and privilege; or with a working-class view (as expressed in Chartism) of a society based on mutual aid and co-operation.

How are the values experienced? In terms of conflicts or complications within one class, or as tensions between classes? Williams arges that the novels and popular fiction teach us something about the ways conflicts are experienced and resolved. The structure of feeling may be more articulated and intensified in literature but it gives a sense of the real relations and of the social conventions which placed limits on what people could do. It has to be admitted that this is only a sketchy illustration, and it only begins to get the problem of cultural analysis into Williams' sights.

But Williams has two more important conceptual moves to make. The first is to explore the relationship between the individual and society; and the second is to consider the significance of different images of society. Both are tasks of classification and critique and point us in the direction of is own ideal of a democratic society. The normative element in this is clearly revealed towards the end of Williams' discussion on individuals and societies. The rabbit, after a number of feints and manoeuvres, comes out of the hat:

> If man is essentially a learning, creating and communicating being, the only social organisation adequate to his nature is a participatory democracy, in which all of us, as unique individuals, learn, communicate and control. Any lesser, restrictive system is simply wasteful of our true resources; in wasting individuals, by shutting them out from effective participation, it is damaging our true common process.
>
> (Williams 1965: 118)

The term 'individual' is famously problematical in social analysis. What Williams does is to draw upon the symbolic interactionist perspective of G.H. Mead: the self is socially created and interacts with others. This is what shapes social experience and character. The self creatively shapes its own being and is shaped by its environment, with which it interacts. Then, in order to refine ideas of conformity and non-conformity to society, Williams draws upon a series of categories, which can be applied to individuals in different situations. Individuals may belong to more than one of these categories during their lives. Again, in typological terms, these social categories are juxtaposed by Williams with how such individuals might perceive society. We can set these down as follows:

Social category of individual	Perception of society
Member	Community
Servant	Establishment
Subject	Imposed system
Rebel	Tyranny
Exile	Absent/lost
Vagrant	Meaningless

What societies are *really* like will depend on their actual forms of organization. For Williams the concept of the individual was, in the first instance, a liberating one, set against the kind of society which controlled and directed people's lives from above. Yet it had come to be seen in restrictive terms – the individualism of selfishness and indifference to others. But it remains the case that the individual as a member of community is a social individual (to use Durkheim's term). The question is how can we identify and encourage a process that sustains and nurtures personal and social growth? For Williams this is nothing less than the quest for a participatory democracy.

If, then, the concept of the individual has to be rescued so that it can be seen as connecting with others in an affirmative, unselfish way, so too does the concept of society have to be reviewed in relation to its democratic possibilities. In discussing images of society Williams again offers some type formations. There is a twofold purpose in this: to delineate actual societies and to show how assumptions behind images of society permeate our language. For example, if we have an image of a feudal society, under the King, there is a sense of order and hierarchy to which the individual is subordinated. It is the basis of absolutism, alongside which develops the concept of the nation state. 'The real question, whether the social order actually serves our needs, cannot be asked when our social thinking is determined by the assumption that it is from the order that we must start' (Williams 1965: 123).

An important contrast is with the emergence of capitalism, where society is an organization for production and trading in the market – the 'free' market. 'With the further development of capitalism to its corporate stage, society was no longer thought of as merely providing a market: the organisation of society itself was essentially a market organisation' (ibid.: 124). And the language changes from one of rights and duties, services and obligations, to one of buying and selling, of labour markets and meeting the needs of the economy.

If societies are so strongly organized in terms of an elitist social order or a market then even the socialist image of society as a possible alternative can in practice be hemmed in and typically find expression in the defensive activities of trade unionism and co-operatives. There are practical and theoretical problems in envisaging socialist societies in terms of meeting human needs on the basis of practical equality, especially given the struggles and power politics that are involved in shifting entrenched positions.

There is a significant fusion of the two types of order – absolutism and society as economy – in the concept of the mass, which, as we have seen, was a strong motif in *Culture and Society*. This becomes a crucial consideration for Williams:

> however elites are composed their practical relations with the 'masses' are then defined as directing and directed, as in other kinds of absolute order. But the idea of mass society also repeats, in a new way, the idea of market. The 'masses' exert their influence on the direction of society, not by participation, but by expressing a pattern of demands and preferences – the laws of a new kind of market – and this, for the elites, is a starting point: to be carefully studied (by such techniques as market research and opinion polls) and then worked on. When these two conceptions are joined, they compose a very powerful image, which obviously corresponds with very important elements of our experience in very large societies: the concentration of political and economic power, but on a basis of a pattern of demand; the centralised control of highly efficient techniques of popular communication, again on the basis of a pattern of preferences. This combination of a wide public reference and a narrow area of actual power is indeed a significant model, but what we most notice about it is its essential impersonality. The elites, necessarily, are not concerned with individuals, but with averaged figures and generalised trends in the mass pattern. This technique which underwrites and

validates these functions becomes, inevitably, an habitual way of thinking about society.

(Williams 1965: 129–30)

We need hardly add that much of this has continued relevance to our own society in the 1980s and 1990s. Indeed the term 'authoritarian populism', coined by Stuart Hall to describe the strong government/free market Thatcher administrations, captures something of the connections implied here (Hall 1988b).

Can socialism generate an alternative image of society that is not contaminated by the older ones? In so far as it does not then its moral claims become suspect, since society would still stand against the individual (whatever the political label) rather than for her or him. Part of Williams' attempt to break the stranglehold of the old categories is to argue that society itself is more than a political or economic order (systems of decision and maintenance, as he calls them). There is also a system of learning and communication and a system of generation and nurture. Only if we think in terms of the complicated relationships between all of these can we begin to glimpse possibilities for an alternative human order: to dwell on politics and economics alone is not enough:

> It is not a question of looking for some absolute formula, by which the structure of these relations can be invariably determined. The formula that matters is that which, first, makes the essential connexions between what are never really separable spheres, and second, shows the historical variability of each of these systems, and therefore of the real organisation within which they operate and are lived. . . . Our contemporary experience of work, love, thought, art, learning, decision and play is more fragmented than in any other recorded kind of society, yet still, necessarily, we try to make connections, to achieve integrity, and to gain control, and in part we succeed.
>
> (Williams 1965: 136)

Williams' strategy, then, is to deal with what he regards as a significant absence in the study of society as compared to our knowledge of the political and economic spheres. It is the study of what he terms our expanding culture and its relationship to a growth in communications. This, for Williams, is a question partly of describing the changes but also of discovering values and commitments and identifying choices that can be made:

Yet whether these means are used for creative growth or merely as new ways of organising older human systems, is an open question. Both the industrial revolution and the revolution in communications are only fully grasped in terms of the progress of democracy, which cannot be limited to simple political change, but insists, finally, on conceptions of an open society and of freely cooperating individuals which alone are capable of releasing the creative potentiality of the changes in working skills and communication.

(ibid.: 141)

Whether the long revolution will lead to the achievement of this aspiration is uncertain because of the struggles between contending values and interests. Williams' intention is first to try and clarify the nature of these changes, and secondly to advocate participation in this cultural struggle towards greater democracy. He is sustained by the hope that change in this direction is possible, yet conscious of the depth and intensity of the struggle.

The second part of *The Long Revolution* consists of seven essays. At first sight they are rather disparate, ranging from 'Education and British society' to 'Realism and the contemporary novel'. They can, perhaps, best be understood as an elaboration of the idea of cultural expansion – its nature and significance for British society.

The connection between education and culture was, as we have seen, addressed in *Culture and Society*, and for Williams this raises qualitative questions about the 'education of desire' and structural questions about access to the means of education. If education is part of culture then we may ask: what is to count as education, for whom, for how long and for what purpose? To examine such matters is to look at the way a cultural resource (education) is defined and distributed and has significance for the appreciation of and access to other cultural resources so far as the nation's population is concerned.

The expansion of education, then, is linked to the expansion of culture. But what has this involved? The rapid changes of the industrial revolution, as in so many other things, led to reforms in curricula and the extension of education at elementary, secondary and tertiary levels. This expansion partly related to the changing needs of industry, and partly to political arguments about the changing role of education in a democracy. The Foster Education Act of 1870, which established the principle of elementary education for all and the role of the state in providing it, came just three years after the extension of the franchise in 1867. But part of Foster's argument had been the necessity of putting elementary education in place quickly in order to ensure industrial prosperity. The growing competitive strength of Germany and the USA was becoming clearer year by year.

However, education is not a simple product and, not surprisingly, its relationship to democracy is not clear-cut. Williams draws attention to three distinct groups who argued about the purposes of education and, therefore, its content and organization, in the nineteenth century. They represent positions that are with us still: the public educator, the industrial trainer, and the old humanists. The first argued the democratic right to education and the role of government in promoting it. The industrial lobby wanted a sufficiently educated workforce to make industry work efficiently and a set of values that would encourage discipline and obedience to authority. The humanists saw such education as the enemy of true learning. While the public educators were sometimes in alliance with the industrial trainers lobbying for the spread of education, they drew upon humanist arguments that education was not to be seen in instrumental terms as simply fodder for the educational system. While education expanded throughout the nineteenth and twentieth centuries, it was contested terrain, and still is. The expansion in opportunity and practice was certainly related to class structure – the Taunton Commission of the 1860s provides simple testimony to that. Twentieth-century concepts of equality of opportunity turn out, on inspection, to be greatly conditioned by class position. Equality of opportunity is a continuing kind of inequality of outcome if there is no equality of condition or access in the first place.

Williams' own interest is in the role of education in a participatory democracy. At a time when issues of national curriculum are once more on the agenda, it is worth noting his own proposals. They were:

1 extensive practice in the fundamental languages of English and mathematics;
2 general knowledge of ourselves and our environment, taught at the secondary stage not as separate academic disciplines but as general knowledge drawn from the disciplines which clarify at a higher stage, i.e. biology, psychology, social history,

law and political institutions, sociology, descriptive economics, geography including actual industry and trade, physics and chemistry;
3 history and criticism of literature, the visual arts, music, dramatic performance, landscape and architecture;
4 extensive practice in democratic procedures, including meetings, negotiations, and the selection and conduct of leaders in democratic organizations. Extensive practice in the use of libraries, newspapers and magazines, radio and television programmes, and other sources of information, opinion and influence;
5 introduction to at least one other culture, including its language, history, geography, institutions and arts, to be given in part by visiting and exchange.

(1965: 174–5)

Williams makes a distinction between the expansion of education in an empirical sense and the contribution education actually makes to the participation in a common culture, that is, the experience of cultural expansion. For him, the second is still limited by class differences and the forms of educational organization which flow from it. What he wants to suggest, as with the curriculum proposals above, is that there is nothing natural or determined about the state of education and we need not see proposals for an educated participatory democracy as utopian:

> It is a question of whether we can grasp the real nature of our society or whether we persist in social and industrial patterns based on a limited ruling class, a middle professional class, a large operative class, cemented by forces that cannot be challenged and will not be changed. It is only a question of whether we replace them by the free play of the market or by a public education designed to express and create the values of an educated democracy and a common culture.

(ibid.: 176)

Williams stands in the tradition of public educators and clearly distinguishes himself from those who associate culture with elites. He wants the cultural products associated with elite minorities not only to be extended – as part of the common culture – but also to dissolve, without abdicating from critical judgements, the categories of high and low culture. So he advocates as early as 1961, that proper space be given to social studies, the history and criticism of music, including jazz, visual art forms, broadcasting, the critical reading of newspapers and magazines, the study of propaganda and advertising, as well as scientific discoveries and their social effects. This culture is common in that it is part of our common inheritance. We should not only have access to it but be able to respond and contribute to it.

These recurring issues – minority/mass, elite/democracy, high/low – inform Williams' discussion of the significance of an expanding culture. These are continued in his accounts of the growth of the reading public, the popular press and of standard English. The underlying question in each case is: what is the significance of growth for cultural expansion? If literacy is a crucial element in understanding and participating in our common culture then, in general terms, the growth of literacy is something to celebrate. Yet this has to be set against those who argue that the growth of a literate population leads to a decline in the quality of literary products or will lead to social disorder because authority will more frequently be questioned. On this Williams writes:

> No issue is more central in the history of our culture, for the argument about quality and the argument about democracy are here so deeply intertwined as to appear insuperable, and this has led again and again to a deadlock in the cultural argument which has been profoundly discouraging and confusing.
>
> (ibid.: 179)

Can this confusion and discouragement be overcome?

First, what the case of the growth of the reading public signifies is that there should be no easy rush to judgement. After all, as Williams reminds us, both Elizabethan popular drama and the nineteenth-century novel were condemned as low and idle but are now part of our standard literature. Tastes and judgements change. Moreover, it would be a mistake to put the issue of quality in simple class terms when the matter has to be seen in a wider context of education on the one hand and capitalist forms of production on the other:

> The whole argument about 'cheap literature' has been compromised by its use as a form of class-distinction whereas the real problem is always the relation between inexperience and the way this is met. Certainly, in a limited way, it would do middle

class people good to remember that these problems did not arrive
with working class literacy; that new middle class groups made
all the same mistakes and were evidently exploited.

(ibid.: 191)

Education can serve a double function here. It can develop critical
sensitivities and awareness of literature, thus taking the reader well
beyond the 'addiction' to ephemeral writing; and it can remind
us of the way literature is produced and distributed. The awareness
of changes in these practices allows us to think of futures which
might assist a reading public in a democracy.

A parallel point arises in relation to the growth of the popular
press, the development of which is treated as of major importance
in Williams' account of cultural expansion. The blame for a
supposed decline in quality – 'giving the readers what they want'
– cannot be put at the door of the newly literate working class. As
Williams points out, the conventional wisdom which compares the
press of the 1890s, addressed to the millions, to that which had
formerly reached a highly educated, politically minded minority,
overlooks the content of that earlier press. There was, after all, a
genuinely radical press including, for example, Cobbett's *Political
Register* and Wooler's *Black Dwarf*, which became the subject of
government attacks and attempts at suppression. There were also
papers which emphasized the scandalous. Sex, drugs and violence
are not new subjects for the press. The *Daily Telegraph*, for example,
founded in 1855, gave its middle-class readership detailed crime
stories: 'Such stories as a three-column description of the hanging
of a woman remind us that a popular old theme in cheap literature
was now establishing itself in the daily press' (ibid.: 219). The
Morning Post, likewise, published full reports of crime.

Williams is surely right to insist that changes in the nature of
the popular press have to be related to their economic, political
and social context. In the late nineteenth century the relationship
between ownership, new technology, production costs and the role
of advertising provided a crucial nexus, out of which the mass
readership was created and sustained. It is a story of a readership
being turned into a market – an expansion that does not intrinsic-
ally serve or contribute to an educated democracy. The outcome
has been the concentration of ownership in few hands:

The process is evidently something other than the incursion of
the 1870 masses, or the 1820 masses if the process is merely

back-dated. It is something that is happening to the whole of society, and all the elements – not only the bad journalism but also the questions of ownership and the relation to advertising – have to be considered if the process is to be understood. We do not solve the critical questions by understanding the history, but still an adequate sense of the history, as opposed to the ordinary functional myths, is the basis of any useful approach.

(ibid.: 236)

These questions, of course, surface in much of what Williams was to write on communications and we will have reason to take them further.

Common culture? Common language? The long revolution has involved a cultural expansion of the English language so that it can be understood beyond the dialects and accents of local communities and regions. The development of an expanded community of speech is a prerequisite for a participatory democracy. Even so, Standard English (or Received Standard) is a product of the public schools and the middle classes. It became a dominant presence in the education system and in broadcasting (sometimes called BBC English). On this Williams has an interesting observation: 'its naming as "standard", with the implication no longer of a common but a model language, represents the full coming to consciousness of a new concept of class speech: now no longer merely the functional convenience of a metropolitan class, but the means and emphasis of social distinction' (ibid.: 243).

Williams is thus acknowledging the importance of extending our language capacity so that we may communicate with a wider range of people. While Received Standard may represent a form of class power, he impresses upon us the constantly changing and creative character of language. The educated and participatory democracy does not depend on the possession of Received Standard for its development. More variation is available and the language will continue to grow in vocabulary and forms of expression. What is implied by this? While Standard English may be a barrier to some who do not possess it, it is nevertheless a barrier that can be transcended and outgrown. It is not a normative model to be endorsed. A common culture can live with more diversity and flexibility in language and will be the better for it. It can, by the same token, become a way of challenging Received Standard in so far as it is an expression of class power.

The remaining three chapters in this section of *The Long Revolution* serve a rather different purpose. Whereas with literacy, the press and language, the focus is on institutional change, with the writer, drama and the novel, the concern is with artistic practice and its relationship to the rest of society.

In the case of drama the crucial observation has to do with the fact that in contemporary society it is more widely disseminated than ever before. This is not so much because of theatres, which can run into financial difficulties, but because of the development of cinema, radio and television. Moreover, the very flexibility of these new media has made new forms of experimentation possible. This makes it a revolutionary period when all kinds of creative response to the new media are possible and when new audiences are being reached by them. Drama can tell us something about our actual social history and can contribute to a heightened social consciousness. Williams draws particular attention to the possibilities of film techniques and expressionist theatre and the role of contemporary music and drama in exploring and contributing to new kinds of experience:

> Complicated as it is by delay, by the unevenness of change, and by the natural variety of responses to change, only some of which achieve adequate communication, the outline surely exists, in which we can see drama, not only as a social art, but *as a major and practical index of change and creative consciousness*.
>
> (ibid.: 299; emphasis added)

We have seen that for Williams culture can sometimes refer to possible common and universal values and can also, through creative activity, articulate formerly inarticulated experiences. In the activity of drama and its new forms and opportunities Williams expressed the hope that it would reach out in a dynamic way and in both these respects contribute to an expanding culture.

We turn now to Williams' discussion of realism and the contemporary novel. His fundamental claim is that a new realism is necessary if we are to remain creative. New in relation to what?

The realist tradition in fiction, which Williams has in mind, is the kind of novel 'which creates and judges the quality of a whole way of life in terms of the qualities of persons' (ibid.: 304). After a brief skirmish with notions of domestic, bourgeois and socialist realism, he offers us a fourfold classification of realism in the contemporary novel. Schematically, we can present this as follows:

Types of realism in the contemporary novel

	Social	Personal
Social documentary	1	2
Social formula	3	4

The general distinction made between the 'social' and 'personal' novel is that the first emphasizes accurate observation of social life and the second accurately observes and describes persons. Each lacks what the other has and neither comes to terms with the indivisible process that constitutes the relationship between individual and society. The distinction between social documentary and social formula is this. The documentary concentrates on looking at a particular context and looks at a defined way of life – a mining town, a ship, or whatever – and the characters are simply illustrations of the way of life. The formula looks at particular social relations against a backdrop of an imagined society. They work with assumptions about the relation of the individual to society.

What is behind this exercise? Williams puts the question: do these four types of realist novel correspond to some altered reality or do they represent symptoms of a deep crisis in experience, 'which throw up these talented works yet persists, unexplored, and leaves us essentially dissatisfied'? In his view it is the latter. Central to the problem is his view that the realist novel needs a community to relate to. In the twentieth century that is easier said than done because of the real changes that have taken place in the world. Yet unless the last word is about identifying fragmentation there remains, Williams thinks, the creative possibility of exploring what kind of world it is we are actually creating, what kind of common effort we are making to live with change, and how we communicate with one another. This new realism, as with drama, will have to be dynamic, not static:

> The truly creative effort of our time is the struggle for relationships of a whole kind, and it is possible to see this as both personal and social: the practical learning of *extending* relationships. Realism, as embodied in its great tradition, is a touchstone in this, for it shows, in detail, that vital interpenetration, idea into feeling, person into community, change into settlement, which we need as growing points, in our own divided time. In the

highest realism society is seen in fundamentally personal terms, and persons, through relationships, in fundamentally social terms. The integration is controlling, yet of course is not to be achieved by act of will. If it comes at all, it is a creative discovery, and can perhaps only be recorded within the structure and substance of the realist novel.

(ibid.: 314)

This, of course, is a strong normative claim and underwrites Williams' own intentions as a novelist. In an expanding culture, the argument goes, we need a literature that can sensitively identify changing structures of feeling. In Williams' view this is precisely the challenge: to develop the realist tradition at a time when old communities are disappearing and new, non-local communities are to be envisaged – imagined communities.

There is, in this chapter of *The Long Revolution*, a passage which connects Williams' view of realism and how this itself has changed as we think through questions of human perception and interpretation in relation to the world of things. In it the concept of culture as lived experience, creative, selectively interpreted, variable, personal and social, is indicated. The centrality of communication is there and the sense of process is rooted in the exposition. It is a key passage:

We know now that we literally create the world we see, and that this human creation – a discovery of how we can live in the material world we inhabit – is necessarily dynamic and active; the old static realism of the passive observer is merely a hardened convention. When it was first discovered that man lives through his perceptual world, which is a human interpretation of the material world outside him, this was thought to be a basis for the rejection of realism; only a personal vision was possible. But art is more than perception; it is a particular kind of active response, and a part of all human communication. Reality, in our terms, is that which human beings make common, by work or language. Thus in the very acts of perception and communication, this practical interaction of what is personally seen, interpreted and organised and what can be socially recognised, known and formed is richly and subtly manifested ... here undoubtedly is the clue we seek, not only in our thinking about personal vision and social communication, but also in our thinking about the individual and society.

(ibid.: 314–15)

No wonder it is a long revolution. Moreover, it is a revolution without any certainty that the desired outcome will be realized. This Williams goes on to discuss in the final section of the book.

The Long Revolution was not without its critics. A notable, if strident, example was Dwight MacDonald, the American social critic, in *Encounter* (1961). Recalling his own period as a Trotskyist in the 1930s, MacDonald offers the thought that Williams is like them in that he supposes that there is nothing wrong with the working class; it is a matter of treacherous, short-sighted or corrupt leaders. He describes Williams' views about the democratization of culture as a nostalgic progressivism: a pre-1914 position, when a belief in democracy was still intellectually possible. He sees Williams as a propagandist – albeit with 'an appalling prose style' – and a preacher:

> The sermon is his literary form. In true preacher fashion, he is forever contrasting the dismal present with the bright future which can easily come into being if only we will hearken, and in true preacher fashion he never seems to suspect that the present, which is merely the tiny tip of the long thick tail of the past, may be the product of historical forces which will continue to affect the future. He constantly insists on the gloom of the present and as constantly extrapolates from it a misty Utopia, throwing across the horrible gulf a gossamer bridge of good intentions.
>
> (MacDonald 1961: 80)

In these postmodern days it is difficult to write of this as a misreading, let alone a wilful one. Yet it is curious. For Williams, the connections between the past, present and future were inherently problematical. Democracy is a contested concept and will always be so. The past tells us something about the struggles for and around democracy in relation to other kinds of societies variously described as aristocratic, elitist, fascist and mass. There is a rooted view in Williams' work that an educated participatory democracy is something worth struggling for because it does allow for human development in community. But there is no inevitability about the outcome and, because modern societies are increasingly complex, many arguments about how this is best achieved. To dismiss this as misty utopianism is, in our view, very wide of the mark. But, as Edward Thompson has well expressed it: 'the past is not just dead, inert, confining; it carries signs and evidences also of creative

resources which can sustain the present and prefigure possibility'
(Thompson 1981: 407–8).

Thompson, himself, had difficulties with *The Long Revolution*.
Twenty years after his extended review appeared in the *New Left
Review* (May–June and July–August 1961) he referred back to it
(Thompson 1981). He felt at the time that his theoretical differences
with Williams were so sharp that to express them fully would
endanger political relations within the New Left. However, with
the encouragement of the editor, Stuart Hall, the full, uninhibited
review went ahead. He was, it must be said, generous in his personal tribute to Williams, especially in recognizing his commitment
to socialist thinking at the height of the cold war in an independent,
critical spirit. And he recognized that, in a significant way, Williams
took over the vocabulary of his opponents in order to outflank and
subvert them.

What then were his reservations? At a surface level it was partly
a matter of tone. Williams, he argued, preferred the impersonal
to the personal, the passive to the active construction. This had
the effect of depersonalizing social forces. We might infer that this
was a study of social change with the people left out. What this
pointed to, for Thompson, was that the element of struggle between
contending groups and the reality of power was insufficiently
stressed. It was too smoothly subsumed under the category of culture
as a 'way of life'. This led to the central criticism that Williams'
attempt to construct a general theory of culture was inadequate.
If culture is in the end a 'way of life' how is it to be distinguished
from society?

> Any theory of culture must include the concept of dialectical
> interaction between culture and something that is *not* culture.
> We must suppose the raw material of life-experience to
> be at one pole, and all the infinitely complex human disciplines
> and systems, articulate and inarticulate, formalised in institu-
> tions or dispersed in the least formal ways, which 'handle',
> transmit, or distort this raw material to be at the other.
> It is this active *process* – which is at the same time *the
> process through which men make their history* – that I am insisting
> upon.
>
> (Thompson 1961: 33)

In an essay written in 1976, 'Notes on Marxism since 1945' (in
Williams 1980) Williams referred to the issue of the role of struggle,

in particular the view that he had substituted an 'extensive' for
a 'conflict' theory:

> I thought I had indicated my own position clearly enough in
> calling the process a long *revolution*. Perhaps the trouble was that
> it was indeed long (as the seventies most bitterly reminded us)
> and that it was much easier to go to a desk or a meeting and
> say it should be short. But then again I did, and still do, find
> extension, transfer, slow development at least as often as I find
> the transitional process, transformation, and as often, also, as
> explicit conflict and struggle. What I would insist on is that this
> is not a shop-counter of theoretical options. It is, or it can become,
> a theory of the historical variations of cultural process, which
> then necessarily connects (has to be connected) with a more
> general social, historical, and political theory.
>
> (Williams 1980: 244)

The relationship between culture and society was one that
Williams continued to wrestle with. In what follows we will see
developed examples of how this worked out, notably in *The Country
and the City* and in *Towards 2000*. In a more formal, conceptual way
he went on to distinguish between dominant, residual and emergent
cultures. The residual, the continuation of earlier values, beliefs
and practices, could sometimes be seen as an alternative to the
dominant forms, for example rural life in opposition to urban
industrial capitalism. The emergent – the development of new
meanings, values and practices, as in working-class movements of
the nineteenth century – could also provide oppositional elements
to the dominant culture. Williams' pervasive concern was with the
capacity of dominant social orders to incorporate residual and
emergent cultures. This was a process which Williams judged to
be very effective and penetrating in advanced capitalist societies.
While this was a personal and political problem for him, it was
never a question of total incorporation:

> What has really to be said, as a way of defining important
> elements of both the residual and the emergent, and as a way
> of understanding the character of the dominant, is that *no mode
> of production and therefore no dominant social order and therefore no
> dominant culture ever in reality includes or exhausts all human practice,
> human energy, and human intention.*
>
> (Williams 1977: 125)

This theoretical position underpins much of his work and sustains, for him, the possibilities of alternatives to the dominant forms of capitalism, whose growth he charted and whose values he rejected.

Chapter 5

The critique of media culture

It is impossible to discuss communication or culture in our society without in the end coming to discuss power. There is the power of established institutions and there is increasingly the power of money, which is imposing certain patterns of communication that are very powerful in the society as a whole.

('Communications and community' (1961), in Williams 1989)

Books, journals, magazines, newspapers, theatre, films, radio, television, records, compact discs, videos and advertising – all of these remind us of the variety of activities that go to make up what we collectively term 'the media'; the media, that is to say, of communication. The connections between communications and society are a preoccupation with Williams, whether it is the significance of Elizabethan drama in sixteenth-century England, or the rise of the press in the nineteenth century, or film and television in the twentieth century. Late in his career, his 1974 inaugural lecture, 'Drama in a dramatized society', he marks the complexity and centrality of new forms of communication and the way these enter into the warp and woof of social existence:

> Till the eyes tire, millions of us watch the shadow of shadows and find them substance; watch scenes, situations, actions, exchanges, crises. The slice of life, once a project of naturalist drama, is now a voluntary, habitual, internal rhythm; the flow of action and acting, of representation and performance, raised to a new convention, that of a basic need.
>
> (Williams in O'Connor 1989a: 5)

That, of course, incorporates drama on the screen as well as other genres. Millions of people can watch more drama in a week on television than they would have seen in their lifetimes in former centuries. Drama itself becomes an habitual experience.

It is crucial to any understanding of the nature of communication to recognize that it is not just some secondary matter at one remove from 'real life' or some marginal activity. In the very fabric of our society are forms and patterns of communication. They are human constructions and so, in principle, subject to criticism and the possibilities of change. But the institutions in which they emerge and flourish can be very powerful. Williams underlines this in many places, including the quotation with which this section began. In that essay he reminded his readers that while critique and evaluation of communication systems is possible, they have the appearance of a wall, made up of stones of power. Williams did not deploy metaphor a great deal. Here he conveys the strong sense he had that the closer you get to the wall, the more you are aware of your own size in relation to its height and strength. As against those who are at the commanding heights of the cultural apparatus, the cultural critic is a person of little power. Nevertheless what the student of communications can do is explore and analyse the nature of communications systems and what they tell us about the kind of society we live in. From this we can think about possible futures and what this signifies for the future of democracy. Social life and patterns of communication are inextricably intertwined, so it is misleading to speak of 'reality' and then communication about reality:

> How people speak to each other, what conventions they have as to what is important and what is not, how they express these in institutions by which they keep in touch: these things are central. They are central to individuals, and central to the society. Of course in a complicated society like ours, it is very easy to lose sight of this, and to discuss the press, or television, or broadcasting, as an isolated thing . . . in the end, we are looking at the communication systems not just to make points against them, but to see in a new way what sort of relationships we have in this complicated society, which way these relationships are going, what is their possible future.
>
> (Williams 1989c: 23)

The continuing preoccupation in so much of Williams' writing is how we can have a democratic system of communications – it is desirable, of that he has no doubt, but is it possible, and what would it look like? From the same essay, 'Communications and community', we can take a summary statement of his value position and then consider how this supports his analysis in a number of places:

> Now in a democratic system of communications, what is the first essential? Surely that communication is something that belongs to the whole society, that it is something which depends, if it is to be healthy, on maximum participation by the individuals in the society. Since communication is the record of human growth, it has to be very varied. It has to disperse itself into many different and independent systems, all of which, however, have to be secure enough to maintain themselves. It has to get rid of the idea that communication is the business of a minority talking to, instructing, leading on, the majority. It has, finally to get rid of the false ideology of communications as we have received it: the ideology of people who are interested in communications only as a way of controlling people, or making money out of them.
>
> (1989c: 29)

With this in mind we will pursue a number of issues raised by Williams concerning communications. The seminal text here is undoubtedly *Communications*. This had a long publishing life. First published in 1962, it was revised and updated in 1966. It was then re-issued in 1976, with further updating and a new section, 'Retrospect and Prospect, 1975'. The original impetus had come from an invitation to contribute to a National Union of Teachers' Conference on 'Popular Culture and Personal Responsibility'. The marks of its origin are evident. We see it in Williams' criticisms of the concept of 'the masses' – it can be used by those who justify what they are producing in the media as simply giving the public what it wants. Education, on the other hand, works on the premise of respect for the person and the recognition that people may change and grow in their tastes and interests. But, argued Williams, when the emphasis in the media of communications is on profit 'there will be a constant pressure to concentrate on things already known and safe, with never enough effort given to the much longer and more difficult job of trying new things and offering new ideas and experiences' (Williams 1976: 108).

This also underlines his challenge to the concepts of mass culture and minority culture. It becomes easy to identify the culture of the masses with that which is popular, undiscriminating, vulgar and inferior – low culture. Those who work with such a contrast may then go on to express the fear that high culture will be overwhelmed by mass culture. The crux of Williams' argument is that we need to reconsider the role of 'the great tradition' in social life. Rather than see it as the exclusive property of elite groups in society, we should see it as a common inheritance which, through education and communication, should be made as widely available as possible. Not only this; the great tradition is a living, developing activity and need not be confined to the minorities of the privileged. In the following quotation, Williams develops this point and, in doing so, also makes a clear distinction between popular culture and synthetic culture:

> If the great tradition is not made generally available, there is often this frightening combination of hostility and a vacuum. What then usually happens is that this is penetrated and exploited from outside. In the worst cultural products of our time, we find little that is generally popular, developed from the life of actual communities. We find instead a synthetic culture or anti-culture, which is alien to almost everybody, persistently hostile to art and intellectual activity, which it spends much of its time in misrepresenting, and given over to exploiting indifference, lack of feeling, frustration and hatred. It finds such common human interests as sex, and turns them into crude caricatures or glossy facsimiles. It plays repeatedly around hatred and aggression, which it never discharges and continually feeds. This is not the culture of the 'ordinary man'; it is the culture of the disinherited. It seems to me that those who have contrived the disinheritance, by artificially isolating the great tradition, bear as heavy a responsibility for these destructive elements as their actual providers.
>
> (Williams 1976: 115)

So here is a theme that has already been considered in *Culture and Society* and *The Long Revolution* . Williams' interest is in how this great tradition can be responsibly extended to more people and in new media of communication, as well as in identifying the blockages to these developments. The categories of high and low culture are, for him, unhelpful ways of doing this; they are, indeed, part of the problem.

However, in the light of this perspective, we can more readily see why he focuses upon systems of control in the media. This is the reason for looking at three types of control systems which affect the way the institutions of communication operate; the authoritarian, the paternal and the commercial. These he eventually compares with a fourth possibility, the democratic system. The authoritarian is seen as part of a more general system of control through which the minority governs society. The system serves as a means of transmitting the ideas, instructions and attitudes of a ruling group. The means of communications and, by the same token, the means of censorship are in the hands of the government and in which alternative or oppositional views are not available. We may remark that such systems, repressive as they are and absolutist in intention, do not thereby obtain credibility. The communist state-controlled systems of Eastern Europe, which were for so long a feature of post-war Europe, are a standing reminder of that. In contrast, the active role of the media, especially television, as a midwife to social transformation in, for example, Romania and Czechoslovakia, calls attention to the latent democratic potential of the means of communication even in such threatening circumstances.

The paternal system works on the basis of seeking to guide and protect its readers, listeners or viewers. Its control is aimed at directing the development of the majority in ways thought desirable by the minority. This is a political and cultural task. The values and purposes of the minority are seen as representing the public interest. So it is that the minority are represented as guardians of the society's central values. Their activities are surrounded by concepts of duty and service. Indeed, the concept of public service historically has this sense of duty and obligation attached to it, as Williams had earlier discussed in *Culture and Society*. Within this framework there can be a place for dissent, which can function as a safety valve. To examine the nature and extent of that dissent is to look at the socially constructed boundaries within which the paternalist system operates. In the context of the communication systems in Britain it is the position of the BBC that most obviously springs to mind. Since this is a crucial element in public debate, and in some respects has been from the early days of the BBC, we will take this a little further. John Reith (later Lord Reith), the first Director-General of the BBC, saw the Corporation as being dedicated to the maintenance of the highest standards and argued that it was better to overestimate it. This is of course a long way from the treatment of audiences as targets for a programme sponsor. Essentially his view was that broadcasting could help to develop an informed and enlightened opinion on the issues of the day. This kind of paternalism was not a simple matter of relaying the instructions and views of the current government and to that extent represents a contribution to the enlargement of democracy in British society. That was precisely why Reith favoured the setting up of a public corporation rather than have it set up under the direct aegis of a government department. He wanted the BBC to be free from state and political interference. But he also wanted it free of commercial pressures. Within such a space and with such institutional arrangements public service broadcasting could, he believed, flourish. It was this general position which informed the idea of a public corporation serving the public interest, with the state only having an indirect role through the licensing system. The general issue had been discussed as early as 1923 by the Sykes Committee on broadcasting and its future uses, where it was argued that the wavebands in any country must be regarded as a valuable form of public property. The public interest was seen as the guiding consideration in contradistinction to private interests (Scannell 1990).

The BBC was not immune to political pressure in practice as *The Reith Diaries* (1975) make clear. At the time of the 1926 General Strike, Reith records that the government was going to set up its own newspaper, the *British Gazette*, edited from the War Office. According to Reith, the editor expected to see the BBC news as an offshoot of that, which Reith refused to accept. An argument developed within the cabinet with Winston Churchill stating that it was monstrous not to use the instrument of radio to the best possible advantage. This view did not prevail. The diary entry for 11 May shows a more subtle policy:

> The Cabinet were to make a decision at long last about the BBC. Davidson was going to it. I primed him up with all the arguments and he came to see me at 7.15. As he was smiling broadly I saw it was all right. The decision was not a definite one, but at any rate we are not going to be commandeered. The Cabinet decision is really a negative one. They want to be able to say that they did not commandeer us, but they know that they can trust us not to be really impartial. Davidson came around again at 9.15 and we were supposed to draft a notice defining the BBC position. I wanted the inconsistencies in our acts so far squared

up, setting us right with the other side. Davidson, however, thought the Cabinet would only agree to a statement that we could do nothing to help the Strike since it had been declared illegal. This does not seem to me straight.

(Stuart 1975: 96)

As Reith pointed out, the BBC was in a very awkward position. He was clear that to turn the BBC into a propaganda arm of the government would have destroyed its credibility, and even more so if it had been commandeered. In seeking to resist that he tried to square the circle. His sense of loyalty to the Prime Minister cut across his uneasiness that impartiality was a cloak concealing the government's position – at the very least by keeping other views off the air. The debate about impartiality, defined as it is as a cornerstone of public service broadcasting, is still very much with us.

We can see that Reith was aware of the inconsistency he had allowed himself and the BBC to get into. But in any case the root of the problem goes deeper because impartiality is essentially a contested concept. When it comes to issues like apartheid, famine or racism, moreover, we do not necessarily see impartiality as the cornerstone of public service broadcasting. This does not prevent us from recognizing that the concept has been tied up with the concern for independence from state control from the time of Reith onwards. This concern is a very proper one when public service broadcasting is at issue: the interests of the state and of the civil society are not necessarily identical. Even if we want to recognize the limitations of the paternalist system as against a democratic communication system and argue that the concept of impartiality has been used to favour the interests of one class over another, the idea of public service broadcasting can encourage pluralist tendencies by postulating broadcasting as part of civil society and not as an arm of the state.

The third category in the Williams typology is the commercial system. At root it is opposed to authoritarianism and paternalism. It exists neither to enable state control over the individual, nor to provide guidance or enlightenment. It is grounded in the notion of market freedom which, ideally, is seen as a way of ensuring freedom of communication. People buy and sell what they want. This freedom enlarges the range of choice for consumers and therefore increases the opportunities for producers. The reality in a capitalist society is that there are impediments to a free market

that in practice constrain human choice in relation to both production and consumption. Production costs in modern systems of
communication are often very high. In Williams' view what tended
to happen was that:

> practical control of the means of communication over large areas
> and particularly in the more expensive kinds, can pass to
> individuals or groups whose main, if not only, qualification will
> be that they possess or can raise the necessary capital. Such
> groups, by the fact of this qualification, will often be quite
> unrepresentative of the society as a whole; they will be, in fact,
> a minority within it. Thus the control claimed as a matter of
> power by the authoritarians, and as a matter of principle by the
> paternalists, is often achieved as a matter of practice in the opera-
> tion of the commercial system. Anything can be said, provided
> that you can afford to say it and that you can say it profitably.
>
> (Williams 1989c: 133)

While the commercial system of communications is in the hands
of those who can afford to buy into it – the owners, the advertisers
and so on – it is typically justified by populist rhetoric: people should
be able to decide what they want and not be told from above
(whether by authoritarians or paternalists) what is good for them.
This can also be done in the name of democracy – the extension
of individual choice – and in the name of public service, but
Williams was deeply suspicious of this, seeing in it the construction of a synthetic culture driven by money and speculation. Despite
the rhetoric of democracy, Williams argued, the cultural apparatus
was falling into irresponsible hands – speculators not interested in
the health and growth of the society but in exploiting the technology
of communication and organizing it for quick profits.

Let us consider the question of commercial television in Britain
in order to tease this out a little further. When the Independent
Television Authority (ITA) was set up in 1954 it was presented
as an extension of public service broadcasting, not an alternative
to it. It was, alongside the BBC, to provide a means of information,
education and entertainment and was charged with maintaining
high standards of programme quality. The extent to which this was
accomplished remains a matter for debate. The Pilkington Report
on broadcasting in 1960 was quite unconvinced that commercial
television was meeting the criteria of public service broadcasting.
Rather it was considered to be committing the 'natural vice' of

television: trivialization. The fear expressed was that it was contributing to the development of a 'mass society' by its unthinking conformism, its erosion of the critical faculties, its failure to recognize the differences in aesthetic tastes, cultural values and moral standards. There was, it was argued, a tendency to equate quality with box office success. In this, we may observe, commercial television could be described as populist but not pluralist. It was not contributing to the development of a democratic society precisely because of its concern with ratings, which in turn was linked with the special interests of advertising, which, in effect, drove the system.

Not surprisingly we get a different range of views from those who were involved with the ITA and later the Independent Broadcasting Authority (IBA). The autumn 1990 edition of *Airwaves*, the quarterly journal of the IBA, was a retrospective issue to mark the end of the IBA and is a valuable source to consult. One example must suffice. Sir Brian Young, in his article 'Programmes above profit', reminds readers that Reith had likened the advent of the ITA to the coming of the bubonic plague and recalls the story of Kenneth Clark being booed in the Athenaeum Club for becoming ITA's first chairman. He then makes the following claim:

> Yet the ITV proved over the years the equal of the BBC in quality programming and in the care of engineers for reaching the most distant of viewers; meanwhile it developed a system of advertising control that confounded eager critics. The key to this was surely the decision to appoint an Authority with wide powers of regulation and control; in the 1960s these powers were strengthened, and later on a more interventionist authority led the companies to realise the very best of which they were capable . . . it was the programmes of ITV on which the Authority as regulator was most often judged; and it was there that the interests of viewers, rather than investors or advertisers, were clearly made paramount, till Independent Television became the only advertising-financed service in the world which put programmes sufficiently above profits to win plaudits from international juries – more indeed than any licensed-based service.
>
> (Young 1990: 8)

Here then is a picture of a commercially financed public service system, although, interestingly, in defending its record Young treats it as a very special case (perhaps the only one), as the last sentence of the above quotation shows. Even so, when we have acknowledged the achievements – from *Spitting Image* to *The South Bank Show*, from *Rock Follies* to *The Naked Civil Servant*, from *Death of a Princess* to *Death on the Rock* – we still must note the necessarily privileged access that advertisers have to the medium. And we are, of course, very conditioned to it. The concept of a 'natural break' for advertising is actually an unnatural break in the flow of what is being shown. We do not go to the cinema and watch a two-hour film with advertising breaks every fifteen minutes. It would be foolish to deny that the schedules are geared to ratings, which takes us back to the advertisers. The point has been made sharply and, as he recognizes, unfashionably, by Nicholas Garnham:

> in my view advertising finance is, and will remain, incompatible with the ideal of public service as I have outlined it. The aim of advertising is not to encourage the rational exchange of information and opinions in search of agreement as to the public good, but on the contrary to exploit the irrational in the admitted pursuit of private interest. Thus for me the fact that the BBC is not financed by advertising, unlike many other broadcasters in Europe, is crucial and, given the level of broadcast advertising in Britain, a remarkable social achievement. Thus for instance the current weakening of the BBC's stance towards sponsorship is not a peripheral housekeeping matter, but absolutely central.
>
> (Garnham 1990: 310)

When Williams was writing a regular television critic column for the *Listener* he devoted one piece to the 'natural break' (August 1972). He reminds us that when the 1953 White Paper was introduced in Parliament, the government position was that no interruptions of programmes could be permitted, but very soon this was altered to read: 'no interruptions unless they occur in natural breaks', through which a coach and horses could be and were driven, so that now 'natural breaks' predictably occur three or four times an hour. But it is not only natural breaks into which advertising intrudes and not only on commercial television:

> Sponsored sporting events have become so natural, even on the BBC, that one has to suppose a high correlation between love of horse-racing, athletics, golf, cricket or similar outdoor pursuits and directorships in beer, cigarette, razor blade and similar companies.
>
> (O'Connor 1989a: 186)

Williams points out that advertisements encircle the boundaries and fences at cricket and football matches, the product of planning, contracts and calculations for profit. He concludes:

> I think it is worth resisting this whole drift. It is in any case necessary to expose its naturalism as a contrivance. And what goes, all along the line, for Commercial Television, goes also for the encroachments and contrivances that has got what is in effect advertising into public service broadcasting.
>
> (ibid.: 187)

Twenty years on, the drift has become a definite movement. We now have, by way of example, the playing areas at the legendary grounds of Lord's, Old Trafford and so on, stamped with the advertising crest of the sponsor. So much for 'sacred turf' we might conclude.

We have entered now into the world of deregulated broadcasting. At the Edinburgh Television Festival in August 1989 Rupert Murdoch, head of News International, gave the MacTaggart Lecture, entitled 'Freedom in broadcasting'. In this he attacked the paternalism of the BBC and also the commercial television of IBA, both for the establishment attitudes they represent and the freedom of choice they hinder by their duopoly. We can at least see where he is coming from:

> I have never heard a convincing definition of what public-service television really is, and I am suspicious of elites, including the British broadcasting elite, which argue for special privileges and favours because they are supposed to be in the public interest as a whole. . . . My own view is that anybody who, within the law of the land, provides a service which the public wants at a price it can afford is providing a public service.
>
> (Murdoch 1989: 8)

So it is competition, in place of monopoly or duopoly, that should be the driving force. Matters of quality are simply judged: they are in the eye of the beholder. Towards the end of his lecture Murdoch describes Sky Television as a destroyer of monopoly power and creator of choice and then complains about the legislation that is beng called for to prevent newspaper companies from participating in the opening up of broadcasting markets:

> The fact of the matter is that in circumstances in Britain, cross-ownership of media is a force for diversity. Were it not for the

strength of our newspaper group, and our human capital resources, we surely could not have afforded to have doubled the number of television channels available in Britain from February 5th.

We might, I suppose, say that – on reading this – monopoly also is in the eye of the beholder. All this from the man who a year later effectively hijacked his rival, BSB, from under the embarrassed eyes of the IBA. The competition we are witnessing is not free competition but the competition of multinational conglomerates: it is not open to 'anybody to provide a service which the public wants'. The choice which flows from this is not consumer choice, but that which is pre-formed by those with the capital to play this game. In place of the 'comfortable duopoly' we have the world of takeovers and mergers, in other words a drift and thrust towards monopoly capitalism. Public service broadcasting in such a world is simply what comes out of these new formations. Its anti-democratic character is camouflaged in a populist rhetoric. The individual consumer, who may or may not be able to pay for access, is not to be equated with the social beings who as citizens discover that life is about co-operation as well as competition, about mutual interdependence and not possessive individualism, and that virtue and quality are not the natural outcome of the free market.

In his discussion of the democratic model of broadcasting, Williams pointed to the existence in Britain of a social device which enabled social institutions to exist in the public sphere with a good measure of autonomy. He used the worlds of science and scholarship to illustrate how it could be for broadcasting:

> It is true that science and scholarship are different from general communications. But their importance is no greater, to a civilised democratic community. The only alternative to control by a few irresponsible men, who treat our cultural means as simple commodities, is a public system. There will always be tension, in any such system, but the precedent of the universities, which could not survive without public money, yet which have retained their academic freedom while accepting it, is important. Theoretically, the state could now dictate to the universities, under the threat of withholding funds. In practice there can be no such dictation, though there can be tension and argument, which in fact are useful. Academic freedom is at least as vulnerable as the general freedom of cultural contribution, but

it has not been killed or weakened by the public system we have. An important element in this, undoubtedly, is that the universities, as bodies, are organised scholars and teachers to whom this freedom is necessary, and who can defend this principle in a collective way.

(Williams 1976: 156)

The lesson we learn from this is, sadly, different from that which Williams imagined. What the state could do theoretically it did do in practice and, as we know, the universities are in the middle of a funding crisis. Moreover the control system has changed from one of arm's length relationships to one of close scrutiny and surveillance with its emphasis on value for money and the cultivation of enterprise. In this, and we could extend the point to funding for the arts and the difficulties now experienced by theatres, what is happening to broadcasting is paralleled in other parts of the cultural sphere. The structure of the cultural apparatus is being attacked in the name of economic realism: the public sphere, civil society, which in the end is the barometer of our democratic health, is under threat. The twin pressures, which Reith was well aware of in the beginning, of state interference and commercial pressures are with us still. The democratic struggle is not for some imagined consensus, which we are all supposed to share, but the struggle for space that allows for a pluralism of perspective and a diversity of contributions; space for critique of the powerful; space for an awareness that takes us beyond our own nation, beyond Europe, to a world which is fragile and turbulent but full of new possibilities; space to celebrate the human project in a mysterious universe.

Chapter 6

Drama and literature
Williams' analytical and theoretical approach

Williams' approach to literary analysis arose from his own creative pursuits, his experience of writing fiction. Many of the keywords employed by Williams in his studies of drama and literature are, as will become clear in the following chapters, those central to his own novels: community; connections; pressure; feeling. The crucial concept of 'structure of feeling', first articulated in *Preface to Film*, is interlinked with Williams' experience of creative writing, a notion which:

> is strongly felt from the beginning, in the way that important actual relationships are felt, but also it is a structure and this, I believe, is a particular kind of response to the real shape of a social order: not so much as it can be documented – though it ought never, I think, to contradict the documentation – but as it is in some integrated way apprehended, without any prior separation of private and public or individual and social experience.
>
> (Williams 1983a: 264)

Further, 'structure of feeling' is not only a characteristic which emerges in the writing as written word but, for Williams, it informs his very experience of writing *per se*. As he describes it:

> I am in fact physically alone when I am writing, and I do not believe, taking it all in all, that my work has been less individual, in that defining and valuing sense, than that of others. Yet whenever I write I am aware of a society and of a language which I know are vastly larger than myself: not simply 'out there', in a world of others, but here, in what I am engaged in doing: composing and relating.
>
> (ibid.: 261)

Thus the concept of 'structure of feeling' is, for Williams, both a practical experience and a theoretical tool. It is a predominant concept throughout all of his work, providing him with a means of examining history not just as product but as *process*. With this concept, Williams attempts to analyse literary developments in relation to patterns of *social* change, rigid determinism being replaced by interrelationship, itself implicit to the concept of 'structure of feeling'.

As a concept, 'structure of feeling' embodies the interconnective approach adopted by Williams throughout all of his work, creating a base from which he can explore various areas and issues, and to which he can continually return. It has similarities with C. Wright Mills' notion of 'the sociological imagination'. Like the former, Mills' concept

> enables its possessor to understand the larger historical scene in terms of its meaning for the inner life and the external career of a variety of individuals. It enables him to take into account how individuals, in the welter of their daily experience, often become falsely conscious of their social positions. . . . The sociological imagination enables us to grasp history and biography and the relations between the two within society.
>
> (Mills 1967: 5–6)

Both Williams and Mills seek for a conceptual means of examining, and simultaneously positing an interrelation between, areas of individual and general experience, private and public processes, and social structures and historical formations.

Applying this concept to cultural theory, Williams argues that 'structure of feeling'

> is a way of defining forms and conventions in art and literature as inalienable elements of a social material process: not by derivation from other social forms and pre-forms, but as social formation of a specific kind which may in turn be seen as the articulation (often the only fully available articulation) of structures of feeling which as living processes are much more widely experienced.
>
> (Williams 1977: 133)

In attempting to provide a 'fully social theory of literature', Williams examines each element as part of a continuous and interrelational process (ibid.: 171). Thus, his theory of literature

involves a dynamic approach, this same dynamic informing the
concept of 'structure of feeling'.

Central to Williams' theoretical approach to literature is his
emphasis upon both 'language as *activity*' and 'the *history* of language'
(ibid.: 21). These concerns illustrate two predominant analytical
methods adopted by Williams throughout all of his work and, more
specifically, in his examination of drama and literature: (1) analysis
of phenomena *in process*; (2) historical analysis. Informing his
methodological approach, both serve to establish a sense of
continuity, of movement, and of connection, qualities characteristic
of Williams' writing on literature and drama.

This perspective itself stems from Williams' conscious attempt
to break away from the influential work of Richards and, more
significantly, of Leavis. Criticizing disciplinary separation of
literature and language studies at Cambridge University, Williams
describes his own approach to literary criticism, a description which
illuminates the processes involved in his analysis of the drama and
the novel:

> Language in history: that full field. But even within a more
> specialised emphasis, language produced in works through
> conventions and institutions which, properly examined, are the
> really active society. Not a background to be produced for
> annotation where on a private reading – naked reader before
> naked text – it appears to be relevant and required. Instead the
> kind of reading in which the conditions of production, in the
> fullest sense, can be understood in relation to both writer and
> reader, actual writing and actual reading. A newly active social
> sense of writing and reading, through the social and material
> historical realities of language in a world in which it is closely
> and precisely known, in every act of writing and reading, that
> these practices connect with, are inseparable from, the whole
> set of social practices and relationships which define writers and
> readers as active human beings, as distinct from the idealised
> and projected 'authors' and 'trained readers' who are assumed
> to float, on a guarded privilege, above the rough, divisive and
> diverse world of which yet, by some alchemy, they possess the
> essential secret.
>
> (Williams 1983a: 189)

Here there is a clear emphasis on language as a social and
historical reality, and also evident is Williams' essential desire to

penetrate received ideas and ideologies. His literary criticism is at once a criticism of orthodox methods and accepted values, and a reassessment of the history of literature which also challenges dominant modes of analysis and dominant definitions. This approach is closely connected to Williams' enthusiasm for 'realism' as a literary and dramatic form, a form which attempts to portray life as it is lived. The kind of realism he encourages is, as Hall observes, realism 'in the Brechtian sense', an artistic method which aims to expose apparent reality and thus, ideally, suggest the possibility for change (Eagleton 1989: 63).

This approach to realism as an artistic form reveals the political dimension of Williams' literary criticism. Allied with his struggle for social democracy, Williams' hopes for the future are an ever-present force in his response to literature. His dedicated examination of language, and of the construction and alteration of definitions, enables him to attack the system of meanings and values generated by a capitalist society from an historical and theoretical vantage-point. In this way, Williams' literary critique is also a social critique.

Williams distinguishes between realism as an artistic method and as a certain attitude towards 'reality'. In 'A lecture on realism' (*Screen* 1977 reprinted in Williams 1990b), he identifies three definitional characteristics of realism in relation to eighteenth-century bourgeois drama:

1 as a conscious movement towards social extension;
2 as pertaining to actions taking place in the present, in the contemporary world;
3 emphasis on secular action, corresponding with the emergence of rationalism.

A similar, if not the same tripartite structure is proposed by Williams in his analysis of English naturalism. Here the three distinctions are identified as:

1 a method of 'lifelike' reproduction;
2 a philosophical position related to science, natural history, and materialism;
3 a movement involving the fusion of (1) and (2) (in Axton and Williams 1977: 203).

Although Williams acknowledges the confusion between 'naturalism' and 'realism', 'especially since later distinctions, of a comparable kind, have usually reversed the terms', the similarity of his analytical approach to both certainly does little to lessen this confusion (Axton and Williams 1977: 217). This is perhaps a difficulty which remains throughout his work.

However, in his analysis of the film, *The Big Flame*, which was made in the late 1960s, Williams adds a fourth condition – that of conscious interpretation in relation to a particular political viewpoint – clarifying the link between his own adherence to both realism and socialism. This final condition of realism is, he argues, a Brechtian technique: an intrinsic quality of Brecht's dramatic form.

This fourth definition of realism highlights the degree of subjectivity involved in the critical process, an element which Williams does not deny. Rather, it forms a significant part of his critical argument, rooted in his concern to reveal the ideological processes in forming traditional methods of literary analysis. Whereas the latter, by their structure, focus and language, tend to *disguise* the judgmental factors underlying the formal 'objective' rules of analysis, Williams argues that if: 'one pushes a judgement about some specific work back to the conditions in which the judgement was made, the result is not relativism because one also judges those conditions' (1981a: 335).

The significance of this process, for Williams, gives rise to his criticism of structuralism for preventing the possibility of judgement, deconstruction becoming the ultimate end of criticism. The political dangers inherent in any theoretical reliance upon 'judgement', however, leaves Williams' own argument exposed to the criticism of relativism.

Let us turn, specifically, to Williams' application of his theoretical arguments to his literary and dramatic critiques. A comparison between *Drama from Ibsen to Eliot* and its revised edition, *Drama from Ibsen to Brecht*, highlights the increasing significance Williams attaches to the concept of 'structure of feeling' and the way in which this idea, as both a theoretical tool and a practical experience, shapes and deepens his response to the drama.

The relation between 'structure of feeling' and 'convention' is first acknowledged by Williams in *Preface to Film*: 'All changes in the methods of an art like the drama are related, essentially, to changes in man's radical structure of feeling' (1954: 23). However, it is apparent in its early stages in *Drama from Ibsen to Eliot*. Although it is not fully articulated, Williams describes his critical approach to modern drama as one formed 'not from a theoretical inquiry, but from responses to particular dramatic works' (1964: 42). Feeling is thus situated as a central and motivating force although the fully developed concept of 'structure of feeling' is absent. In this early work, Williams' focus is upon the relationship between drama and literature, a relationship which is later replaced by the crucial connection between 'structure of feeling' and 'convention'.

In *Drama from Ibsen to Brecht*, analysis of this latter relationship is posited as the first critical task. The notion of 'convention' involves the interplay of two definitions: convention as 'tacit agreement', dramatic methods requiring audience acceptance, 'the necessity of experiment', the development of new dramatic methods corresponding with raw forms of experience. Changes of experience, or feeling – arising from social crises, technological developments, new patterns of experience, and so on – lead, in Williams' argument, to the establishment of new conventions, alterations in accepted standards. This process often involves struggle, friction and pressure, previous conventions being supported by a strong material base. However, as Williams asserts in *Culture and Society*, repeating his earlier claim made in *Preface to Film*, 'changes in convention only occur when there are radical changes in the general structure of feeling' (1961: 156).

Although his approach is clarified in *Drama from Ibsen to Brecht*, in both this and in the earlier *Drama from Ibsen to Eliot* Williams is anxious to demystify the notion of 'the tradition', to analyse developments in drama through a reassessment and revaluation of received ideas. In his analysis of the drama of Ibsen he attacks the orthodox interpretation of Ibsen's work provided by the 'Ibsenites', Shaw being a prominent voice in this group. Williams insists that, 'we should not let biography usurp the functions of criticism' (1964: 97: 1973: 66). Instead, Williams attempts to examine Ibsen's work as a totality, with new, or previously unacknowledged, connections being suggested between Ibsen's later plays and his earlier work, connections arising from the continuity of theme, form, language and dramatic imagery.

The argument for criticism as opposed to biographical details is particularly crucial for Williams' reading of Strindberg. His analysis is deliberately *non*-biographical in an attempt to displace 'orthodox' accounts of Strindberg's work. Williams focuses on the variety of dramatic methods and purpose, and the range of technical experiments, found in Strindberg's drama. Describing his approach to Strindberg's drama, Williams refers to his reaction to 'reading truly appalling "biographies of the artist", which tell you which of his wives or girlfriends is which character, which episode is transcribed into which scene, and reduce every work to the neurosis of the author' (1981a: 196). Williams accepts the criticism that by intentionally abstracting Strindberg's drama from the playwright's non-dramatic writing on politics, class, sex, society and religion he has undermined the substance of the drama itself. By adamantly rejecting the dominant biographical approach, Williams claims to have provided space 'for exploring the real conditions of dramatic practice'.

The more developed critical perspective adopted by Williams in *Drama from Ibsen to Brecht*, compared with *Drama from Ibsen to Eliot*, results in certain differences in conclusion. Of Strindberg's *The Road to Damascus*, Williams initially writes that, 'The only limitation of the work, as I see it, is a heritage of the nineteenth-century divorce of drama and literature' (1964: 132). However, the central problem later becomes 'the practical integration of word and scene' (1973: 99). What Strindberg was attempting to achieve, Williams argues, was an integration which could not be contained within the available theatrical forms, an integration awaiting the development of film. This new perspective itself corresponds with Williams' developed interest in film and television between the original and revised versions of his dramatic critique.

Whereas in his earlier book Williams argues that Strindberg never succeeded in establishing an appropriate dramatic form, his main achievement lying in isolated achievements, a more positive analysis is offered in *Drama from Ibsen to Brecht*. Here Williams regards the new conventions deployed by Strindberg as directly related to a particular 'structure of feeling'. As opposed to 'isolated successes', Williams now concludes that in Strindberg's drama, 'the power, the creation, the astonishing invention, are authentic and lasting: an achievement and unforgettable dramatic word' (1964: 140; 1973: 107).

This altered response to Strindberg's drama, relating to Williams' different critical perspective through his introduction of 'structure of feeling' as a critical tool, is also evident in his examination of Chekhov's plays. In both versions of this book Williams writes that 'One's doubts about even the best of Chekhov's plays are doubts about the strings' (1964: 149; 1973: 114). In the first version Williams then proceeds to explore the practice of self-dramatizing qualities of Chekhov's characters, concluding that his drama remains 'completely characteristic of the naturalist theatre', with Chekhov being unable to exceed the limits of naturalism and thus failing to explore the unexamined experience which is hinted at in his plays (1964: 153). In *Drama from Ibsen to Brecht*, Williams explores the same drama in a very different way, looking at the convention: 'of an explicit self-revelation, at times awkward and sentimental, at other times negotiated as satire or farce – and Chekhov's actual structure of feeling. And what we then see is an important change, from both Ibsen and Strindberg' (1973: 114).

In Chekhov's drama, Williams now observes the emergence of a new structure of feeling. What was previously regarded (from a different or less developed critical perspective) as a weakness is later viewed as an achievement. This change of outlook derives from his analysis of Chekhov's drama in relation to the concept of structure of feeling and, in turn, the relationship between this structure of feeling and the conventions available to Chekhov. Chekhov is no longer placed in 'Stanislavsky's camp, and of the camp too of the decadent naturalism' (1964: 152–3). Rather, Williams now regards Chekhov's achievement as being:

> to invent a dramatic form which contradicts most of the available conventions of dramatic production ... a writer of genius beginning to create a new dramatic form, but in ways so original and so tentative that it is in constant danger of breaking down, and another kind of art has to be invented to sustain it. It is now seen as the crisis, of the naturalist drama and theatre.
>
> (1973: 120)

In *Drama in Performance* this same crisis is described as involving a problematic disruption between drama and performance. Again this is seen as a process in which the naturalist form, here specifically the naturalist form of presentation and representation, can no longer contain or adequately express the content, style and meaning of the emerging drama. Williams' concern with the interrelation of text and performance leads to his assertion that: 'the serious and exploring drama, from Ibsen and Chekhov and Strindberg to Brecht and Beckett, was faced always with a contradiction: that what it seemed to make real, in theatrical terms, was what it wished to show as a limited reality, in dramatic terms' (1991a: 126).

Returning to the comparison between *Drama from Ibsen to Eliot* and the revised version, perhaps the most obvious change of outlook can be observed in Williams' approach to the plays of O'Casey. Whereas in the first book, analysis of O'Casey's plays is limited to a couple of pages within a chapter devoted to the drama of Synge, in *Drama from Ibsen to Brecht* Williams allocates O'Casey's work to a separate chapter in the section on 'The Irish Dramatists'. Having previously reacted 'very bitterly' to the language of O'Casey's drama, Williams now realizes that 'the real point is more complex' (1973: 165). Williams extends his previous analysis, examining the various constituents of O'Casey's plays in relation to the structure of the drama as a whole, an extension facilitated by incorporation of the concept of 'structure of feeling'.

This later analysis focuses on a problem which is significant in much of Williams' work, in particular in relation to his own fiction: that of articulation. This is one of the central motivating factors shaping Williams' changed response to O'Casey's drama. The language spoken by O'Casey's characters is no longer dismissed as 'the language of the novelette' but is now understood as the voice of 'the exposed and deprived who cannot understand what is happening to them; who can talk, within limits, in their own idiom, but then fall for an alien rhetoric' (1964: 190; 1973: 168).

Not only is Williams involved in a reassessment and revaluation of orthodox views on drama, in *Drama from Ibsen to Brecht*, he is also engaged in a reassessment of his own previous critical outlook and methodological approach. Between the two versions of this book, Williams' writing style and critical approach to drama matures, his analytical concepts acquiring greater precision and meaning. This development reflects Williams' commitment throughout his work to the nature of process. Rather than looking at the work of a specific dramatist as a settled, finished, given product, Williams examines drama in terms of a continuous, while interconnected, movement of styles, themes, methods, language and, perhaps above all, of feeling. The development of Williams' critical perspective mirrors his analytical outlook.

This development can be observed in relation to Williams' use of language. In *Drama from Ibsen to Eliot* Williams describes Synge's dramatic discourse as 'a naturalist language' (1964: 176). In the revised version, however, the term 'naturalist' is absent and instead Williams concentrates on the variations in Synge's dramatic use of this language, recognizing the importance of the relationship between language and action. This more detailed attention to language, one which, as already observed, radically changed his approach to O'Casey's drama, is a positive and necessary (in terms of Williams' altered critical perspective) addition to his former work. Language is, for Williams, an active *social* process, and a careful examination of labels attached to dramatic forms – 'naturalist', 'realist', 'expressionist', 'absurdist' – itself involves an examination of ideological processes. By analysing these descriptions themselves, 'we can go back behind the names, and make our own history, in our own terms' (1973: 382).

Alongside the concept of structure of feeling is that of community and the later notion of the 'knowable community', a concept central to Williams' contemplation of the relation, or lack of relation, between the individual and society as this is expressed through the drama. New ways of thinking about and experiencing the world give rise to changes in this relationship. Ibsen's drama, for example, displays the perceived influence of the environment upon the individual, expressed as a deterministic relationship. Strindberg's belief in certain universal *a prioris* is reflected in his depiction of the impossibility of sexual harmony. Social, cutural and historical factors inform the mode, nature and content of dramatic expression. In the same way, the dramatist is engaging with a particular audience, the significance of this arising, for Williams, with reference to a 'community of sensibility' (1964: 31):

> The artist's sensibility – his capacity for experience, his ways of thinking, feeling, and conjunction – will often be finer than that of his audience. But if his sensibility is at least of the same kind, communication is possible. Where his sensibility is of the same kind, his language and the language of his audience will be closely and organically related; the common language will be the expression of the common sensibility.
>
> (1964: 31)

Although Williams does not elaborate on this in his analysis of drama, the implications of this idea continue through the concept of structure of feeling. In *Preface to Film* he defines 'structure of feeling' as that which attempts to express 'a complex whole', to convey the totality of life as it is lived and experienced, the totality which provides material for the artist, 'only realisable through experience of the work of art itself, as a whole' (1954: 21; 22). Through the use of this concept, Williams' dramatic criticism becomes an analysis of social conditions, of social structures and the conditions of production in which writing occurs, and of the available means of communication. It is a concept which enables him to examine problems of *experience* confronting the dramatist as well as problems of form. It also allows him to expand connections *between* the various works which he studies.

In *Drama from Ibsen to Brecht* Williams provides a detailed description of his understanding of 'structure of feeling', using it as a term to convey 'the continuity of experience from a particular work, through its particular form, to its recognition as a general form, and then the relation of this general form to a period' (1973: 9). Implicit in this concept is the act of connection, embodying both the description and analysis of developments in dramatic form, these developments themselves being related to widespread movements and change. In *Drama from Ibsen to Brecht* Williams adds to his initial definition provided in *Preface to Film*, writing that:

> It is as firm and definite as 'structure' suggests, yet it is based in the deepest and often least tangible elements of our experience. It is a way of responding to a particular world which in practice is not felt as one way among others – a conscious 'way' – but is, in experience, the only way possible. Its means, its elements, are not propositions or techniques; they are embodied, related feelings. In the same sense, it is accessible to others – not by formal argument or by professional skills, on their own, but by direct experience – a form and a meaning, a feeling and a rhythm – in the work of art, the play, as a whole.
>
> (1973: 10)

Here, continuing from the initial methodology proposed in *Preface to Film*, Williams is essentially concerned with a process of overlapping movements, the interrelationship of 'structure of feeling' and 'convention', neither element being cited as a causal factor of change. It is this interrelational approach which sometimes poses problems for the comprehension of Williams' work. Yet it relates to, and arises from, Williams' attempt to capture the nature of life as it is experienced.

Williams describes his continuing concern to relate literary analysis to life as arising from his experience of analysing drama, a process in which, for him, new perspectives emerged on both drama *and* society:

> I learned something from analysing drama which seemed to me effective not only as a way of seeing certain aspects of society

but as a way of getting through to some of the fundamental
conventions which we group as society itself. These, in their turn,
make some of the problems of drama quite newly active.

(1983a: 20)

Williams' approach to literary analysis, which involves a total
overview, has similarities with Simmel's conception of society, which
views all aspects of life as structured through various forms of mutual
interaction of individuals who are themselves structured through
relationships with each other (see Frisby and Sayer 1986). Simmel's
preoccupation with the transitory nature of social life permeates
his own writing style. It can sometimes result in problems of
comprehension similar to those encountered in Williams' work.
However, in both cases, any attempt to describe processes of
movement and change is necessarily restrained by the fixed nature
of the written word. Through his continual attention to the processes
of definition and redefinition, Williams manages to convey the sense
of language as an active social process, his writing style reflecting
the ideas and concerns of its content.

Gorak, in his attempt to situate the concept of alienation as the
key to Williams' work, describes Williams' dramatic analysis as
'a body of work that freezes history into one endlessly reverberating
alienated moment' (Gorak 1988: 32). Yet through the concept of
'structure of feeling' – the very concept upon which Gorak's
criticism relies – Williams sustains a sense of continuity and
consistency, both in terms of developing interrelationships between
the works which he studies and in relation to his overall
methodological approach. The only alienation involved here seems
to arise from the rigid attempt to apply one single term (and, in
Gorak's case, an ambiguous one) as an all-pervasive and essen-
tialist description of Williams' work. Such a self-limiting approach
seems to contradict the subject-matter of Williams' work as a whole:
a wide-ranging and interdisciplinary field of analysis.

As has been emphasized throughout this chapter, Williams'
dramatic criticism and literary analysis provide a social critique,
extending beyond biographical and stylistic details to consideration of material conditions and changes in the relationship between
the individual and society. This kind of critical attention, one which
already informs *Culture and Society*, *The Long Revolution* and *Modern
Tragedy*, is illustrated by Williams' analysis of Synge's *Playboy of
the Western World*. He studies the community portrayed by Synge's

drama in relation to the social and economic conditions of Ireland
at the beginning of the twentieth century. Williams argues that the
'starved community' depicted in Synge's play:

> has at once alienated and launched its destructive and confus-
> ing fantasy. The fantastic deception is separate from them; lost
> to them; gone out into romance. It is a bitter comment on the
> poverty, which required other experience and other actions. It
> is also a bitter comment, as we now look back, on the real relation
> between the Irish drama and the Irish people of this period. What
> the writers found, in their own medium, was 'richness', but the
> richness was a function of a more pressing poverty, and this was
> at times idealised, at times compounded; in *The Playboy* faced
> but then confidently superseded: the poverty and the fantasy,
> always so closely related, seen now as bitterly nourishing each
> other; grasped and projected into an exiled orbit.
>
> (1973: 148)

This examination of social and material conditions in relation
to dramatic analysis is a reflection of Williams' conception of culture.
His understanding of 'structure of feeling' as 'an experience com-
municated in a particular form, through particular conventions',
as an existential concept which extends from the particular to the
general, incorporates the same sense of totality, of a whole way
of life, as does his description of culture as one which 'becomes
almost identical with our whole common life' (1973: 12; 1961: 249).

Returning to the comparison between *Drama from Ibsen to Eliot*
and the revised version, an important introduction to the latter is,
as the title reveals, the work of Brecht. Despite the commonly held
view of Brecht's drama as revolutionary, Williams regards it as
presenting not the means for transformation but 'modes of evasion,
necessary to protect yourself against an oppressive society' (1981a:
216). Brecht is seen as dramatizing, and thus externalizing, forms
of alienation in an already alienated world which had previously
been dramatized primarily from the inside, or internally, producing
what Williams terms a 'dramatic negative' (1973: 332).

Although he is not the final playwright to be studied, the
addition of Brecht provides a more interesting finishing point for
Williams' analysis of the development of naturalism because, unlike
Eliot, Brecht is so frequently separated from the dramatic tradition which precedes him. By demonstrating the continuity of
dramatic devices, Williams uses the apparent radical changes

and innovations introduced by Brecht to emphasize previous conventions and developments:

> Looking back from Brecht, we see the drama of the last hundred years differently: see its consciousness and its methods from the outside, in a fully critical light. We do not, because of that, at all lessen our respect: the power of the masters is what it was. But the power of this different master is conclusive. With this last shift, a particular dramatic world – that of the individual against society – is now wholly seen. Without the substance created by others, Brecht's critical epilogue – his dramatic negative – could not have been written. But now that it has been written, in two or three great plays and in a wider achievement of a powerful and unforgettable dramatic consciousness, we have to struggle to enter, as Brecht himself insisted, a new kind of world.
>
> (1973: 332)

This 'new kind of world' means, for Williams, overcoming the distinctions between individual and society, and family and environment, film and television playing a crucial role in this process. The future of a new realism, involving a political (socialist) and class (working-class) struggle, lies, for Williams, in the combination of three factors, the camera providing the central power of transformation:

1 'the more mobile dramatic forms of the camera';
2 'direct relationship with more popular audiences';
3 'development of subjunctive actions'.

(1981a: 224)

Although Williams does not dismiss the radical innovations occurring in theatre, it is the media of film and television in which he places his hopes for change. However, his analysis of literature likewise reflects his deep commitment to democratic socialism. His writing style and his continual attempt to challenge orthodox opinions are part of his political intention to extend the understanding of literature and its relationship to society. In his essay, 'Art: freedom as duty', Williams argues 'that the need for freedom in the arts is, above all, a *social* need' (1988d: 89). Viewing the arts as a material process, Williams looks at the notion of artistic freedom in relation to the freedom of society as a whole. The freedom of a writer, for Williams, is the freedom to prolong the moment at which a writer hesitates because 'the words can come all too easily' (ibid. 94). If this hesitation precipitates the writer's adoption of more difficult procedures, then linguistic innovations become possible. It is this point of hesitation, with the possibility of moving beyond it, which Williams views as 'the only kind of duty that I think writers ought in the first instance to recognise' (ibid.). This position is integral to Williams' argument for democratic socialism:

> the claim for the freedom of the artist is necessarily a claim for quite new kinds of freedom, an acknowledgement of the need for freedom for everyone in society. This sense connects with the deepest notions of an educated and self-managing democracy as the best cultural and political model, distinct from the received models with which other ideas of art have been so commonly associated.
>
> (ibid.: 89)

So Williams' attempt to challenge the literary tradition is also a political endeavour. By examining artistic processes and products in new ways, Williams suggests the possibility for alternative social formations. This approach informs *Modern Tragedy*, written between *Drama from Ibsen to Eliot* and its revised version. Here Williams attempts, in many ways, to rewrite the 'Tragic' tradition, once again situating his analysis within personal experience, his experience of tragedy as 'the life of a man driven back to silence, in an unregarded working life', and as 'the loss of connection built into a works and a city, and men and women broken by the pressure to accept this as normal, and by the deferment and corrosion of hope and desire' (1966: 13). On a wider scale, the concept of tragedy is applied to an action of war and, crucially in the context of Williams' book, to social revolution.

Modern Tragedy is an attempt to relate common experience of tragedy, or what is now frequently referred to as 'tragic', to tragic literature and theory. Williams explores historical changes in the definition of 'tragedy', arguing that 'it is to these pressures, of contemporary ideology and experience, that we must relate the idea of tragedy which is now temporarily dominant, but which is offered as at once historical and absolute' (1966: 45).

Although Williams describes the creation of *Modern Tragedy* as akin to the virgin birth (see 1981a: 211), the central idea behind the book was introduced more than a decade before its publication. In *Preface to Film*, Williams writes that if:

we seek to understand *tragedy*, we need to take a number
of particular works, which have at different times and in
different places been called tragedies, and, on a basis of the
facts of each, see how far it may be possible to generalise
about them. Even then, we should not suppose that we are
seeking to distil from these works some absolute essence called
Tragedy, which is independent of any of them. We are more
likely to do justice to the works themselves if we say that our
enquiry is into varieties of dramatic experience that have been
called tragic.

(1954: 4)

Tragedy, indeed drama as a whole, should not be analysed,
Williams argues, in relation to some notion of absolute essence;
it is a name applied to different kinds of activities, occurring at
different times and in different places. Tragedy, for Williams, is
both historically and culturally specific and this recognition is itself
a rejection of received definitions. This rejection gives rise to his
criticism of the academic separation of 'Tragedy' from ordinary,
human experience of suffering, a separation which he regards as
an ideologial distinction. In contrast to this, Williams attempts to
expose the 'radical connections' in modern tragedy 'between event
and experience and idea' (1966: 9). However, the only obvious
such connection he makes is that between tragedy and revolution.
He argues that liberalism, with its emphasis on the individual, is
especially responsible for the opposition between the concept of
tragedy and the idea of revolution. Instead, Williams replaces conceptions of a permanent human nature and a fixed social order with
his belief in the possibility of human and social transformation.
It is from this position, he argues, that the modern sense of revolution finds *its* origins. Concepts such as Fate, Destiny and Fortune,
significant to the received definition of tragedy, conflict with the
notion of revolution. For Williams, however, the dichotomy
between tragedy and revolution cannot be sustained, as revolution
involves

the inevitable working through of a deep and tragic disorder,
to which we can respond in varying ways but which will in any
case, in one way or another, work its way through our world,
as a consequence of our actions. I see revolution, that is to say,
in a tragic perspective.

(1966: 75)

Modern Tragedy is criticized by Stein for establishing its own deterministic framework, 'a tendency to equate the problem of "modern tragedy" more and more totally with the problem of "tragedy and revolution"' (Stein 1969: 187). Also criticized are Williams' writing style and his method of argument. Kermode dismisses both as 'a personally satisfying "stucture of feeling"', while Hampshire describes his own response to *Modern Tragedy* as one of 'wandering around in a circle, from the imagined social experience to the dramatic literature, and from the literature to the social experience' (Kermode 1966: 85; Hampshire 1966: 169). Both criticisms arise from Williams' use of concept of 'structure of feeling' as a critical tool. This concept is essential to Williams' analytical approach – enabling him to analyse specific issues while incorporating and implying related factors – as well as to his writing style, the precision over definitions sometimes appearing to contrast with the seemingly endless ramifications of his arguments. This can, as Hampshire suggests, result in the sensation of dizziness on the part of the reader. However, the pendulum-like movement between the literature and the social experience is an inevitable aspect of Williams' methodological approach. When writing about one, he is, as implied by the concept of 'structure of feeling', writing about the other. As he makes clear in *The Long Revolution*, 'all the acts of men compose a general reality within which both art and what we ordinarily call society are comprised' (1965: 69).

Although such an approach can give rise to difficulties – inter-relational analysis causes greater confusion than subject-specific examinations – one significant outcome, itself enabled by such an approach, arises from Williams' concern with language. Williams' analysis of tragedy involves consideration of the way in which linguistic separations evolve, separations which, in turn, affect our consciousness, actions and beliefs. Through his study of tragedy – looking at developments in 'tragic' drama and literature while continually questioning dominant interpretations of form, content and concept – Williams attempts to redefine standard academic usage of the term and thus suggest connections which have been lost or hidden. The cold war is, from this perspective, placed in a 'tragic' light, with Williams describing the nuclear arms race and the nuclear 'deterrent' as 'a tragic illusion' (1966: p. 79). The whole concept of tragedy is, for Williams, a predominant characteristic of our contemporary world, although here the name changes to that of revolution:

The tragic action, in its deepest sense, is not the confirmation of disorder, but its experience, its comprehension and its resolution. In our own time, this action is general, and its common name is revolution. We have to see the evil and the suffering, in the factual disorder that makes revolution necessary, and in the disordered struggle against the disorder. We have to recognise this suffering in a close and immediate experience, and not cover it with names. But we follow the whole action. . . . We make the connections, because that is the action of tragedy, and what we learn in suffering is again revolution, because we acknowledge others as men and any such acknowledgement is the beginning of struggle, as the continuing reality of our lives. Then to see revolution in this tragic perspective is the only way to maintain it.

(1966: 83–4)

Rather than attempting, as Kermode asserts, 'to relate our fictions of action or suffering to a systematic revolutionary view of history' (Kermode 1966; 85), Williams' main concern is to restore the interrelated concepts of tragedy and revolution to the realm of the ordinary, in a way that can relate to our experience of the modern world. The importance of this is, we think, the attempt to uncover the underlying ideological processes informing traditional analysis of tragedy and the reintegration of tragedy and experience.

In *Modern Tragedy*, Williams explores the development of tragedy in both the drama and the novel, observing changes in form and, interlinked with this, in 'structures of feeling'. During this process Williams recognizes continuities between the works he examines. He also focuses on developments from a specific angle: the changing relations between the individual and society as these are reflected in literature, and the view of human nature depicted by writers at particular times and within specific social conditions. This perspective is integrally related to the whole concept of 'structure of feeling'.

Looking at the work of Sartre and Camus – the former being described as a 'tragic humanist', the latter as a 'tragic revolutionary' – Williams argues that common to both is a lost sense of a common process or a common life (1966: 188). In relation to this, Williams views their work as an analogue of individualism, as: 'the latest and most notable struggle within the deadlock which has, historically, taken over our consciousness. The conclusions they draw, whether of revolt or revolution, are convincing only to the extent that one's own mind remains within the deadlock itself' (1966: 189).

The entire thrust of *Modern Tragedy* negates such a literary deadlock. In the very act of examination, Williams connects themes, expression, form and 'structures of feeling' within and between different literary works. In this he uses humanism as a sort of yardstick against which to measure any developments.

Williams' historico-humanist reading of literature is influenced by his reading of Brecht, with Brecht's desire to create 'complex seeing' through the use of *Verfremdungseffekte* (alienation techniques), bearing close similarities with the intent behind Williams' 'structure of feeling'. For Brecht, the distinguishing feature of *Verfremdung* is the integration of form and content. The same could be said of Williams' 'structure of feeling'. Conversely, it is the overtly Brechtian tone of Williams' *Koba*, inserted at the end of *Modern Tragedy*, which serves to weaken this play.

Koba is essentially a dramatization of the Stalinist 'tragedy', Joseph being the central protagonist. The two main concepts of *Modern Tragedy* – tragedy and revolution – are brought together in this play, as if a creative illustration of theory in practice. Similar keywords and ideas to those found in Williams' novels are present in *Koba* – 'generation', 'settlement', 'pressures', 'community' – but the language and tone of the play bear such marked resemblance to Brecht's recognizable style, particularly that of his *Lehrstücke* that Williams' drama remains uncomfortably like a Brechtian pastiche, ironic given Brecht's own frequent use of pastiche. The sharp, clipped, rhetorical prose – 'It is the voice of the party, which can never be broken. It is the voice of the people, which can never be mastered' – and the use of poetry are too obviously Brechtian for any originality of thought or feeling to be successfully conveyed (1966: 252).

Returning to the central text, Williams summarizes his main argument in *Modern Tragedy* as focusing 'on the deep relations between the actual forms of our history and the tragic forms within which these are perceived, articulated and reshaped' (1989d: 95–6). In his essay 'Afterword to *Modern Tragedy*', Williams writes of what he describes as a strengthening of one of these 'tragic forms' which, he argues, has become temporarily dominant and, at times, overwhelming. This arises from the sense of 'a widespread loss of the future', something he sees as being prevalent during the years following his completion of *Modern Tragedy* (ibid.: 96). This 'tragic' structure of feeling is viewed as a reflection of a dying social order (capitalism) and a dying class (the capitalist class), despite the divergent and alternative responses emerging within this structure of feeling.

Williams observes a theoretical distinction between previous forms of subjective expressionism, the work of Strindberg in particular, in which the conditions giving rise to struggle and conflict were seen as inevitable and unalterable, and a new form of radical private tragedy in which connections are explored between destructive personal or sexual conflicts and social conditions which are now seen as capable of change. This new form, and new perception, of tragedy has, Williams argues, been expressed in a variety of ways, all of which reflect a sense of shock and loss of hope, feelings which arise alongside the disintegration of an established social order.

Shock, loss and disturbance are, in the early work of Brecht and the 'theatre of cruelty', converted into conscious abuse, attacks, insults, in an attempt to expose that which is being attacked. Beckett's work, in Williams' view, involves an even deeper form of degradation in which the consistent reduction and depravity of all represented forms of human life has led to the emergence of a new contemporary form. The total breakdown of communication – the theme and dramatic method of Beckett's later work – completes, Williams argues, 'more deeply than could at all have been foreseen, the long and powerful development of bourgeois tragedy' (1989a: 101). However, Williams insists that Beckett's dramatic form is not the dominant one. The predominant dramatic form of our contemporary existence is not rooted in notions of a public world or of a private feeling but in our inability to communicate:

> People still assemble or are assembled, meet or collide. A given collectivity is in this way taken for granted. But it is a collectivity that is only negatively marked. A common condition is unsuspected, intimated, glanced at but never grasped. The means of sociability and of positive relationship are fundamentally discounted, but not as actual isolation; merely as effective isolation within what is still unavoidable physical presence. This group or that group exists, but always negatively. There is no effective identity either within it or outside it. And this is not some

invitation; it is a worked form. The skills of dramatic composi-
tion, within this dominant form, are now employed to render,
that is to say produce, a negative incommunicability which is
then presented to be overheard.

(ibid.)

The inability to communicate is, as it must be for Williams, the
real end of hope. Our present situation becomes incapable of change
if the very means of change have themselves been absorbed by a
formal–dramatic and social form being firmly interlinked – which
in itself denies any possible future. The dominant dramatic form,
Williams insists, is an ideological distortion, involving a complete
rejection of the historical and continued diversity of tragic theory
and practice. He traces the origins of this new and pervasive
structure of feeling to the Russian Revolution, maintaining that
the Stalinist era, crushing the original aspirations behind the political
actions, led to stasis. Including his own experience of this, Williams
argues that the dynamics of a long and complex history, and recognition of current struggles elsewhere, were forgotten in the focus
on this historical era. To break this perceived deadlock, Williams
proposes the dramatic (in every sense of the word) connection
of past, present and future struggles, a form 'which follows
the whole action and which is thus again profoundly dynamic'
(ibid. 105).

Communication and community are central components of this
proposed form and they remain predominant and interrelated
concepts throughout all of Williams' work. This can sometimes be
done in unexpected ways as in his discussion of Joyce's *Ulysses*
(1922), which, significantly, he sees as a realist novel. Joyce had
created new structures of language which made possible new ways
of seeing the city. Williams comments:

But what must also be said, as we see this new structure, is that
the most deeply known human community is language itself.
And it is a paradox that in *Ulysses*, through its patterns of loss
and frustration, there is not only search but discovery: of an
ordinary language, heard more clearly than anywhere in the
realist novel before it; a positive flow of that wider human speech
which has been screened and strained by the prevailing social
conventions: conventions of separation, reduction, in the actual
history. The greatness of *Ulysses* is this community of speech.

(Williams 1984: 167–8)

We may compare this with a passage in *The Long Revolution*, where communication and community are seen as synonymous:

> Since our way of seeing is literally our way of living, the process of communication is in fact the process of community: the sharing of common meanings, and thence common activities and purposes; the offering, reception and comparison of new meanings, leading to the tensions and achievements of growth and change.
>
> (1965: 38–9)

Community, and in particular the concept of the 'knowable community', occupies a central position in *The English Novel from Dickens to Lawrence*. Here, Williams traces the development of 'the novel and community; the novel and the city; the novel of "acting, thinking, speaking" man' (1984: 168). During the 1840s, Williams maintains, the whole concept of 'community', in terms of the way in which people experienced it, defined it and related to it, became increasingly uncertain. This resulted in 'the crisis of the knowable community' (ibid.: 16). By *naming* this crisis, Williams argues, it becomes possible to examine its relationship to changes articulated in the novel. Once again Williams is reassessing the literary 'tradition', restoring several writers rejected by Leavis, in particular the work of Hardy, which becomes Williams' central focus in his attempt to undermine 'orthodox' analysis.

Williams cites several significant factors which contributed to the 'crisis of the knowable community', such as the industrial revolution, urban expansion, the institutionalization of urban culture, legislation on public health and factory working hours. During the 1840s the novel became the major form in English literature, but:

> It was not the society or its crisis which produced the novels. The society and the novels – our general names for those myriad and related primary activities – came from a pressing and varied experience which was not yet history; which had no new forms, no significant moments, until these were made and given by direct human actions.
>
> (1984: 11)

The 'crisis of the knowable community' is understood not simply as a result of socioeconomic changes but arises at the level of consciousness and at this point, Williams asserts, the problem 'interlocks with the method derived from the new historical consciousness; the new sense of society as not only the bearer but the active creator, the active destroyer, of the values of persons and relationships' (ibid.: 26). It is this perspective which informs Williams' analysts of the English novel from Dickens to Lawrence. It is also this double correspondence – an increasing uncertainty about the nature of community being experienced and expressed alongside a changing understanding of society – which is implicit in his understanding of the 'crisis of the knowable community'.

O'Connor maintains that the concept of 'knowable community' 'describes a strategy in discourse rather than immediate experience of an "organic" community' (O'Connor 1989a: 68). While methods of discourse are unquestionably involved, with the notion of community relying on particular form(s) of communication(s) for its very existence as such, the concept of 'knowable community' does embrace immediate experience, as is perhaps most clearly revealed in Williams' fiction. The 'knowable community' concerns perceptions of self and others, ways of comprehending one's place within a social context. Alongside this, the concept embodies a sense of relationships – between people, between people and place, and between people and possibilities. Thus, immediate experience is implicit in Williams' concept of the 'knowable community', both words arising from and being rooted in, available experience. As Williams makes clear, 'Those novels which can attain an effective range of social *experience* by sufficiently manifest immediate relations possess a knowable community' (1981a: 247).

Williams employs the idea of a 'knowable community' in relation to a specific form of narrative, referring to the 'knowable community' of the novel as 'that form predicated on the general reliability of direct observation and disclosure and therefore on a narrative completed in time' (1987; 4). In this essay, he observes the changes occurring between the novels of Austen, Eliot and Hardy, in terms of what he describes as an extension of the 'knowable community'. Whereas Austen's work focuses on a particular social class, Eliot's writing includes craftsmen and small tenant farmers, while Hardy's novels extend to a rural poor who are presented not as an undifferentiated stereotype but as sharply individualized people. This extension, with the novel beginning to depict and incorporate a variety of social classes, led to increasing pressure on the formal structure of the novel. Williams argues that, corresponding with this extension of the 'knowable community', the more clearly and disturbingly it was seen as divided, even conflictual, and the narrative was then not only a matter of recognition and disclosure but of a necessary history: a history producing indifference as well as cruelty; exploitation as well as an overseeing, overlooking patronage; separation, real separation as well as the physically and immediately knowable.

(1987: 5)

The extended knowledge acquired by different communities, and by individuals in these communities, and the increasing recognition of a wider social order which both directly and indirectly shapes and influences communities and individuals, led to the idea of given, knowable relationships becoming problematic as, too, did the actual social basis in which such relationships were formed. Thus the experience of change, which Williams examines through the concept of 'knowable community', is an experience which, he argues, is visible in the form and structure of the novel.

Williams uses his literary analysis as a means of examining culture, his focus being on the 'radical culture' and the 'anonymous culture', areas largely ignored in academic work. In his study of Dickens he explicitly rejects the critical criteria established for analysing novels belonging to the so-called 'great tradition'. Instead, Williams insists upon the *newness* of Dickens' work, in which a new kind of reality is realized: the reality of a new kind of city. However, in *Politics and Letters* Williams is criticized for giving credit to Dickens' abstraction of a non-social human quality and thus contradicting his emphasis on the interconnection of the personal and the social. Williams' response reveals the predominant concern throughout his work: his concerted effort to analyse and reveal the oppositional elements to, and in, a dominant culture:

> My present position, which I develop in *Marxism and Literature*, is that however dominant a social system may be, the very meaning of its domination involves a limitation or selection of the activities it covers, so that by definition it cannot exhaust all experience, which therefore always potentially contains space for alternative acts and alternative intentions which are not yet articulated as a social institution or even project.

(1981a: 252)

Although not denying the criticism of his approach, Williams acknowledges a difficulty he has encountered in his own literary analysis: how to define and deal with forces present in a writer's work which do not neatly coincide with a recognizable calculus of socioeconomic factors; how to treat such forces in a non-metaphysical and rational manner. For Williams: 'the problem of these non-traceable, or not immediately traceable, liberating impulses is in the most emphatic sense not only a question of literary analysis, but a very urgent contemporary political issue' (ibid.: 256).

This relationship between literary analysis and politics is implicit to both the concept of 'structure of feeling' and to that of the 'knowable community'. Both are used as tools of literary analysis which enable any critical examination to incorporate some form of social critique. Both are also conceptual methods for examining phenomena in process as well as in totality and this is further emphasized by Williams' reference to 'the voice'. This term, employed in his analysis of changes in the novel, creates a simultaneous sense of narrative and writing style, and of the specific consciousness apparent in the novel.

Williams' interest in the work of Hardy is rooted in Williams' sense of a shared personal experience. Yet it is a personal experience which is extended to that of a common condition. Referring to Hardy, Williams asserts that:

> He writes more consistently and more deeply than any of our novelists about something that is still very close to us wherever we may be living: something that can be put, in abstraction, as the problem of the relation between customary and educated life; between customary and educated feeling and thought. This is the problem we already saw in George Eliot and that we shall see again in Lawrence: It is the ground of their significant connection.
>
> ((1984: 97)

This observed experience of conflict is regarded by Williams as specific to a generation as well as being relative to more general changes in Britain, increasing mobility leading to new crises at both the social and individual level.

Williams' analysis of Hardy's work provides a clear example of his overall approach to literary and dramatic criticism. He rejects what he views as dominant social stereotypes of Hardy's work: descriptions of his novels as 'regional' or 'rural'. In contrast, Williams argues that the significant pattern of Hardy's novels:

is the relation between the changing nature of country living, determined as much by its own pressures as by pressures from 'outside', and one or more characters who have become in some degree separated from it yet who remain by some tie of family inescapably involved.

(ibid.: 102)

The feeling of 'pressure' which, as will be further examined, is a significant force in Williams' own fiction, pervades his analysis of Hardy's work, stemming from his understanding of the novelist as 'both the educated observer and the passionate participant, in a period of general and radical change' (ibid.: 106). Despite the pressures of mobility experienced by Hardy, his major novels are rooted in the ordinary processes of life and work, and it is this which Williams heralds as Hardy's most significant achievement. For it is this 'ordinary' culture which Williams is himself attempting to restore through his revaluation of the literary 'tradition'.

Throughout his analysis of the development of the novel from Dickens to Lawrence, Williams is attempting to 'connect and continue' (ibid.: 185). The process of making connections is integral both to his revaluation of received ideas and to his understanding of this 'tradition' itself:

It isn't something handed down. What's handed down with some weight is an establishment, and in every creative generation one of the first jobs is getting rid of those connections and then of course finding others.

(ibid.: 185–6)

The overall importance of this process is integrally related to Williams' concern to promote an awareness, an historical awareness, of our social experience and social inheritance. There are obviously similarities between this kind of project and the implications of Marx's 'demystification process'. Paradoxically, however, in Williams' analysis of the development of the novel in relation to the 'knowable community' a considerable *lack* of alienation is observed, with received definitions often being cited as *the* great alienator. Further, Williams criticizes the widespread dichotomy, often inherent in Marxist theory, between the public and the private. The idea is that the novel is, or should be, concerned with the private because it is a product of individual creativity is not one to which Williams adheres. The very concepts of the 'knowable community' and, indeed, of 'structure of feeling', are, as analytical and methodological tools, themselves contradictions of this public/private dichotomy.

Reintegration of processes frequently regarded as separate is the focus of *Drama in Performance*, the central concern being to establish an interrelationship between literature and theatre. The theme of drama in performance is considered in three ways:

1 in terms of the development of a method of dramatic analysis;
2 in relation to accounts of particular performances;
3 in terms of the consequences of general ideas concerning the relationship between dramatic text and performance for dramatic theory.

Once again, the underlying implications of 'structure of feeling' are asserted, with Williams arguing that 'Drama is always so central an element of the life of a society that a change in its methods cannot be isolated from much wider changes' (1991a: 171).

This continued insistence on the interrelationship of drama and society is, for Williams, reinforced by the development of film and television as popular and widespread forms of communication. Indeed:

> The slice of life, once a project of naturalist drama, is now a voluntary, habitual, internal rhythm: the flow of action and acting, of representation and performance, raised to a new convention, that of a basic need.
>
> (1991b: 13)

This interconnected perspective, which Williams employs in his analysis of contemporary drama, linguistic formations, social structures and consciousness, arises from, and is articulated through, his concept of 'structure of feeling'. This central concept informs and constitutes his analytical and methodological approach to drama and literature, an approach which in itself incorporates a sociocultural, historical and political critique. This is made clear in his definition of 'structure of feeling' as concerned with:

> meanings and values as they are actively lived and felt, and the relations between these and formal and systematic beliefs are in practice variable (including historically variable), over a range from formal assent with private dissent to the more nuanced

interaction between selected and interpreted beliefs and acted and justified experiences.

(1977: 132)

The public and the private, the personal and the political, the individual and the general, are forever interwoven in Williams' literary and dramatic analysis. Although film and television displaced the novel from its previously unchallenged position of artistic dominance, Williams maintains that the development of the novel from Dickens to Lawrence still provides us with the strongest connections, the 'deepest sense of the problematic, in community and identity, in knowable relationships' (1984: 191). It is this central problematic which structures Williams' own fiction. In his fiction, the keywords which characterize his literary and dramatic analysis – structure of feeling, connection, community, pressure – remain central to the content, form, structure and expression. It is through his fiction that the practical implications of these theoretical concepts are most clearly revealed.

Chapter 7

The trilogy

Where they were standing, looking out, was on a border in the earth and in history: to north and west the great expanses of a pastoral country, where the iron and coal had been worked, the crowded valleys, the new industries, in their turn becoming old. There had been a contrast, once, clearly seen on this border, between an old way of life and a new, as between a father living in his old and known ways and a son living differently, in a new occupation and with a new cast of mind. But what was visible now was that both were old.

The pressure for renewal, inside them had to make its way through a land and through lives that had been deeply shaped, deeply committed, by a present that was always moving, inexorably, into the past. And those moments of the present that could connect to a future were then hard to grasp, hard to hold to, hard to bring together to a rhythm, to a movement, to the necessary shape of a quite different life. What could now be heard, momentarily, as this actual movement, had conditions of time, of growth, quite different from the conditions of any single life, or of any father and son.

(Williams 1988c: 206–7)

Starting, paradoxically, at the end of Williams' trilogy, the above paragraph captures the 'structures of feeling' arising throughout the three novels. It contains the key words, images, themes and ideas of the trilogy as a whole. 'Border', 'an old way of life and a new', 'pressure', 'past', 'present', 'future', 'connect', 'father and son' – it is these interrelated concepts which become the continuing focus of attention in Williams' fiction, their thematic predominance shaping his approach to both the structure and language of his work.

Williams discusses his own approach to fiction in his essay 'The tenses of the imagination'. Here he analyses different interpretations of, and values attributed to, the concept of the imagination, a concept which has, he writes, 'a structure, at once grammatical and historical, in the tenses of past, present and future' (1991b: 259). For Williams, these tenses provide the greatest challenge to both writer and reader, involving, for both, an examination of contemporary structures of feeling alongside possibilities for discovering the new. It is these three tenses which form the structure of Williams' trilogy and, in this way, his fiction can be understood as theory in practice. His creative writing reflects his theoretical response to literature, and this relationship is continually explored both throughout this chapter and in the later Chapter 6; which is devoted to Williams' analysis of literature and drama.

From the outset, a series of interrelated connections can be observed as central to Williams' trilogy, connections which arise at both the thematic and the structural level. It is these connections or relationships which contribute to the recognizable 'structure of feeling' arising from the trilogy as a whole and which form the focus of our analysis of the three novels. The central connections can be understood as those:

1 between the past, present and future;
2 between memories and current experience/feelings;
3 between generations;
4 between the child and the adult;
5 between the individual and the social;
6 concerning language and communication.

Analysing these also clarifies, and is clarified by, the concept of 'structure of feeling', thus re-establishing its conceptual predominance within Williams' methodology. It is a concept which, as a theoretical and practical tool, embodies a sense of the past, present and future, so vital to the themes, structure and mood of Williams' trilogy, indeed to *all* of his fiction.

'Structure of feeling' is a term which Williams employs to describe process and product, individual and general, the new and the old, the concrete and the fluid. Eagleton describes this concept as mediating, 'between an historical set of social relations, the general cultural and ideological modes appropriate to them, and the specific forms of subjectivity (embodied not least in artefacts) in which such modes are lived out' (Eagleton 1984: 110). From this perspective, 'structure of feeling' both describes and analyses the kinds of connection visible throughout Williams' fiction.

Rooted in the relationship between the individual and the social, a relationship Williams perceives as emerging out of continual interaction, 'structure of feeling', as a sociohistorical description and development, is integral to his understanding of 'community'. A sense of community pervades all of Williams' work, fact and fiction, with his insistence upon the influential, if not deterministic, position of the social, political and economic environment in terms of individual development. The significance of community, at both a personal and political level, and the related consequences of change and disintegration, are central areas of exploration in Williams' fiction.

Fundamental to Williams' understanding of community is the process of communication by which interaction becomes possible. Their interrelationship forms the basis of his cultural analysis in *The Long Revolution*, in which he insists upon 'the process of communication' as 'the process of community' (1966: 38–9). This interrelationship, which is both implicit to his concept of 'structure of feeling' and is explored throughout his cultural and literary analysis, becomes a thematic and linguistic focus in Williams' fiction.

Returning to the three tenses perceived by Williams as fundamental to imaginative creativity – the characters of the trilogy, their relationships to each other and to their environment, the thematic interests interlinked with the characters' lives, thoughts and experience, the imagery, writing style and setting of the novels, are combined to create the sense of an interconnected, and almost coexisting, past, present and future. Williams' characters speak and, more importantly, *feel*, these different tenses and this is often described as a pressure (one of the keywords in the trilogy) or a 'pull'. As Matthew Price remarks, 'I feel the pull of the past so strongly, but I think there's something else that belongs to this country: a pure idea, a pure passion, for a different world' (Williams 1988c: 98).

As with Matthew, the awareness and experience of the continued tension between past, present and future often leads Williams' characters towards a new way of seeing and/or feeling, resulting in the familiar appearing strange or the strange becoming familiar. In *Border Country*, the separation between Matthew, as an adult now distanced from Wales, and Wales, as the country of his birth and upbringing, is at the heart of this disparity between the unfamiliar and the known. When Matthew returns to Wales this incongruity is both expressed and resolved, the resolution involving a realization of both past and present. Waiting to board a train to Glynmawr, Matthew realizes that:

> It was no longer a crowd that he saw, but the hurrying, actual people. He went slowly down the steps, watching the people who passed him. It was as if, for the first time, he was able to know them as himself, and this was like a change in the weight of his body, a deep flowing back of energy. He was feeling the recovery of a childhood which at the moment of recovery was a child's experience no more, but a living connexion between memory and substance.
>
> (1988c: 317)

This connection between 'memory and substance', or between the past and the present, is central to the structure and plot of *Border Country*. Focusing on Matthew's return to his home country, this novel is constructed as a process of recollection, resulting in a fusion of the past and the present. The use of flashback, either (as in the above example) in the form of a personal experience or (as in the overall structure of the book) as an account of the past accompanying the description of the present, provides Williams with a device by which to continually connect his contemporary milieu with its historical origins. The use of flashback enables him to focus emphatically upon those tenses which he regards as central to the creative process and, simultaneously, to extend the reality of his fictional characters. This extension further corresponds with Williams' theoretical insistence on historical analysis as the basis for any examination of the present and the future.

Border Country is a novel formed out of the continuous movement of past and present, both having implications for the future, a future which is here suggested and then more fully explored throughout the trilogy as a whole. This movement is articulated by Matthew's dying father, Harry, telling his son:

> I get it clear, Will. Then it goes, of a sudden. Only the clear isn't what I started with. You could say the dream isn't real at all. Bringing together things you didn't know were there. . . . You get these connexions.
>
> (Williams 1988a: 318)

These sentiments reflect the structure of the novel, Williams' writing moving between the past and the present, following the fluctuating process of his characters' memories and feelings. Also implied is the effort involved in making connections, the problematic nature of fusing seemingly disparate elements. This difficulty confronts both the theoretician and the writer as well as posing problems in the everyday world. It is certainly inherent to the utility and comprehension of 'structure of feeling', given the multifarious ramifications of this concept. In this sense, Williams' characters are representative of a struggle which Williams views as an arduous, yet necessary, factor of human life: the task of making connections.

In *Border Country* the interrelationship of the first four connections outlined on p. 140 can be observed both through the character of Matthew and through this character's relationship with his father. Indeed, the represented father/son relationship bears a striking resemblance to Williams' interpretation of Arthur Miller's *All My Sons*. Williams observes that:

> In both father and son there are the roots of guilt, and yet ultimately they stand together as men – the father both a model and a rejected ideal; the son both an idea and a relative failure. But the model, the rejection, the idea and the failure are all terms of growth, and the balance that can be struck is a very deep understanding of relatedness and brotherhood.
>
> (Williams 1973: 309)

Matthew's return to Wales involves a contradiction between memory and present experience, itself arising alongside his growth from child to adult, with his father's imminent death reinforcing the distance and simultaneous intimacy between the past and the present. Wales, as the setting for both the past and the present, is obviously central to this process of recollection and reassessment. As the social location of this novel, Wales thus becomes the symbolic and represented lived reality of the relationship between the individual and the social milieu.

Wales provides Williams with the basis from which to explore his interconnected thematic interests: community; self-identity; generation movements; alienation; work; the nature and consequences of industrialization. As observed in the previous chapter, the problematic status of the 'knowable community' is central to *The English Novel from Dickens to Lawrence*. Here it is perceived as corresponding with changing social relations, altering familiar patterns of communal life and resulting in 'the crisis of the knowable community' (1984: 16). This, for Williams, is ultimately a crisis of consciousness and it is this level which finds expression in his fiction.

Detachment and separation inform Matthew's response to his home country. His experience simultaneously emphasizes the interrelationship of community and communication:

> he heard the separate language in his mind, the words of his ordinary thinking. He was trained to detachment: the language itself consistently abstracting and generalising, supported him in this. And the detachment was real in another way. He felt, in this house, both a child and a stranger. He could not speak as either; could not really speak as himself at all, but only in the terms that this pattern offered. At the same time, and quite physically, the actual crisis took its course.
>
> (1988a: 83)

The physical distance between Matthew and his home community here becomes a linguistic separation, which is further highlighted by his very name: 'Always, when he had lived here, he had been Will, though his registered name was Matthew, and he had used this invariably since he had gone away' (ibid.: 14). This duplicity mirrors Williams' personal experience; he adopted the name Raymond in place of Jim when he reached university. As he remarks, 'The two names in the novel, and in my own experience, point up the problem of being two persons to know, and of negotiating between two different worlds' (1981a: 283). The fictional representation of the Will/Matthew dichotomy, one rooted in Matthew's troubled sense of self-identity, reflects Williams' own experience of the related problematic between identity and community, between the individual and the social.

Aware of the distance between himself and his home country, Matthew resents this isolation. For him, it is a consequence of generation changes; he insists that:

> a part of a whole generation has had this. A personal father, and that is one clear issue. But a father is more than a person, he's in fact a society, the thing you grow up into. For us, perhaps, that is the way to put it. We've been moved and grown into a different society. We keep the relationship, but we don't take over the work. We have, you might say, a personal

father but no social father. What they offer us, where we go, we reject.

(1988a: 281–2)

From this example we see the way in which Williams attempts to connect the theme of generation movement with the relationship between the father and the son, itself a cyclical representation of that between the child and the adult, and one extended to the association between the individual – the 'personal father' – and society – the 'social father'. These connections are established throughout Williams' fiction with the political/public sphere continually impinging upon the lives of his characters.

In *Border Country*, the General Strike provides the crucial illustration of this process. Williams portrays the polarization of the community that results from positions adopted towards strike action. Morgan Rosser, a lifelong friend of Matthew's father, is most clearly affected by the miners' eventual defeat and this is expressed in relation to his sense of identity as well as his communal affinities. For Rosser:

A struggle had been lost; a common effort had failed. And it was not only the failure that broke him, but the insight that this gave, or seemed to give, into the real nature of society. . . . He had lived in his ideas of the future, while these had seemed in any way probable, and they had seemed probable until now. And a man could bear to lose, but the sudden conviction that there was nothing to win – that the talk of winning was no more than talk, and collapsed when the real world asserted itself – this, deeply, was a loss of his bearings, a change in the whole structure of his life.

(1988a: 153)

However, despite his initial fears of its capitalistic overtones, Morgan establishes himself as a local entrepreneur, his new position representing the gradual encroachment of external factors upon the small Welsh villages. This symbolizes the increasing recognition of a wider social life. Depicting this expansion at a personal level, Williams employs the same character to articulate its implications for the tight-knit Welsh communities, warning that:

what they don't realise is there's far stronger things, not like people at all, breaking in from the outside. If a man digs hard enough he'll eat: that's all they see of it. But a miner digs, just as hard, and it isn't the same. It isn't just what they grow, but what happens out there, places they've never seen and know nothing about.

(ibid.: 180)

Despite such foresight, Morgan's socialist ideals are contradicted by his entrepreneurial status and this juxtaposition is contrasted with Harry's authenticity. This authenticity is expressed by Morgan as a consistency between self, thought and deed; he regards Harry as an example of connective realization:

He took his own feelings and he built things from them. He lived direct, never by any other standard at all. . . . What we talk about, Will, he's lived. It all depends on a mind to it, a society or anything else. And the mind we're making isn't the society we want, though we still say we want it. The mind he's got is to the things we say really matter. We say it, and run off in the opposite direction.

(ibid.: 287–8)

This distinction between life as it is lived and life as 'talked about' is again related to the problematic nature of communication, which, in Williams' fiction, is expressed as the disconnection of the feeling from the word. Feeling as thought is an image central to his characterization. His characters' speech patterns frequently imply their struggle to articulate emotion. This concern with the nature of communication and the analysis of language, found throughout Williams' work, provides him with a basis for a social critique. In his essay, 'You're a Marxist, aren't you?' (Williams 1989c: 65–76), Williams argues that in order to break free from the dominant definitions asserted by capitalist society, new relationships must be grasped, in particular the connections between the political and the economic; the cultural and the educational; and formations of feeling and relationship. In a system constructed by separation, such connections, Williams maintains, remain hidden.

In *Border Country* Williams portrays the struggle to retain these connections through his characters. Throughout the novel, this experience is predominantly expressed as a linguistic dilemma, arising from a discontinuity between the feeling and the word. A sense of desperation is experienced by Matthew following the death of his grandfather. He asks himself:

when will the voice come? When, to take away this weight, will the feeling rise where it can be seen? We can stand and sing on the formal occasions, but now, when the pressure is desperate, we cannot even speak. The house is quiet, the patch quiet. And the valley quite still, the mountains dark. When will the cry come? Let it come now, let the voice come. In silence now, taking the strain, we risk being broken. Let the cry come, let the son cry.

(1988a: 260)

This need 'to find the voice' relates to Williams' theoretical and political concern with notions of commitment and alignment, positions which, he maintains, are integral aspects of the writing process. Examining the historical development of the concept of 'commitment', Williams argues that alignment precedes any form of commitment. Indeed, 'born into a social situation with all its specific perspectives, and into a language, the writer begins by being aligned' (1989c: 86). Williams' search for 'the voice' corresponds with an unmasking of deep-rooted ideologial processes, as he argues for the need to become 'conscious of our own real alignments' (ibid.). Williams' expressed commitment is to discover 'the sound of that voice which, in speaking as itself, is speaking necessarily, for more than itself' (ibid.: 87).

Through Williams' fiction, certain unvoiced emotions *are* articulated – with difficulty, with hesitation – and this in itself enables him to express and develop those relationships which he regards as crucial to any process of social change. This is ignored by Pinkney, who argues that the literary form adopted by Williams negates the author's political perspectives. Pinkney maintains that: 'In *Border Country* the formal structure of the novel is exactly congruent with the structure of the political defeat at the book's heart – to the point, indeed, where one is inclined to posit causal relations between them' (in Eagleton 1989: 25).

For Pinkney, this novel illustrates the failure of realism as a means of extension or transformation. Yet both processes are depicted in *Border Country*, as crucial aspects of individual and social experience. Further, as the beginning of Williams' trilogy, this novel forms the first stage in a sequence which, both conceptually and through narrative, reaches towards the future. Focusing on the past and its consequences in the present, *Border Country* contains the seeds of possible change.

Criticizing Williams' commitment to realism, Pinkney argues that, as an artistic form, it necessarily excludes 'the *desire* of the individual socialist writer' (in Eagleton 1989: 25). For Pinkney,

Williams' failure adequately to reinstate the definitional terms of realism foreshadows the resulting failure of his novels. Rooted in the realistic mode, they are restricted by formal parameters.

Disputing Williams' attempt to redefine realism, Pinkney's criticism undermines the interrelationship of Williams' theoretical practice and its implications for his creative writing. Although, in his later book, Pinkney makes a valid attempt to analyse Williams' fiction 'precisely as *novels* by George Eliot or Italo Calvino' (Pinkney 1991: 14), this similarly serves to leave Williams' fiction lying fragmented on the postmodernist bookshelf.

Throughout his literary analysis Williams distinguishes between 'the naturalist form' and 'the naturalist habit' (1973: 191) and, similarly, between realism as a particular artistic method and as a recognizable attitude towards reality (see Williams 1990b: 226–39). Indeed, in *Preface to Film* Williams argues for the understanding of realism as a critical term to refer to the representation of psychological reality:

> *Realism*, in this sense, is being used to describe the author's conception of his theme, and the result in the minds of his audience, and cannnot refer, in any definitive way, to the particular means by which the experience has been com-municated from the one to the other.
>
> (1954: 31)

Taken as a whole, Williams' understanding of, and analytical approach to, naturalism and realism involves a reinterpretation of their established definitional status. By so doing, Williams establishes an interrelationship between literary forms as conventional practices and as illustrations of a particular 'structure of feeling'. If, as he maintains, the underlying consciousness cannot be defined by the *means* of expression adopted by the artist, then, correspondingly, his own realistic writing style does not determine the *feelings* that are being expressed.

Pinkney's observations on the futurist qualities of Williams' work seem to contradict his earlier criticism of Williams' commitment to realism:

> there seems in Williams to be an inheritance from futurism itself – though he remains wary of the epithet, which for him denotes an abstract utopianism ungrounded in the actual social tendencies of the present. Only, the Futurist celebration of speed, mobility,

power, technology is in him invested, not in the forces or sites
of production, not in their dynamic products ... but rather in
the democratic process itself – in its complex circuits of referral,
its speed of recall, its sophisticated communications technology.
(Eagleton 1989: 31)

From this perspective, Williams' fictional framework and literary
mode, describing, through character and theme, the long and
difficult processes of connection and communication are consistent
with his understanding of the gradual nature of sociopolitical
development. In addition, Williams' emphatic insistence on locality
as significant to political consciousness is disregarded by Pinkney
despite Williams' expression of the interrelationship of the two: 'I've
always been very aware of the complicated relationships between
class and place. I've been enormously conscious of place, and still
get an extraordinary amount of emotional confirmation from the
sense of place and its people' (in Eagleton 1989: 180). By situating
his trilogy in Wales, Williams is confirming not, as Pinkney implies,
the failure of socialism but his own understanding of the complex
interrelationship of the personal and the political as being con-
textually specific. Dai Smith provides a thorough description of
the significance of Wales in Williams' fiction and its continuing
importance throughout his work:

This fusion of personal and public histories is located in
that Border Country which sent Raymond away from Jim ...
only to force Matthew to discover Will (as in *Border Country*).
The way out of Wales, as he probed in *Second Generation* was,
for him and so many others, literally through emigration and,
maybe, social mobility later. Since 1960 he has been exploring
another 'way out of Wales'. This route is circuitous yet not
circular. It insists that Wales is rediscovered through understanding the social process of its past. It argues that this is the
only real exit from a timeless, mythical Wales which will
otherwise suffocate the living Welsh. It embraces change rather
than the dynamics of modernism, for it sees change as growth
that is rooted, pruned and fostered by communities who strive
to make choices for their culture in their own local and national
terms. The vehicle for this route is working class struggle. The
map is history.

(in Eagleton 1989: 38)

Using his home country as the predominant setting for his trilogy, Williams describes both his own experience of alienation from a 'knowable community' and more widespread issues of sociopolitical development. Consistent with his stated belief in the relationship between person and place, the two are, as in his fiction, fundamentally interconnected.

The problematic status of the 'knowable community' reappears throughout the trilogy. Like Matthew, Kate Owen, in *Second Generation*, experiences an extreme level of alienation. Not only does she suffer a detachment from her own community but this becomes a separation of her personal feelings from what she perceives as dominant 'structures of feeling'. This is itself described as a crisis of identity:

> It was like being two persons in one world. Every scrap of English belittling, of narrowness, of philistinism, she felt quite active in herself. All the destructive derision, pettiness, complacency of this English world kept coming back to the surface as her own thoughts. But at the same time there was this quite different drive, towards belief, energy, action. The one mocked the other, perpetually, but not in any external conflict. What might have been a division in the world was in fact the ebb and flow of her own mind.
>
> (Williams 1988b: 109)

Kate's sense of alienation remains unresolved by her affair with Arthur Dean, a university lecturer. This relationship is pivotal to the central thematic issue explored in this novel: the relationship between the personal and the political. It is the lack of connection between the two which, for Kate, results in the breakdown of her relationship with Arthur. Later she views their affair as an attempt to realize a fantasy, the 'fantasy of the personal break-out, through sex. . . . The old bourgeois fantasy. That you can do what you like. Pretend society doesn't exist. Dismiss all the consequences as the old wisdom' (ibid.: 272).

The 'old wisdom', conventional morality, dominant terms of reference, exert powerful control over all of the characters in *Second Generation* despite the discrepancy between these predominant 'structures of feeling' and their own experience. The character of Kate most clearly symbolizes this conflict. She is the central medium through which Williams explores the issue of sexual freedom, the relationship between the personal and the political, dissatisfaction with dominant and restrictive codes of social conduct, and so on.

Failing to achieve her academic potential due to financial restrictions, Kate uses her intellectual abilities to help and encourage her husband's career: 'Kate wrote the exercises and essays, but Harold copied them out and they were submitted in his name' (ibid.: 37–8). Kate subjugates her own ability to her husband's trade union activities, and her frustration and Harold's insensitivity result in marital difficulties. Much of her adult life has been lived through her husband and son, both being an outlet for her intellectual energy. But, as Kate realizes, 'the time comes, as your husband's work settles, as your son grows away, when you know you can't live for ever through others, when the restlessness defines itself and it is your own life you consider' (ibid.: 38). This 'restlessness' leads to Kate's affair with Arthur, a so-called radical thinker on sexual politics.

Refusing to accept the subordinate female role, Kate attacks the traditional forms of male/female relationships, conventions which are at the centre of this novel. Her affair with Arthur is a means of rejecting the conventions which those around her seem to accept. For Kate, Arthur is:

> her last chance. If she rejected this, she would die in Goldsmith Street, knowing that all her life she had been cheated and deprived. And she would have for company, in that bare street, all the other grey restless people; the shadows of what could have been men and women, the huddling survivors of a generation that had seen every chance of a new life deferred, and had acquiesced in the deferment. This is what it meant to be born into the deferred generation, into war, into the slow collapse of hope.
> (ibid.: 126)

Deferred generation? Hopeless generation? The concept of 'second generation' extends beyond Kate's own generation to that of her son, Peter, who experiences an equal sense of disillusionment and despair. Although his political convictions about sexual relations strive towards greater equality between the sexes – 'the lies go on, and the men make them go on. If only somebody, for once, would just tell the truth' (p. 16) – the exposure of Kate's affair with Arthur reveals the contradiction between his political beliefs and his personal morality or security. This is expressed as a crisis of 'settlement', another key word in Williams' fiction.

The discovery of Kate's affair leads Peter to reflect upon issues of sex, marriage, fidelity, identity and conventions, realizing that 'even in the routine there was no security' (ibid.: 225). It also leads to the contemplation of generational differences, themselves involving problems of communication. Standing outside his house, having witnessed a fight between his parents, Peter sees his uncle, Gwyn:

> standing there, his back to the fire. He was looking down and talking. Peter could see his face quite clearly. Gwyn was never interested, but he's all right, you can count on him. The lean, tired unassuming face. From their generation, meeting them in their generation. Able to speak in a known voice, to speak and to intervene. But at this distance, beyond the lighted glass, no words, no connections.
>
> (ibid.: 214–15)

The 'distance' between Peter and his parents is not only a physical but a cultural one. Aware of these barriers, which are emphasized by the outside/inside division, Peter, like Matthew in *Border Country*, is conscious of his alienation:

> From here, from myself, I cannot step into that circle, cannot intervene in that relation. She would be sitting there, drawn up close, her face turned away. And his hands drawn back, limp, resting loosely in his lap. The hands that had torn at their hair, forcing the head back and down. The darkness in the hands, forced suddenly into the light.
>
> (ibid.: 215)

This final image of light from the darkness relates to the thematic and structural progression of this novel, with conventional standards and lifestyles, sexual relationships, political issues and questions of identity being forced into the forefront for re-examination and reassessment. For Peter, his parents' conflict is interlinked with his own crisis of identity, reflected in his indecisive and deeply uncertain attitude towards his research. Attempted resolution of this conflict leads him to return to Wales.

While he is there, he drives to the Holy Mountain, a prominent landmark in this trilogy. As he is driving:

> the ordinary pressures seemed unimaginably distant. On this empty road, which seemed a mere accident of the mountain, there was hardly any possibility of meeting or traffic, and the silence and emptiness had passed through into his mind. It was

a cancelling, an annihilation, through which he could still feel
the sharpness of the wind on his skin.

(ibid.: 220)

Although the 'ordinary pressures' are alleviated, this new, harsh,
rural environment evokes a force of its own. The crisis of identity
alters in this unfamiliar milieu.

Continuing on his journey, Peter drives through Glynmawr, 'past
the railway station, which was closed to passengers though the
signalbox was still open, and a signalman stood at the window,
leaning on the single black bar' (ibid.: 222). This fleeting observation presents no point of connection for Peter, yet it vividly connects
with Williams' previous novel, interlinking the first two parts of
the trilogy.

During his time in Wales, Peter meets his uncle and it is their
interaction which articulates the central themes of *Second Generation*.
The two characters climb together, their physical ascent symbolizing
the departure from 'ordinary' life. Throughout the trilogy, physical
height accompanies heightened consciousness and altered
perspectives.

In this scene Williams creates a contrast between the two men:
Gwyn, older, more experienced though less well educated than
Peter, struggles to articulate deep-rooted feelings; Peter, equipped
with political knowledge, suffers from the confusion of his dichotomy
between the personal and the political. Whereas Peter views
his mother's affair as a 'sort of extension of the politics, and
that's damnable' (ibid.: 229) – here attempting to separate
the personal from the political – Gwyn adopts a wider perspective.
The hesitancy of Gwyn's articulation both illustrates and expresses
the central themes of the book, Williams' dialogue itself reflecting
the difficulty of 'finding the words', of making the connections.
As Gwyn says:

I've not got the words, Peter. . . . But the life and the sex aren't
separate, that's what I'm trying to say. What you do in the one
you do in the other. . . . There's so many ways, Peter. That's
where I stop, every time. Just in the few of us there's so many
ways, and I don't really know. It's just I feel the connections
. . . you've got to face it Peter. . . . Not just about your Mam.
About yourself.

(ibid.: 230)

Again, the emphasis is upon *feeling* the connections, this being an acknowledgement that the connections are there. For Gwyn, this feeling is embedded in experience, suggesting the conflict between individual behaviour and dominant morality.

Returning home from Wales, Peter, too, becomes conscious of this contradiction. Once again, this involves the familiar appearing strange. Observing the traffic, Peter contemplates the separation between convention and individuality, the public and the private:

> The general movement seemed clear and confident, through a conventional world. But the individual movements, individually seen, were almost always uncertain, unfinished. The general voice was confident, moving from point to point, but the personal voices, where they could be plainly heard were uncertain, inarticulate, struggling still with original experience. The acknowledgement of another reality was continually made, at the edges of the ordinary network. And yet, collectively, this network was the reality; here, and here only, was society confirmed. . . . Everyone knew, in a private way, how much was left out, by these familiar definitions, yet still, in common practice, they seemed daily more absolute and more relevant. This was the network by which the society lived, and through which it moved and communicated. The rest, ineradicably, was private.
>
> (ibid.: 234)

As in *Border Country*, Williams explores a series of interconnected issues in *Second Generation*. One of the central relationships considered is that between the production system and its social base. Mirroring the General Strike of the previous novel, Williams depicts an industrial dispute at the car factory where Harold works. Personal problems and working relations become intertwined, the breakdown of Harold's family life adding to his disorientation:

> All the words had gone, and he was left with the pain of fact. For years, he had known, things had been far from right, in the home and family on which he depended. Yet today, forced back into the familiar routine, he would have given anything to recover the state of a year, even a few months, earlier. He and Kate had been drifting apart, and Peter, growing up, had become like a stranger, but still, within some normality, he had felt his connections with them, known some underlying assurance. That,

now, had been broken, and could not be recovered.... There
was no available life, now, against which the work could be
measured.

(ibid.: 276)

The connection between 'the work' and the 'available life' is
one continued from *Border Country*, a theme reflecting Williams'
political concern with the relationship between individual and social
processes. This concern is expressed as a crisis of settlement, one
interlinked with crisis of identity. In Williams' fiction, this results
in a breakdown of communication.

Although the problems raised in *Second Generation* remain
unresolved, its closing pages suggest the beginning rather than,
as in *Border Country*, the end of a journey. We feel a push towards
the future, a push which involves struggle, pressure and learning.
It is the shape of this future which becomes the predominant theme
in *The Fight for Manod*.

The structure of the trilogy mirrors the distinction or continuation
of past, present and future. *Border Country* is constructed out of
memories of the past and the significance of this past upon the
present; *Second Generation* focuses largely upon the present situation
of an ongoing strike and personal difficulties; *The Fight for Manod*
concentrates on the future shape of Manod, a small town in mid-
Wales suffering from industrial decline and depopulation.

Central characters from both *Border Country* and *Second Generation*,
Matthew and Peter, are appropriately brought together in the final
part of this trilogy. With Wales once again the setting, the
predominant themes of the previous novels culminate in the final
part of Williams' trilogy. The struggle, by both Matthew and Peter,
to relate their academic work to the reality of lived experience is
provided with an empirical basis. The connections between
generations, between past, present and future, between local
and international issues, between the personal and the political,
and between feeling and expression are central themes in *The Fight
for Manod*.

Several changes have occurred in the nature and occupation of
Williams' characters. Robert Lane, a university teacher in *Second
Generation*, is now working for the governmental Department of the
Environment, in charge of the investigation into the viability of
Manod as the site for the experimental construction of a new city.
Matthew Price is now 'A man of fifty-eight. Tall, heavy-boned,

with thinning dark hair. .... A deep, broken voice, perhaps Welsh. A hard, set face, almost carved' (1988c: 9). This description echoes that of Harry Price in *Border Country*, Williams' imagery signifying generational continuity. Matthew has completed his book on population movement (which he was writing in *Border Country*) and, according to Lane, has succeeded in *living* his work. Indeed, it is because of Matthew's perceived ability to 'make a history human and yet still a history' that he is employed by Lane to carry out 'a lived inquiry' (ibid.: 14).

The correlation between life and work is attributed to Williams himself by Eagleton, who asserts that 'Long before the slogan "the personal is political" became fashionable, Williams was living it, in the complex, intimate relations between his life and work' (Eagleton 1989: 3). This interrelationship is clearly established through his fiction, in which Williams brings together his personal experience, theoretical insights and political convictions. The thematic and structural orientation of the trilogy also correspond with Williams' approach to literary and dramatic analysis, illustrating the interdisciplinary nature of all of his work.

The difficulty of relating work to lived experience is one confronted by Williams' characters throughout the trilogy. However, the previous talk of reconciling the two spheres of existence becomes *actualized* in *The Fight for Manod*, providing the central thematic and situational framework for this novel. Here, Williams provides a fictional illustration of the possibility of connecting academic research with lived experience, a possibility which he suggests throughout his theoretical writing and one informing his conceptual reference to 'structure of feeling'.

As in *Border Country*, Matthew returns once more to Wales, again experiencing the strangeness of the familiar: 'What he saw in this country, which he believed he knew, was very deeply unfamiliar, a waiting strangeness, as if it was not yet known what would come out of these shadows, what new world, that begins every day' (1988c: 20).

The image of this 'new world' provides the central structural, thematic and linguistic focus of *The Fight for Manod*. It is the shape of this future, in whose interests this future should be conceived, and its relationship to both the past and the present which Williams explores through the characters of Peter and Matthew.

For Matthew, there is an inherent difference between his work as an historian and his current research activities, a difference rooted in the structure of past, present and future:

> In all the years between he had worked on the past. That learning was now a habit, to make a single experience common. But where there has been past life there is no problem in finding substance; that kind of attention has a natural hold. To work on the present and on the future is a different kind of attention: at once alert and hesitant, intent and open.
>
> (ibid.: 37)

Whereas, from this perspective, the past can be analysed as a completed entity, the present and future involve unknown experience, remaining in the realm of possibility.

The character of Matthew is central to Williams' exploration of the interrelationship of past, present and future. Indeed, Matthew symbolizes or embodies all three tenses. His consciousness of the past arises both from his professional status and, more importantly, from his personal memories of Wales. This consciousness shapes his perception of the present which, in turn, influences his attitude towards the future of Manod. At the same time, Matthew's character reveals the conflicting impulses of the three tenses, a dichotomy arising between his professional and personal response to the past, and between his present position and his personal past. The future of Manod, for Matthew, thus incorporates the divisions between the personal and the political, the individual and the social, the emotional and the theoretical.

Change and continuity have been persistent themes throughout the trilogy but here, with the sense of an impending and possible future, they acquire a predominant position, the concept of a planned future enabling Williams to concentrate more exclusively on these issues. This thematic focus is at once specific to the novel and arises from the fictional structure of Williams' trilogy, developing a personal structure of past, present and future through his literature. In this way, Matthew recalls his past, a past already depicted by Williams in *Border Country*, memories evoked by his physical position on the hillside where he stood as a boy. Matthew's recollection encompasses the central themes of the trilogy and asserts the significance of the unwritten life underlying the recorded history:

not sculpted beyond him in the shapes of the land but a pressure, a shaping, a long movement and settling and unsettling of ground, behind the watching eyes. He saw his father standing at the window of the signalbox. He saw Morgan Rosser's van along the narrow country road, which had now been straightened and widened, making a long clear run for the lorries. Glynmawr station, now, was not only closed but flattened, obliterated: the platforms and waiting rooms bulldozed down into hard core. Morgan Rosser's factory, local food and local work – 'a bit of country quality' – had lasted twenty years as a branch of a large corporation and then been closed as uneconomic; it was now a tyre depot. None of it felt like change; it felt like cancellation. Yet within all these movements there were still particular lives. They had a lasting closeness, though their bodies had died. In himself, still, in this other valley, he could feel his father's experience. There was a connecting, unnerving persistence, in movement and voice.

(ibid.: 36)

As had been observed, such heightened consciousness is familiar to Williams' characters, providing the central medium through which his themes are expressed. Involved in this expression are both the necessity of articulation and the inherent difficulties of voicing the thought. In addition, the articulation of alienation and distanciation corresponds with an increasing awareness of underlying connections. Thus, in Williams' fiction we find a focus on communication as a problematic process which, during struggle and uncertainty, becomes communication in its fullest sense.

Williams' writing style captures these contradictory yet corresponding processes. His characters express their struggle to 'find the words', thus articulating this difficulty and, through articulation, giving expression to the thought. This is evident during Matthew's attempt to describe his emotional responses to his environment, when he tells Peter that he feels:

Something different: Something other. Some altered physical sense. . . . What I really seem to feel is these things as my body. As my own physical existence, a material continuity in which there are no breaks. As if I was feeling through them, not feeling about them.

(ibid.: 97–8)

Peter replies, 'I can hear that you feel it. But . . .' 'Yes,' responds Matthew, 'But. There's usually nothing to be said.' This acknowledgement of the continual difficulty of expressing the inexpressible is in itself its articulation.

One fundamental *lack* of communication established in this novel arises from the division between the community of Manod and the characters of Matthew and Peter. This directly relates to the distinction between Manod 'the actual place' and Manod 'the project' (p. 181). Recognition of the former involves consideration of *lived* experience and it is this level which engages Matthew's energies, as it informs Williams' own theoretical inquiries.

However, Matthew's emotional responses, deriving from his personal attachment to the physical location of his work, at times conflict with his theoretical perspective, although, in accordance with Williams' own assertions, the two can never be wholly detached. During his first conversation with Peter, Matthew talks of his initial reaction to the proposed plans for Manod when confronted by its physical reality, saying, 'I just stood there looking and I found myself saying: leave it alone, leave at least this place alone' (ibid.: 75). Yet this feeling, arising from a sense of nostalgia and the weight of memories evoked by the familiar landscape, is also questioned by Matthew, with the recognition that 'I still get my living elsewhere. I made that choice long ago. This place is good to look at but people still have to leave it' (ibid.). Even here, Matthew perceives a lived reality which contradicts his personal response.

Again, Williams' emphasis on feeling is paramount, but the feelings he attributes to his characters are always situated in relation to a given context. Although the characters frequently experience alienation, he describes that which they are isolated *from*: a particular way of life; a specific community; a certain environment; a social order. . . . In this way, Matthew's recognition of the need to relate feeling to perceptions of life as it is lived reflects the descriptive and linguistic structure of Williams' fiction. The concept of 'structure of feeling' implies feeling as a crucial human response to existing social relationships rather than as an emotion solely experienced and articulated at the subjective level.

Related to the emphasis on the lived reality beneath the theoretical inquiry is 'settlement', a theme which, although central to the previous novels, acquires increasing urgency in *The Fight for Manod* amidst the uncertainty of the future. Alongside the changes occurring in Manod and the continual contemplation of its future, Williams' characters voice their persistent desire for settlement.

Certain forms of personal settlement do occur – the birth of Peter and Beth's baby, the marriage of Ivor and Modlen – but an uncertainty about the future taints these occasions with insecurity. On the other hand, the nature of these events themselves suggests new possibilities. Death, marriage and birth provide a symbolic parallel with the structure of past, present and future, evoking the thematic concern with the movement of generations.

In relation to the structure of past, present and future, the notion of settlement becomes tenuous and problematic. If, as Williams portrays in his fiction, these three tenses exert a continual and conflicting pressure, how can settlement, with its connotations of certainty and persistence, ever be attained? Is it merely an idealistic desire or is it grounded in some form of available social reality?

At a theoretical level, Williams' concept of 'settlement' requires the reconciliation of the dichotomies which form the thematic focus of his trilogy: past/present; individual/social; personal/political; local/international; feeling/expression. All of these issues are brought together in Matthew's final speech at the decisive government meeting concerning the future plans for Manod:

> The feeling in Manod, in that whole district, is against being used from outside. That is also, I needn't say, a very general feeling in Wales ... the crucial factor – you must really appreciate this – is who the people are to be. For this is a country bled dry by depopulation. Not far away, in the valleys, there is a ravaged and depressed old industrial area. If it can clearly be seen that in these new ways, bringing the two needs together, a different future becomes possible, a future that settles people, that gives them work and brings them home, then through all the dislocation, through all the understandable losses and pains of change, there could still be approval, significant approval: not just the design of a city but the will of its citizens ... I don't mean nationality. I mean that the storms that have blown through that country – storms with their origin elsewhere – should now be carefully and slowly brought under control. In one place at a time, one move at a time, we should act wholly and consistently in the interests of that country, and those interests, primarily, are the actual people now there, caught between rural depopulation and industrial decline, the end of two separated orders, and

there in Manod, if we could see it, is a real way beyond them. But only a real way if it belongs to the people on whose land it is being made.

(ibid.: 193–4)

As well as expressing Williams' personal concern with problems confronting his home country, Matthew's speech describes a vision of the future which clearly corresponds with Williams' socialist perspective, as described in the essay, 'You're a Marxist, aren't you?' This simultaneously reflects Williams' defence of artistic freedom as an essential constituent of democratic socialism, arguing that: 'the claim for the freedom of the artist is necessarily a claim for quite new kinds of freedom, an acknowledgement of the need for freedom for everyone in society' (1989: 94).

Such a process, in itself establishing the interconnection of cultural and political formations, is attempted in the theme, structure and imagery of Williams' fiction. Further, it is a process which, as observed in the previous chapter, continually informs the methodology adopted in his analysis of literature and drama.

For Williams, 'the writing of prose is a sharing of experience which, in its human qualities, is both affected by and can transcend the received social relations' (1991b: 72). This perspective informs the thematic focus and the structure of his trilogy. The interconnection of past and present is expressed both as a personal experience – Matthew's relationship with his father and to Wales – and as a more general concern in *The Fight for Manod*. Continually, Williams' emphasis is upon the nature, articulation and significance of experience within the overriding structure of past, present and future. Through his fiction Williams explores experience as both a process and a pressure, one which involves continued struggle. Nevertheless, in the trilogy, connections *are* realized and, thus, some form of 'settlement' is suggested. In relation to the themes, structure and writing style of Williams' fiction, the trilogy corresponds with Williams' definition of the theory of culture as 'the study of relationships between elements in a whole way of life' (1965: 46). Williams' fiction provides him with a medium through which to illustrate both the problematics and the possibilities of his theoretical perspective.

Chapter 8

The Volunteers and *Loyalties*

The significance of the structure of past, present and future, so vital to the trilogy, is reasserted in *The Volunteers*. Published in 1978, the action of the novel takes place in the then future of 1988. It is a political thriller, the only novel in which Williams writes in the first person, with the main character, Lewis Redfern, working as an investigative reporter for Insatel, an international television satellite service. At the beginning of the novel, Lewis is commissioned to investigate the shooting of Buxton, Secretary of State for Wales, a Wales which has long since been given its Assembly. This incident provides the first strand in a series of connections, the uncovering of which, both by Lewis and ourselves as readers, forms the structure of the novel.

As in the trilogy, place is central to *The Volunteers*, with Wales once more providing the significant location, at both the descriptive and the political level. Just as the characters in the trilogy frequently experience the familiar as the strange, so, too, does Lewis sense a juxtaposition between scene and action, between the setting in which the shooting occurs and the political motives behind the attack:

> The full improbability of the whole scene struck me very forcibly. What a place, after all, for an event like this! A political shooting, from the raw hard world of industrial struggle, had taken place here, in a folk museum. The very incongruity, after the first surprise (which looking down from that terrace at the peaceful trees and the water kept returning, mysteriously, as if only these things were real and all the rest was nightmare) had, in the end, a certain point. It was just the improbable conjunction, the bringing together of apparently separate parts of our life, that

made it significant. What this place offered, after all, was a
version of the life of a people: a version, characteristically, that
attracted official visits. And then what had poured into it, roughly
and incongruously, with this lingering shock of surprise, was
another version, another practice, of the life of the same people.
The clash of scene and action was then the first thing to grasp.
To understand that would be to begin to come nearer.

(Williams 1985a: 26–7)

This initial *dis*connection becomes the means through which
connections are gradually made, a technique familiar in the trilogy
and one informing Williams' cultural and literary analysis. While
in his fiction Williams explores this process through the lives of
his characters, his theoretical inquiry uses a similar conceptual
approach. In *Drama from Ibsen to Brecht*, for example, his analysis
proceeds: 'from the recognition of two apparently contradictory
facts: that an important work is always, in an irreducible sense,
individual; and that there are authentic communities of works of
art, in kinds, periods and styles' (Williams 1973: 8).

In both his fiction and his theory, a similar methodological
structure is developed, which revolves around the examination and
discovery of interconnected areas of experience.

Writing in the style of the popular thriller, Williams employs
a literary form which easily lends itself to such an exploration.
Reliant upon the nature and process of connection for its structure
and expression, this genre provides Williams with an appropriate
medium through which to expose:

crimes and disloyalties now happening everywhere around us
which really need to be tracked down, not in the enclosing
rhetoric of an already unknown political statement, but in the
complex and surprising ways in which they actually happen and
within a social order of which any serious investigator will come
to know he is a participant as well as the idealised observer.

(1989d: 118)

This attempt situates *The Volunteers* in what Williams refers to
as the 'subjunctive action', which he regards as appropriate to
matters of fiction rather than theory (*Screen* 1982: 148). Further,
he argues that the fact that complicated processes can be revealed
through the subjunctive mode distinguishes it from futurism. His
own comments on the novel illustrate his approach and intentions

towards the future tense in contrast with *The Fight for Manod*. This
in itself results in a change in Williams' writing style:

> I wrote *The Fight for Manod* in one style at the same time as I
> was writing *The Volunteers* in another and *The Volunteers* is precisely
> a subjunctive one, because not only is it placed ahead in time,
> but it does pre-suppose actions which not only haven't occurred
> because of the date, but haven't yet occurred because of the stage
> of social development, of saying if these things happened, then
> what would occur? And in *The Fight for Manod* ... there was
> a very strong sense ... of something new about to happen, which
> people wanted to happen, and then of finding the very compli-
> cated blockages which prevented it happening, blockages at all
> sorts of levels, which seemed to me the difference between a
> subjunctive action and simple futurism.
>
> (Williams 1982: 148)

Although stylistic differences exist, there are many similarities
between *The Fight for Manod* and *The Volunteers*. Both involve an
investigation throughout which connections are continually made,
the Inquiry into events at Pontyrhiw (*The Volunteers*) providing a
parallel with the government meeting at the end of *The Fight for
Manod*. Just as Matthew Price, initially an observer of Manod,
experiences conflictual pressures from his increasing participation
in the community, so, too, does Lewis find himself 'living' his
investigation. Gradually, he becomes part of the activities he is
investigating – 'the line between observer and participant, that I'd
always theorised, had been turned so effortlessly' (1985a: 179) –
and despite disagreeing with the ideas and tactics of the underground
activists, the Volunteers, he still recognizes, and desires for himself,
'the cement that keeps so many lives together: the experience of
belonging to something, of confirming an identity in the identification with others' (ibid.: 165–6). As in the trilogy, the concept of
community is a central issue, the 'knowable community' being
beyond Lewis' reach. His personal sympathies alienate him from
his professional duties while his professional status and individual
beliefs preclude his full membership as an underground activist.

Another thematic focus continued from the trilogy is that of
generation. Mark Evans, a leading member of the Volunteers, an
oppositional force attempting to infiltrate the system from within,
refers to himself as being part of 'a failed generation', his political
failure being judged not 'a personal failure but a historical failure':

The opposition is still opposition, the system is still there and
you have not changed it. Then you start to see what must happen,
the one last way. But what you contemplate as theory is suddenly
practice, and your son is engaged in it, your son and your sons.
A failed generation is contemptuously pushed aside. A new force
emerges. A force that is strange to you but in it you can recognise
your own features, your own language, your own being. Changed
but connecting, father to son.

(ibid.: 176)

The connection between father and son is integral to Lewis'
response to his investigation, a detail which only emerges fully at
the end of the novel. Lewis relates his father's death as a national
service soldier in Kenya, 'one of the very worst of the last colonial
wars' (p. 195), with the murder of Gareth Powell by the army on
the picket-line at Pontyrhiw: 'the fading chalk bullet-marks were
still on the walls along the street. A street in Pontyrhiw. A dirt
road in Kenya' (p. 207). This connection, made quietly and simply,
overrules any distinction between the personal and the political.

As in the trilogy, this distinction is explored in *The Volunteers*.
It is interlinked with a continual return, made conscious through
the character of Lewis, to the ordinariness of life. Here, a contrast
is made between the nature and scale of Lewis' investigation,
emphasized by the public profile of the media organization for which
he is working, and the 'ordinary' lives coexisting with this. This
juxtaposition is highlighted by Lewis' visit to, and subsequent
rejection from, the home of Gareth Powell's widow. This provokes
Lewis' realization of the contradiction between news coverage and
life *as experienced*. Buxton, following the shooting:

was now recovering satisfactorily, in the hospital at Cardiff, while
Gareth Powell was dead and his wife and child were without
him in that tidy back garden at Pontyrhiw, with her brother
coming round, looking after her, trying to see her through it.
On any real estimate, that was the case, but nothing works like
that. The public story, in any available dominant version, was
still the shooting of Buxton. A public version against my private
feelings; was that now the problem? I don't know about private
feelings: all I could touch was the rawness, and of course the
resentment, of being turned out, seen off, from that private
garden.

(ibid.: 98)

The more involved Lewis becomes in the lives of those whom he is investigating, the more problematic becomes the distinction between private and public, preventing any simple dichotomy being asserted between the two. The interrelationship of the private and the public, the individual and the social, creates the development structure of *The Volunteers*.

As in *The Fight for Manod*, the ending of *The Volunteers* leaves us with the sense of possibility, of future in the making. The Inquiry into Pontyrhiw resolves one problem, with Lewis providing conclusive evidence of Buxton's leading role behind the army intervention. However, Lewis resigns from his post at Insatel and is now aware of the multifarious ramifications of the connections which have been both made and denied. As he realizes, 'no action ever runs a single course' (ibid.: 206). For him the connection between the events at Pontyrhiw and the shooting of Buxton at the Welsh Folk Museum must itself be understood in relation to wider actions. Despite the complexity of this process, Lewis senses it as a necessity:

> There was only, now, the deep need to connect and the practical impossibility, for unregrettable reasons, of making the connections, even the known connections. Yet then, all the time, within this impossibility, were the inevitable commitments, the necessary commitments, the choosing of sides.
>
> (ibid.: 207)

These 'necessary commitments', seen as corresponding with the process of connection, involve the question of alignment and of loyalties, a question which, evident by the title, is at the centre of Williams' last completed fictional work, *Loyalties*, *People of the Black Mountains* remaining an unfinished project.

Like *Border Country*, the structure of *Loyalties* follows a movement from the present to the past. Spanning the years from 1936 to 1984, *Loyalties* encompasses the Spanish Civil War, the Second World War and the miners' strike of 1984. Unlike the earlier novel, however, the connection between the young researcher, Jon Merritt, and the unfolding tale of espionage which constitutes the bulk of the story, is only very gradually revealed. The central action of *Loyalties* is framed by the devices of prologue and epilogue, or 'First' and 'Last'. The opening section describes the research project on which Jon Merritt is about to embark: a television programme investigating a new lead into post-war espionage by British scientists, an investigation which is ultimately to reveal direct links between this past, his own past and so, necessarily, his present.

The first connection observed between this opening sequence and the ensuing story appears in the name of Alec Merritt, Jon's father, a Labour politician and 'a television celebrity: a man to be brought forward into the statutory circle of uncomfortable armchairs to be stared at and interrogated and display radical dissent' (Williams 1989a: 215). Alec Merritt is married to Alex Braose, daughter of Norman Braose, a British scientist and double agent working for the USSR who is a central character in this novel. By descent, Jon Merritt is directly related to Norman, involving him, once the research has been carried out and the connections realized, in 'quite different questions of loyalty' (ibid.: 378). As in the trilogy, the theme of generation is once again predominant, forming the central connection between the characters of the novel.

Coexisting with this is a conscious recognition of class divisions, highlighted by the relationship between Norman Braose, son of a diplomatic family and educated at Cambridge, and Nesta Pritchard, daughter of a working-class Welsh family. Marked by class and cultural differences, their relationship is further viewed by the Communist Party, of which Norman is a member, as a clash of commitments, for 'sex outside the Party would be a division of loyalties' (ibid.: 43).

The notion of loyalty involves issues of morality, necessitating decisions and choices. Loyalties *to* whom, *for* whom, and *by* whom are all questions arising in this novel. One man's loyalty is another man's betrayal and this is intensified by espionage activities. Different kinds of loyalty are explored by Williams: personal, political, sexual, family, class, national and international. Out of these different forms of commitment arise conflicts. For example, Norman's personal, sexual and, with the birth of Gwyn (his illegitimate son by Nesta), family loyalties are subordinated to his political and class alignments.

The image of the Communist Party portrayed by Williams is that of a party dominated by a hegemonic upper class, which dictates a specific code of conduct to its members. The party condemns the relationship between Norman and Nesta with the excuse that Nesta is politically naive. However, it is the class difference between the two which provides the underlying motive for discrimination. Nesta is a member of the class which the party ostensibly seeks to encourage. Yet, in Williams' novel, political dogma and personal interaction are viewed by the party as radically different issues.

Norman's involvement in espionage is portrayed as lacking any loyalty to a level of tangible reality. An ideological loyalty to communism, which excuses certain practices enacted in its name, is depicted, as in *Koba*, as meaningless. For Williams, the ensuing lack of openness results in the impossibility of loyalty, settlement or community.

Williams succinctly captures the class and cultural differences between Norman and Nesta during the following interchange in which Norman, as an outsider to Wales, displays a generalized and simplistically romantic attitude to the country, telling Nesta that:

> you should realise you come from a famous people. When the Romans came up against you, you shocked them. ... If you knew the times we did it at school! You're the Silures didn't you know? The Romans learnt to respect your ferocity in battle, but what impressed them even more was your extraordinary independence. One of them said, I remember translating it: *Neither punishment nor kindness can turn them from their ways.*
>
> (1989a: 30)

For Nesta, however, 'All I remember of history was I had to draw an elephant. It was about Clive of India' (ibid.). Although both accounts are rooted in an imperialist interpretation of history, the simplicity of Nesta's recollection contrasts sharply with Norman's elaborate and depersonalized tirade. This distinction of tone involves different terms of reference, different accents, a different response to, and experience of, a radically different form of early education. Through the tone, style and content of his characters' speech, Williams evokes a wealth of material about their background.

The time-span of this novel provides an important structural link between both the historical eras and the characters themselves. The history of the first generation – Norman, Nesta, Bert, Emma, Monkey – is continued through the experience of the second and third generations – Gwyn, Alex Braose and Jon Merritt.

The central thematic issue in *Loyalties* concerns the struggle for socialism, various aspects of this struggle being analysed within a fictional framework. Two principal characters are used to represent opposite ends of this political struggle, with Bert, Nesta's eventual husband, being contrasted with Norman. Bert is a working-class Welshman whose socialist beliefs lead him to fight in the Spanish Civil War and the Second World War, in which he is badly wounded, before returning to his work as a miner and active union member. Norman, on the other hand, is born into a wealthy family, acquires his socialist principles at Cambridge University and becomes a spy for the USSR. Neither of these positions is presented as achieving a satisfactory solution. Bert's life is arduous and he receives no reward for his efforts. His final days are spent as a dependant, his children helping to feed him in a reversal of the child–parent role. Norman's espionage activities are presented, more emphatically, as misguided. In order to maintain his counter-position he is forced to lie and deceive.

The contrast between these two characters is reflected in their physical attributes. Whereas Bert's active part in the struggle for socialism leaves him scarred, Norman's appearance – tall and golden-haired – symbolizes his physical and political distance. This distinction is captured by Nesta's portraits of the two men. Her painting of Norman conveys the impression of a god rather than a human being:

> It was a clear two-colour portrait of Norman, his head and shoulders with the face half-turned forward. The likeness was startling although the colours were so strange. The ground of face and hair was bright yellow, with small marks of bright blue for features. All around the head was blue, with lines of yellow down into the shoulders, and some other yellow marks in the top left-hand corner.
>
> (ibid.: 75)

This bright, radiant, idealistic image presents an unmistakable contrast to Nesta's portrayal of Bert:

> It was immediately Bert: the face was never in doubt. The oils were streaked and jabbed to the domination of the damaged eye: hard pitted lines of grey and silver and purple pulling down the staring dark socket. The whole face, under the cropped hair, was distorted around these lines which pulled from the dark hollow. Angry streaks of crimson and purple pulled beyond the hard shoulder.
>
> (ibid.: 346)

The portrayal of Bert is brutally realistic, displaying 'human flesh broken and pulped'. Bert fought and 'was damaged and made ugly by it'. Nesta's portrait reflects the horror of this experience, its physical harshness which she herself has had to confront throughout her life. Nesta's loyalty to Bert has not been an easy one, compounded as it is by the difficulties of coping with his physical disfigurement. Taken together, the portraits serve as visual reminders of her own suffering. They represent the possibility and the actuality, the ideal and the reality. Although the possibility itself became ugly, with Norman's accusations of Nesta's affair with Bert, there was still a time in Nesta's life when the reality appeared as radiant as the portrait. However, the lived reality became her marriage to Bert, a life which, far from glamorous, involved struggle and pain, culminating in Bert's death from silicosis. This is the nature and consequence of Nesta's loyalty to Bert.

Returning to the notion of political loyalty, which structures Williams' depiction of Bert and Norman, the substance of this loyalty provides the predominant question throughout the novel. Exploring the issue, Williams describes two clear and contrasting worlds of experience. On one side, there is Norman, his sister, Emma, and their friend Monkey Pitter, members of a well-educated upper class, attempting to deviate from the values associated with their social position through their participation in the activities of the Communist Party. Their political loyalty is an acquired affiliation and is partly a reaction against their social status, a means of rebellion. They are, in Bert's words, 'Runaways from their class' (p. 256). Yet their manners, attributes and lifestyles are still rooted in the dominant class. They continue to accept the advantages bestowed upon them by birth and Williams makes a sharp distinction between this kind of life and that experienced by Nesta and Bert. It is Nesta who voices the dichotomy between the two expressions of political loyalty, saying, 'I didn't choose my politics. they was chosen for me, by the family I was born to and the place I grew up in. More like a religion, and I had that too. I don't really understand much more of one than the other' (ibid.: 29).

Nesta's political loyalty is rooted in lived experience; it is an unquestioned adherence to a particular way of life rather than a position arising through academic debate. This distinction, which divides Norman from Nesta and Bert, is interrelated with a further contrast: between those characters who remain true to themselves – yet another form of loyalty – and those, like Norman, who rely on a false, or misconceived, sense of responsibility. Norman's spying activities leave him alienated. Although he remains true to his political convictions, he evades social commitment and thus lacks any sense of settlement: he ends his relationship with Nesta and simultaneously refuses the father–son relationship with Gwyn.

However, the father–son relationship, as in *Border Country*, is central to the thematic structure of *Loyalties*. The movement of generations encompassed by the timescale of this novel is depicted as both a personal (in terms of the individual and interconnected lives of Williams' characters) and a historical progression. Parallels are drawn between the historical conflicts encompassed by the novel. As Gwyn asserts, 'Vietnam is our Spain', although this is qualified by his awareness that 'it was both for our Dad's generation. . . . The struggle in the pits and the struggle for Spain' (ibid.: 220). While drawing historical parallels, parallels which are rooted in the temporal structure of the novel, Williams also maintains distinctions, distinctions of experience. At a general level, the Vietnam War may evoke memories of the Spanish Civil War but for those with direct experience of the latter, the former is qualitatively different, in both political and, more significantly, existential terms. For the older generation the Vietnam War involves different allegiances, altered commitments; it is a different kind of struggle.

This contrast between general observation and individual experience is rooted in the objective/subjective dichotomy, a central thematic focus in *Loyalties*. It is intimately connected to the relationship between the personal and political, which are presented as deeply complex and, ultimately, indistinguishable. The character of Gwyn provides the central medium through which Williams explores this issue. A product of a relationship precipitated by political affiliation – Norman's initial visit to Wales arises from his membership of the Communist Party – and broken by political affiliation – Norman's personal/social commitments are subjugated to his political allegiance – Gwyn's problematic sense of identity reflects the subjective/objective dichotomy. His personal experience conflicts with his objective, inherited history. In addition, this alternative history is integrated with his own experience, his Cambridge education being manipulated by Emma, illustrating upper-class influence in action.

Gwyn is the living product of Nesta's relationship with Norman and this generational/genetic continuity sustains the relationship.

As Bert observes, 'it was to be kept going. . . . Kept going in you. By you knowing who you was. . . . And by letting Emma come and watch over you. . . . To turn up when you was ready and get you back to Cambridge where you belonged' (ibid.: 256). Although Gwyn tries to deny this account of his history, his genetic inheritance alienates him from the family in which he was brought up. Like Matthew Price in *Border Country* and Kate Owen in *Second Generation*, Gwyn feels isolated from his home community. Gwyn's education and later occupation result from his status as the son of Norman rather than Bert and this is depicted in the contrast between Gwyn and Dic, Bert's natural son. Whereas Dic, like Bert, remains in Wales as a miner, Gwyn leaves for Cambridge, following in Norman's footsteps.

The motivation behind Gwyn's progress is observed by Mark Ryder, an admissions tutor at Cambridge. He tells Emma: 'it was you brought young Lewis to Cambridge. You picked him up from that Welsh valley, and decided he should come here' (p. 157). This in itself evokes an image of disruption, displacement, unsettlement. Gwyn's isolation from his home community becomes a spatial and physical separation – measured by the experiential distance between Wales and Cambridge.

For Gwyn, the process of self-discovery is enacted at two levels. For much of the novel, Gwyn has never met his natural father; his working-class upbringing alienates him from his father's class. Yet Gwyn retains a powerful sense of 'his own complex history', corresponding with a disturbing awareness of life's contingencies (p. 218). Reflecting on the circumstantial nature of his birth, Gwyn voices his thoughts, articulating both the distinction between, and fusion of, the subjective and objective:

> Perhaps after all there are two quite different traditions. . . . And not only different traditions, but quite different people carrying them. . . . They find common cause, at certain times, and objectively, always, they have need to. But still through people who are basically different from each other. . . . Like if Vietnam is our Spain, objectively that is quite clear. And even the sectarianism can then be incidental. But still the different people. . . . In effect, different classes. . . . It's what follows those moments of temporary fusion.
>
> (ibid.: 223)

Gwyn's awareness of the precarious nature of life and, implicitly, of loyalties, also reflects the pressure of the past upon the present, at both a general and individual level. This pressure is also experienced by Jon Merritt following the connections uncovered between his research and his immediate family. As he says, 'The whole thing comes too close, the pressures and then the decisions. And some have helped to form us. We all say we have our own lives but many of us have been formed by this kind of past' (ibid.: 373).

This pressure is explored throughout all of Williams' fiction, shaping the themes, style and structure of his writing. In *Loyalties* the examination of the past leads to a reassessment of the present. The past, for Jon, is a process of conflicting loyalties and decisions. His thoughts are reminiscent of Matthew and Peter's hopes for their work in *Border Country* and *Second Generation* respectively:

> I want to know what the whole shape was. The whole shape and pressure of that life. And not just what was done but its actual doing, day by day. . . . What I'm saying is that we can only start at all if we really know what was done: not as error, not as scandal, though in the end it might be either, but by people in real and uncertain situations: people rather than figures in a history . . . the question I'm also putting is how someone like myself should live and act now, in as much danger and as much uncertainty.
>
> (ibid.: 374)

The expressed desire to understand history as experience informs Williams' theoretical analysis and is embodied in the concept of 'structure of feeling'. In this way, Williams' fictional researchers reflect his own academic aims and interests. He is able to depict the process of this academic inquiry by providing a clear structure of past, present and future to which his characters are related and, often through struggle, relate. Williams' fictional history is delineated at the level of experience and it is at this level that its implications for the present and future arise.

In his fiction, Williams provides practical illustration of his concept of 'structure of feeling'. Integrally related to the analysis of past, present and future, this concept emerges as the central structural force beneath the themes, characterization, shape and expression of Williams' writing. This literary approach is itself crucial to Williams' consideration of possible forms of action in the struggle for democratic socialism, as he consistently situates his social critique within an historical framework, creating the sense of 'structure of feeling' as a living process. His novels are the creative basis from which he explores a number of interrelated themes through a process of description and discovery. Within this process, the concept of the 'knowable community' becomes a crucial issue, one which is thematically linked to the notion of 'settlement'. The push towards settlement is frequently felt and expressed by many of Williams' characters and the movement of the action reflects this, often involving, amidst wider forms of change and continuity, the search for self-identity. This quest itself necessitates an examination of past, present and future, often symbolized by the thematic and temporal depiction of generation movements. The latter provides Williams with an accessible method by which to create a solid connection between three different periods of time. Throughout his fiction, new generations suggest new possibilities and this further reflects a central conflict familiar to Williams' characters: the distinction between life as it is lived and life as it is hoped for. This, again, is inherently related to the continual and questioning contemplation of the shape of the future and the means by which it can be achieved.

The interrelationship of Williams' fictional and theoretical writing perhaps rests, above all, in the commitments common to both. 'Commitment' is a concept that Williams views as central to the writing process and it informs his analysis of drama and literature. In both his fiction and his theory, he explores different forms of commitments, relationships, possibilities and connections, and the relationship between writing, politics and sociocultural processes, as illustrated by his own creative work, is clearly expressed in his assertion that:

> real social relations are deeply embedded within the practice of writing itself, as well as in the relations within which writing is read. To write in different ways is to live in different ways. It is also to be read in different ways, in different relations, and often by different people. This area of possibility, and thence of choice, is specific, not abstract, and commitment in its only important sense is specific in just these terms. It is specific within a writer's actual and possible social relations as one kind of producer. It is specific also in the most concrete forms of these same actual and possible notations, conventions, forms and language. Thus to recognise alignment is to learn, if we choose, the hard and total specificities of commitment.

(1977: 205)

Chapter 9

The Country and the City
Hidden and knowable communities

I have never written a book where I was more surprised by the directions in which it led.

(Williams 1981a: 305)

The Country and the City is a remarkable study, involving as it does a wide-ranging engagement with literary sources – from Virgil to modern authors, from pastoral poetry to science fiction – and an attempt to situate the writing in particular times and places. Interwoven with this is a deep interest in actual historical societies and an attempt to recover the real relations between town and country. The literary record, Williams shows, could sometimes clarify and sometimes hide the reality of social relations. Williams' task is to bring a discriminating judgement to bear on the literary and historical record. And, as elsewhere, there is a preoccupation with the choices and alternatives which our national – and international – history has presented.

The Country and the City takes up issues about temporal connections – between past, present and future – as well as geographical connections – between town and country, metropolis and province, advanced industrial societies and the Third World. It is more explicitly Marxist than some of Williams' other writings (we will return to this) but without question there is a good deal of continuity in the issues he faces and the procedures he adopts. There is the contesting of received images, of received wisdom about the significance of the literary record (particularly here with reference to pastoral poetry) and the attempt to make visible hidden connections, so that our understanding of society is enhanced. As he comments in *Politics and Letters*:

If you look at the implied relationships of nearly all the books I have written, I have been arguing with what I take to be official

English culture. I have done that in different ways in different places, but always the people in my sights, whether to agree or disagree with, have been within this other tradition.

(Williams 1975a: 316)

Moreover, as Williams makes very clear at the beginning of *The Country and the City*, the problems he addresses in the book came out of personal pressures – commitments that were a product of his early life in a Welsh valley, on the border with England. Not only the national differences but the range of settlements were reflected around him: the villages based on land, the industrial villages and towns of mining and steel production, as well as the market town and the cathedral city:

Before I had read any descriptions and interpretations of the change and variations of settlements and ways of life, I saw them on the ground and working, in unforgettable clarity. In the course of education I moved to another city, built around a university, and since then living and travelling and working, I have come to visit, and need to visit, so many great cities of different kinds, and to look forward and back, in space and time, knowing and seeking to know this relationship, as an experience and as a problem.

(1975a: 11)

The opening chapter of *The Country and the City* almost has the character of a meditation on the many meanings of country life in different times and places – the physical character of the countryside and the livelihoods to which working on it gives rise. Yet there were the connections with towns and cities which were never static. So within the experience of Williams' own family it was a story of movement and change:

We were a dispersed family, along the road, the railway, and now letters and print. There were altering communications, the altering connections, between country and city and between all the intermediate places and communities, the intermediate or temporary jobs and settlements.

(ibid.: 13)

Yet Williams had come to the city for his education and in some respects had learned, in a codified and literary way, about the country through what the city had made available to him – literary sources, alternative perspectives. And his own networks became more cosmopolitan – London, New York, Moscow, and so on. He can see the irony of this and it stops him from making easy contrasts between the country and the city. Some contrasts can be made to the advantage of one and the disadvantage of the other:

> On the country has gathered the idea of a natural way of life: of peace, innocence and simple virtue. On the city has gathered the idea of an achieved centre: of learning, communication, light. Powerful, hostile associations have also developed: on the city as a place of noise, worldliness and ambition; on the country as a place of backwardness, ignorance, limitation. A contrast between country and city, as fundamental ways of life, reaches back into classical times.
>
> (ibid.: 9)

For Williams it is the variety and the interconnections which fascinate him when he reflects on the relationships between country and city to which his own family history and experience pointed. This, for him, is the site on which the personal and the political interact. This is well encapsulated at the end of his opening chapter:

> whenever I consider the relations between country and city and between birth and learning, I find this history active and continuous: the relations are not only of ideas and experiences, but of rent and interest, of situation and power; a wider system. This then is where I am, and as I settle to work I find I have to resolve, step by slow step, experiences and questions that once moved like light. The life of the country and the city is moving and present: moving in time, through the history of a family and a people: moving in feeling and ideas, through a network of relationships and decisions.
>
> (ibid.: 17)

What we have in *The Country and the City* is a skilful reconsideration of literature as it relates to both the personal and the political, and also a committed perspective on the historical record (to which literature stands in varying relationships – from representation to misrepresentation, from myth to reality, from illusion to clarification). It is the awareness of the actual variety of human settlements and the differing functions of literature – which may celebrate and criticize what the authors see or purport to see and which can, on occasion, subsume or embody ideological positions, including class interests – that informs Williams' whole approach. We will try and indicate the lineaments of this, bearing in mind that a subtle interplay exists between class analysis and the idea of community.

An initial puzzle about the countryside can also serve as a clue. Williams cites the view of an unnamed contemporary commentator that a way of life has ended which has come down to us from the days of Virgil. This leads him to reflect on a more general tendency in writing about rural England. Commentators, writing about their own times, will see them as unsettled and subject to disruptive change. They compare this with the past, sometimes only a generation before, when things were stable and ordered and, in the more glowing accounts, an Eden or a golden age. Williams offers the image of the escalator. Each time one gets off at the period referred to as the golden age, there will be a contemporary writer to greet us and tell us that such an age has passed. One could start with Leavis and Thompson in *Culture and Environment* (1932) telling us that the organic community of Old England had just died and then trace witnesses back generation by generation: George Sturt's *Change in the Village* (1911); Hardy's novels of the late nineteenth century and George Eliot's a little earlier; Cobbett's *Rural Rides*, written in the first part of the nineteenth century; back to Goldsmith's *Deserted Village*, written in 1769, to Thomas Moore's *Utopia*, to Langland's *Piers Plowman* of the late fourteenth century. The journey could take us further back to the days before the Norman Yoke and so on. 'Where indeed shall we go', asks Williams, 'before the journey stops?' (ibid.: 21). One response would be to push back to the myth of the Garden of Eden, before the Fall:

> How beautiful the World at first was made
> Ere Mankind by Ambition was betrayed.
>
> (Anon. Seventeenth Century)

This would, however, make it difficult to use the concept of an organic society against which to contrast urban, disturbed, mobile societies. Another would be to try and develop a historical perspective. What are the religious, humanist, political or cultural elements that lead writers to criticize their society by looking back to a settled 'Old England' and its rural virtues? If literary forms and products are to provide us with clues then we must try and place them in their historical context. This is truly a difficult matter, as Williams knew only too well. In *Politics and Letters* he summarized the intention behind *The Country and the City*: 'My project . . . was to try to show simultaneously the literary conventions and the historical relations to which they were a historical response – to see together the means of production and the conditions of the means of production' (1981a: 304).

Williams' point of entry for such a project was a strategic choice (even though in principle he could have alighted at different stages from the escalator): the English country-house poems which, if taken as straightforward historical record, would give the general impression of a golden age – the organic society later to be destroyed by capitalism. But what was life actually like at the time when poetry was written celebrating the country house in the England of the seventeenth century? Williams takes Ben Jonson's 'Penshurst' and 'To Sir Robert Wroth', and Thomas Carew's 'To Saxham', and compares their picture of what they represent with that provided by other historical witnesses.

Jonson on Penshurst writes:

And though they walls be of the countrey stone,
They are rear'd with no man's ruine, no man's grone,
There's none that dwell about them, wish them downe ...
(Williams 1975a: 41)

Nature itself is there to supply the needs of the estate:

To crowne thy open table, doth provide
The purpled pheasant with the speckled side:
The painted partrich lyes in every field
And, for thy messe, is willing to be kill'd.
(ibid.: 42)

Likewise Carew on Saxham:

Thou has no Porter at the door
T'examine, or keep back the poor;
Nor locks nor bolts; thy gates have been
Made only to let strangers in.
(ibid.: 41)

Friendly providence supplies all needs:

The Pheasant, Partridge and the Lark
Flew to my house, as to the Ark.
The willing Oxe, of himselfe came
Home to the slaughter, with the Lamb.

And every beast did thither bring
Himselfe to be an offering.
The scalie herd, more pleasure took
Bath'd in the dish than in the brook.

(ibid.: 42)

Even allowing for hyperbole, the point being made is the personal
and direct coexistence of a natural world of abundance with a social
order of sharing.

But what were Saxham and Penshurst? Whence did they spring?
Saxham was a product of agrarian disturbance at the beginning
of the sixteenth century. It was closely connected with the court
and provided a port of call for hospitality and entertainment for
the social circle who attended the races at Newmarket. Penshurst
was a crown manor, again with strong court associations. In other
words they are founded on patronage and there are precise
references to the nature of the social activities that took place. What
the poetry does is to treat them as though they were timeless and
idealize them as though they were not exclusive. It reflects a moment
of domination by particular social groups in an ongoing story of
the few who control the many. From this perspective it is part of
the story of the long corruption in which even the natural order
is subsumed as part of the social order. Reflecting on this and the
period it represents – the break-up of feudalism, the enclosure
movement and the growing application of capitalist methods to
agriculture – Williams argues that what we are confronted with
is a mystification to which poetry contributes:

> a moral order is abstracted from the feudal inheritance and
> break-up and seeks to impose itself ideally on conditions which
> are inherently unstable. A sanctity of property has to co-exist
> with violently changing property relations and an ideal of charity
> with the harshness of labour relations. . . . An idealisation based
> on a temporary situation and on a deep desire for stability, served
> to cover and evade the actual bitter contradictions of the time.
>
> (Williams 1975a: 60)

The country-house poetry, therefore, is not to be analysed just
in terms of the convention of the literary text but is to be socially
situated and evaluated in its historic context. Then we can ask:
is it realistic or is it a form of mystification? This strategy of
demystifying and dispelling illusions so that we may better glimpse

the reality of particular societies and social changes is one which Williams develops in a number of ways throughout *The Country and the City*. Take, for example, the depiction of the country as innocence and the city as corrupt. Jonson's poem contrasts the country gentleman with the worldly man of the city. Such separation in practice will not do. After all, so much time was spent by city lawyers on land titles. The movement and the linkage between city and country is strong and continuous. It is a two-way affair:

> The greed and calculation, so easily isolated and condemned in the city, run back, quite clearly to the country houses, with the fields and their labourers around them. And this is a double process. The exploitation of man and of nature, which takes place in the country, is realised and concentrated in the city. But also, the profits of other kinds of exploitation – the accumulating wealth of the merchant, the lawyer, the court favourite – come to penetrate the country, as if, but only as if, they were a new social phenomenon.
>
> (ibid.: 64)

This kind of analysis continually prompts the exploration of the social functions of literature and the interest that individual authors of the genre might represent. So the 'town and country' contrast and comparison needs to be unpicked and restructured:

> If what was seen in the town could not be approved, because it made evident and repellent the decisive relations in which men actually lived, the remedy was never a visitor's morality of plain living and high thinking, or a babble of green fields. It was a change of social relationships and of essential morality. *And it was precisely at this point that the 'town and country' fiction served: to promote superficial comparisons and prevent real ones.*
>
> (ibid.: 71; emphasis added)

Yet the relation of fiction to fact, of poetry to social reality, need not always obscure our understanding of social processes. The writing may contain ambiguities, tensions and allusions which, when referred to the times in which they were written, can be revelatory. Goldsmith's 'The Deserted Village' (1769), which Williams refers to as 'that baffling poem', is an instructive case in point. While there are conventional treatments of lost innocence and simplicities of rural life, there are precise references to clearance, eviction and

evacuation so that 'One only master grasps the whole domain.'
What follows from this?

> ... the man of wealth and pride
> Takes up a space that many poor supplied;
> Space for his lake, his park's extended bounds
> Space for his horses, equipage and hounds.

(ibid.: 96)

Since the older settlement had been equated with a time and
place when poetry could flourish, such changes also heralded the
death of poetry. There is a juxtaposition between an idealized
pastoral economy (whose destruction is the destruction of poetry)
and the real material facts of dispossession. Williams' comment
on this is instructive and indicates the way in which he conceives
the relationship of literary to social analysis:

> The present is accurately and powerfully seen, but its real
> relations to the past and future are inaccessible, because the
> governing development is that of the writer himself: a feeling
> about the past, an idea about the future, into which, by what
> is truly an intersection, an observed present is arranged. We
> need not doubt the warmth of Goldsmith's feelings about the
> men driven from the village: that connection is definite. The
> structure becomes ambiguous only when this shared feeling is
> extended to memory and imagination, for what takes over then,
> in language and idea, is a different pressure: the social history
> of the writer.

(Williams 1975a: 99)

But not only is the past idealized by referencing the poet as
central, the future is not grasped. It was not, after all, a move from
fertility to desert, but from relatively unproductive to increased land
use and fertility that actually took place, notwithstanding the human
price that was paid by those who were evicted. Poetry then, as it
were, goes into exile to mount its protest against industry and trade
and to speak for nature. This is, for Williams, an anticipation of
the Romantic structure of feeling to be found in Blake, Wordsworth
and Shelley.

This mixture of myth and reality, which can imbue writing about
country and city and their supposed connections – and the valuations
of past, present and future – provides a way for Williams to explore
the notion of settlement. This term appears in many places, not

least, as we have seen, in his fiction. In *The Country and the City*, it surely has a pivotal place. Typically, Williams tries to handle it in personal and analytical terms. For him, the issue has to do with the idealization of the past with its treatment of community as the organic or 'natural' society. Settlement in such a place would be desirable and right – no need to move out, on or up. The idea of settlement can be coloured by this myth of the past, whilst, at the same time, actual communities in which we grow up do shape our sense of self and personal identity. The contrast between settlement and movement is, of course, one way of distinguishing types of existence in country and city.

In *The Country and the City* there is a passage that is at once personal and generalizing. Williams refers to the structure of values around the idea of settlement. They have to do with a sense of place, of relationships, of identity. This he recognizes as important to his own experience and inner life but does not want it idealized in a way which ignores power relations and exploitation and, by extension, judges those who move away. This is not the special pleading of an exile, although perhaps he had to experience exile in order to articulate the point. Referring to the Black Mountain village in which he was born, Williams writes:

> When I go back to that country, I feel a recovery of a particular kind of life, which appears, at times, as an inescapable identity, a more positive connection than I have known elsewhere. Many other men feel this, of their own native places, and the strength of the idea of settlement, old and new, is there positive and unquestioned. But the problem has always been, for most people, how to go on living where they are. I know this also personally: not only because I had to move out for an education and to go on with a particular kind of work, but because the whole region in which I was born has been steadily and terribly losing its people, who can no longer make a living there. When I hear the idealisation of settlement I do not need to borrow the first feelings; I know, in just that sense, what neighbourhood means and what is involved in separation and leaving. But I know, also, why people have to move, why so many moved in my own family. So that I then see the idealisation of settlement, in its ordinary literary-historical version, as an insolent indifference to most people's needs. ... Settlement is indeed easy, is positively welcome, for those who can settle in a reasonable independence.

For those who cannot – and under the pressure of change from a new mode of production these became the majority – it can become a prison: a long disheartening and despair, under an imposed rigidity of conditions. And the point of the acts of settlement was to maintain this rigidity, this implacable hold on men. From the feudal grip on the serf to the more complicated machinery of the poor law, this control is evident. The consequences of what is idealised as a moral economy can then be plainly read. You fitted where you were; if you went out, you were harried.

(1975a: 106–7)

Such historical settlements were imposed settlements with systems of control through law and property rights manifested in the treatment of tenants, the old, the widowed, the orphan and the poor. Whether the reference is to pre-enclosure or enclosed villages, they are not marked by equality of condition so that the question can be put: was there ever a genuine community in such villages in spite of economic and social inequalities? In overall terms Williams thinks not – not in the feudal system and certainly not in the country-house economy. These very houses were, after all, the fruit of exploited labour as the very disproportion in scale between them and the surrounding farms and cottages suggests. They form the physical expression of a class society. They are:

a visible stamping of power, of displayed wealth and command: a social disproportion which was meant to impress and overawe. Much of the profit of modern agriculture went not into productive investment but into that explicit social declaration: a mutually competitive but still uniform exposition, at every turn, of an established and commanding class power.

(ibid.: 133)

What the process of enclosure did, in Williams' view, was to increase the pressures on and controls over the subordinate groups. One might find there a mutuality of the oppressed, or people finding some margins for living which control systems did not wholly penetrate. Again, without idealizing the matter, some evidence could be encountered for what Williams terms 'effective community' – interests of settlement where mutuality and neighbourliness can transcend class differences. Such space is always under pressure in a system that produces, and tightens through the enclosure movement, the economic system of landlord, tenant and labourer – the system, in short, of agrarian capitalism. This undermined the very possibility of community. Only in contesting it, Williams felt, could an active community be identified. What is important about this, however, is that community (and culture) becomes identified not as terms of a way of life but a way of struggle. This, incidentally, stands as a response to E.P. Thompson's critique of *Culture and Society* (Thompson 1961) which we noted earlier. Williams writes:

> In many parts of rural Britain, a new kind of community developed, as an aspect of struggle against the dominant land-owners, or in the labourers' revolts in the time of the Swing machine-smashing and rick burning or in the labourers' unions from Tolpuddle to Joseph Arch, against the whole class system of rural capitalism. In many villages, community only became a reality when economic and political rights were fought for and partially gained, in the recognition of unions, in the extension of the franchise, and in the possibility of entry into new represent-ative and democratic institutions. In many thousands of cases, there is more community in the modern village, as a result of this process of new legal and democratic rights, than at any point in the recorded or imagined past.
>
> (Williams 1975a: 131)

Such communities, in the English context, could find alternative forms of dissent in the chapels of nonconformity. Church versus chapel was the religious version of landlord versus labourer. The link between chapels and trade union activity and organization has been well documented and is symbolized in the well-known account of the Tolpuddle martyrs. What Williams is pointing to is a community grounded in resistance – as in the practices of rick-burning and machine-breaking – and a community based on alternative values of mutuality, co-operation and equality of condition. These are formed as collective responses to pressure from the dominant class, in circumstances where individual responses on their own, however courageous, could not have changed or modified the system. The new communities reject the values and contest the power of the dominant class and point to a future grounded in democratic values. The energy and intelligence that went into this kind of activity is celebrated by Williams and described as a 'shadow culture': 'Working hard all their lives at a hard and ill-paid employment, they worked second lives for their own people' (ibid.: 232).

Yet it remains true in important respects that the struggle for economic justice and democracy in a capitalist economy was not simply a rural matter. There is an extending connection in which country and city are inextricably related.

But Williams writes also of 'knowable communities', and this has connotations to which we must now turn. In *Politics and Letters* he tells us that the term is used with irony because what is known is shown to be incomplete and, after the industrial revolution and the growth of cities, some things seem to be darkly unknowable (see Williams 1981a: 171). If we had not already acknowledged Williams' strictures on the rural community and its mythologies we might have imagined that the contrast – in reality and in literature – was between the rural community that can be made visible and therefore known, and the life of the city, which in its size, complexity and anonymity remains unknown. Such a stark contrast cannot be sustained. On the one hand, accounts of small communities can leave things out and can be presented from specific points of view; on the other hand, we may come to understand things about cities, both through the imaginative power and insight of the novelist and through methods of statistical analysis, which can draw attention to general features of activity and organization involving large numbers of people.

There is, in any event, an epistemological point about the role and position of the writer:

> For what is knowable is not only a function of objects – of what is there to be known. It is also a function of subjects, of observers – of what is desired and what needs to be known. And what we have then to see, as throughout, in the country writing, is not only the reality of the rural community; it is the observer's position in and towards it; a position which is part of the community being known.
>
> (Williams 1975a: 202–3)

In fact, Williams uses the idea of the knowable community to caution against thinking that literature on rural society tells us more than it does and, conversely, to suggest that literature on the city can reveal connections that were previously unknown. What Williams does is to take examples from both to illustrate his argument. In addition, he takes examples of the border country, where relationships between town and country are explicitly addressed.

In the novels of Jane Austen, for instance, the knowable community shown to the reader is that of a network of propertied houses and families. Her well-observed, shrewd, perceptive writing is done from within that milieu. Her previous knowledge of social relations – of what is expected in and from people within those social circles – and her awareness of the importance of property in the scheme of things, enables her to tell her stories with much wit and irony from within an established framework. But other classes are simply not present: the country exists as a background for walks and views. It is in this way a selective view of reality. But even here the reality referred to is not a traditional, settled reality. There is the mix of aristocracy and bourgeoisie, the fluctuations which lead to changes of fortune, in which codes of conduct are being tested and challenged: 'The paradox of Jane Austen is then the achievement of a unity of tone, of a settled and remarkably confident way of seeing and judging, in a chronicle of confusion and change' (ibid.: 144).

Austen's position as writer and observer is within the network of the propertied groups. As Williams puts it: 'She is concerned with the conduct of people who, in the implications of improvement, are repeatedly trying to make themselves into a class. But where only one class is seen no classes are seen' (ibid.: 146).

'Improvement' carries with it here the double connotation – of agricultural improvement and of the improvement that leads to the 'cultivated' society. Once we set a writer into their social context we do not thereby account for their greatness but we can begin to appreciate what is present and what is absent in their writing and why it might be so.

The case of George Eliot is instructively different, especially in formulating a distinction between a knowable and a known community. Unlike those of Austen, Eliot's novels do include the craftsmen, the labourers, the poor. At the same time, however, she is writing for another audience, with different interests and values. She wants to draw the attention of this known community (the public, her readers) to this knowable community. In Williams' view, this leads to a defensive, placatory treatment of the knowable community, even while it is done with sympathy. Thus, from *Adam Bede*:

I am not ashamed of commemorating old Kester: you and I are indebted to the hard hands of such men – hands that have long ago mingled with the soil they tilled so faithfully, thriftily making the best they could of the earth's fruits, and receiving the smallest share as their own wages.

(cited ibid.: 211)

As Williams puts it, concerning Eliot:

The knowable community is this common life which she is glad to record with a necessary emphasis: but the known community is something else again – an uneasy contrast in language, with another interest and another sensibility.

(ibid.)

In a formal sense, perhaps, we might say that in considering such writing the issue is: who is speaking to whom, in what voice and tone and for what purpose? Language is at the centre of the matter. Eliot, for Williams, serves as a prototype of the problem, which he, as writer and teacher, also experienced as a personal problem. But this is also a reminder of an alternative and continuing cultural tradition with which he identifies and which is seen as in antagonistic relationship to what elsewhere he terms 'official English culture'. It is education which creates an awareness of the problem, since in a sense it is to move into enemy territory. Yet it also provides the possibility of contesting elitist versions of knowledge and culture:

to many of us now, George Eliot, Hardy and Lawrence are important because they connect directly with our own kind of upbringing and education. They belong to a cultural tradition much older and more central in Britain than the comparatively modern and deliberate exclusive circuit of what are called the public schools. And the point is that they continue to connect in this way into a later period in which some of us have gone to Oxford or Cambridge: to myself, for instance, who went to Cambridge and now teach there. . . . It is a question of a relation between education – not the marks or degrees but the substance of a developed intelligence – and the actual lives of a continuing majority of our people: people who are not, by any formula, objects of record or study or concern, but who are specifically, literally, our own families. George Eliot is the first major novelist in whom this question is active.

(ibid.: 209)

The novelist in this tradition becomes more aware, as a result of his or her mobility and education, that the knowable community is different from the known community, and is faced with the problem of how to present one to the other. Because of this tension, an over-concern, even deference to the known community (educated Oxbridge), the knowable community may be presented in inauthentic, stereotyped, sentimental ways, which detracts from the realism of actual life in those communities.

Thomas Hardy serves as a more successful example in that he depicts the knowable community of his Wessex novels in the context of their whole way of life. He is aware of his metropolitan reading public, but also of the real changes that are taking place in rural communities. He is a man of the borders: not only in his own changing position in and connection with Dorsetshire, but also in his links with town and country. What was going on in the wider society – its laws, its economy, its communications, its education, its politics – was relevant to, impinged upon and contributed to change in rural society.

It is the awareness of connections between town and country which impresses Williams. Among the myriad examples that could be cited here is Tess arriving at the little country railway station to deliver the milk for the London train:

'Londoners will drink it at their breakfasts tomorrow, won't they?' she asked. 'Strange people that we have never seen? . . . who don't know anything of us, and where it comes from, or think how we drove two miles across the moor tonight in the rain that it might reach 'em in time?'

(cited ibid.: 252–3)

Here are new real connections between country and city, made possible by trains, and connected to a market economy – existing outside and inside the moral society with its system of ownership, rent, trade, tenancy and wage labour. The novels themselves show awareness of large impersonal forces as well as individual personal histories. The successes and failure, continuities and changes depicted in the novels relate to the experience of actual societies in change and conflict and not to some seamless, timeless country way of life. It is not the tradition of the country versus the change of the city but the interaction of changes in each sphere which makes Hardy much more than a 'regional novelist'.

But there was also with Hardy the interior life, the mental border country; 'the real Hardy, we soon come to see, is that border country so many of us have been living in: between custom and education, between work and ideas, between love of place and an experience of change' (ibid.: 239).

What impresses Williams about Hardy is that, subject to tension between the knowable and the known community, he manages to centre his novels on the ordinary processes of life and work. In doing so he is faithful in his communication of the pressures the characters themselves experience, sometimes to breaking point. So it is that: 'People choose wrongly but under terrible pressures: under the confusions of classs, under its misunderstandings, under the calculated rejections of a divided separating world' (ibid.: 258). Yet by staying close to his characters – Marty, or Tess or Jude – he also affirms them in their struggles and defeats as worthy of the reader's attention – not for the reader's sake but for theirs, since these characters signified the problem of real people in a real world in a particular time and place. They needed neither the defence of their author nor the patronage of their readers.

Williams expresses a sense of kinship with Eliot, Hardy and Lawrence, not only in terms of personal experience of mobility and education, but precisely because of the centrality of the issues of transition in their writing. While it is conventional to distinguish 'regional' or 'country' writing from that which focuses on the city, it is the sense of a connected history between the two that these writers exemplify. For Lawrence, the sense of transition was mediated through his social background, his expectations and his mobility. What does it mean to exist in a borderland and to contemplate the crossing of frontiers?

> Lawrence lived in a border which was more than that between farms and mines. In his own development ... he was on a cultural border. The choice was not only between mine and farm, but between both and the opening world of education and art. In this directly he is a successor of George Eliot and Hardy, but the crisis of mobility, and the history of which it is a part, are in the end very differently seen.
>
> (ibid.: 316–17)

In the end, Lawrence is for Williams a sad case, though this is not offered as a harsh judgement. Williams refers characteristically to Lawrence's 'knot of a life under overwhelming contradictions and pressures' (ibid.: 325). What happened? Lawrence could write of the loveliness of the countryside, contrasting it with the ugliness of the towns. He was not, however, pointing back to some rural English idyll but was concerned with the things that frustrated the instinct of community, 'which would make us unite in pride and dignity in the bigger gesture of the citizen, not the cottager' (cited ibid.: 319). It was, for Lawrence, the spirit of possessive individualism that had fostered the ugliness of English towns and cities. What should have been opportunities for renewal and regeneration and new community have been lost. What Lawrence loses – and here Williams makes an illuminating comparison with Grassic Gibbon's trilogy *Scots Quair* – are the struggles for independence and renewal, both of which existed in the countryside, despite all the pressures, and which were carried into the towns and cities. Lawrence arraigned the capitalist system but then, in the names of independence and renewal, opposed democracy, education and the labour movement. With some anger Williams sees Lawrence's own problems permeating the conventions of literary education and becoming, in effect, a weapon for use by them. This is precisely what Williams is contesting on a general front. By contrast with Lawrence, the less well known Scottish writer, Gibbon, offers a narrative account of transition that embodies both struggle and hope, which neither idealizes nor diminishes the rural experience. Although Williams only deals with the matter briefly there is, we think, a crucial issue at stake for him since he saw the Gibbon trilogy as dealing with an actual phase of history. Though it is not much addressed in direct terms, it is in fact part of the 'long transition', with an emphasis on long. Comparing Lawrence with Gibbon, Williams writes about a 'decisively different structure of feeling':

> The spiritual feeling for the land and for labour, the 'pagan' emphasis which is always latent in the imagery of the earth (very similar, through its different rhythms, to the Lawrence at the beginning of *The Rainbow*), is made available and is stressed in the new struggles: through the General Strike, in the period of *Cloud Howe*, to the time of the hunger marches in the period of *Grey Granite*. Even the legends sustain the transition, for their spiritual emphasis makes it possible to reject a Church that has openly sided with property and oppression. More historically and more convincingly, the radical independence of the small

farmers, the craftsmen and the labourers is seen as transitional to the militancy of the industrial workers. The shape of a whole history is thus decisively transformed.

(ibid.: 323)

Trying to do justice to the life and experience of the country without idealization is then part of Williams' project. The other part is to look at the negative connotations of the city and consider whether they represent the death of community in principle and in practice. What he draws attention to in the literary record is the sense that the city is both dangerous and yet open to new possibilities for human unity and experience, because, and not in spite of, the diversity. There is the coexistence of vice and virtue, chaos and order, wealth and poverty. London was at the apex: 'the astonishing creation of an agrarian and mercantile capitalism, within an aristocratic political order' (ibid.: 181).

Blake and Wordsworth stand as perceptive observers of the life of the city, London in particular. For Blake, London born, there was the organization of trade and finance and work, the conventions of church and marriage – the family coexisting with child labour, prostitution, poverty and human misery. To bring these things together was to challenge hypocrisy and offer a new perspective on the city as a whole:

It is the making of new connections in the whole order of the city and of the human system it concentrates and embodies. This forcing into consciousness of the *suppressed connections* is then a new way of seeing the human and social order as a whole. It is, as it happens, a precise prevision of the essential literary methods and purposes of Dickens.

(ibid.: 184; emphasis added)

The essential point to be made, however, is that Blake's purpose was to consider how *new* cities could be built in England's green and pleasant land: how could the existing contradictions be overcome? For Wordsworth, in the *Prelude*, London is a strange and wonderful place. Neighbourliness is a difficult thing to envisage since there is a perpetual flow, an 'endless stream of men and moving things'. There is transience, unfamiliarity, anonymity and a loss of connection. There is alienation from self and from others. Williams cites the following passage which appears to be central for his expository purposes:

O Friend! one feeling was there which belonged
To this great city, by exclusive right;
How often in the overflowing streets
Have I gone forwards with the crowd, and said
Unto myself, 'The face of every one
That passes by is a mystery!'
Thus I have looked, nor ceased to look, oppressed
By thoughts of what and whither, when and how
Until the shapes before my eyes became
A second-sight procession, such as glides
Over still mountains, or appears in dreams.
And all the ballast of familiar life
The present, and the past; hope, fear; all stay.
All laws of acting, thinking, speaking man
Went from me, neither knowing me, nor known.

Where then the knowable community? Incredibly, given the strangeness, confusion and the unknowing multitude, Wordsworth also sees new possibilities, new promises, which can enrich human experience: a new unity. The idea is set forth:

. . . that among the multitudes
Of that huge city, often times was seen
Affectingly set forth, more than elsewhere
Is possible, the unity of man
One spirit over ignorance and vice
Predominant, in good and evil hearts
One sense for moral judgments, as one eye
For the sun's light.

(cited ibid.: 186–7)

In Dickens, there is a great sense of the immensity of the city, into which people are pulled and swallowed up, as into a great monster. There is the city of the day and the city of the night. There is the fog that really hangs over the city, but which also stands as a metaphor for opaqueness and obscurity. Yet social relationships are established in this precarious world. Dickens reveals the relationships and the institutions in which they are formed to us: the school, the work house, the country house, the family, the law courts, and so on. While much will remain unknown in the city because of its size, Dickens insists upon the possibility of mutuality and neighbourliness in such a world. While things might seem impersonal and people subject to forces they cannot control, Dickens shocks his readers both by showing them something of their own world through fresh eyes and then by reminding them that it is a human construction. To that extent the future is open with possibilities for change in which human values are more consciously taken into account. As Williams puts it:

> It is not only power that is ambiguous – the power to create new worlds. There is also a choice: a choice of the human shape of the new physical environment. Or there can be a choice – we *can* be in a position to choose – if we see, physically and morally, what is happening to people in this time of unprecedented change.
>
> (ibid.: 198)

What makes the city important for Williams in this analysis is first that it provides an alternative site for democratic struggle, to the more restricted, local communities. There are new resources and potential to be mobilized for this end, which, if successful, can feed back into rural areas and on an international, not simply national, scale. The possibility of co-operation democracy and socialism and the role of education in developing a shared consciousness that the rule of the few over the many, whether in town or country, is not the best way forward, is what Williams wishes to emphasize. It is agrarian and industrial capitalism that has to be contested if effective communities are to be realized. To see beyond the blockages, huge as they are, in our society and others is to require and call upon considerable resources of hope.

There are two negative positions to be resisted. One is to peddle unreal views of the countryside, whether in fiction or political nostrums; and the other is to project images of the urban future, in fiction or in versions of political planning, that offer us insoluble problems, from global pollution to individual stress:

> The industrial and agricultural balance, in all its physical forms of town and country relations, is the product, however mediated, of a set of decisions about capital investment made by the minority which controls capital and which determines its uses by calculations of profit. When we have lived long enough with such a system it is difficult not to mistake it for a necessary and practical reality, whatever elements of its process we may find objectionable. . . . The competitive indifference or the sense of social isolation in the cities can be seen as bearing a profound

relation to the kinds of social competition and elimination which just such a system promotes. These experiences are never exclusive since within the pressures and limits people make other settlements and attachments and try to live by other values. But the central drive is still there.

(ibid.: 354)

These 'other values' and 'other settlements' against dominant tendencies are what Williams seeks both to identify and to encourage. The weight of these pressures and the worldwide nature of the dominant tendencies can scarcely leave scope for complacency. But since the struggle is one of values, it is both political and cultural. That is precisely why Williams is so concerned with language. It is, after all, both a means of socialization into dominant, taken-for-granted values and also a weapon for cultural struggle. Through it, meanings are challenged and the interests promoting those meanings made more visible. He reminds us that 'the most deeply known human community is language itself' (ibid.: 294). And that is why we must take seriously modern systems of communication, not least because they are in minority hands and serve to define reality for us.

Modern communications reach out from city to country, encompassing both. In Williams' view, much of the content of modern communications serves to form a shared consciousness, serving as substitute for more direct relations in small communities but qualitatively different.

For in its main uses it is a form of unevenly shared consciousness of persistently external events. It is what appears to happen, in these powerfully transmitted and mediated ways, in a world with which we have no other perceptible connections but which we feel is at once central and marginal to our lives.

(ibid.: 355)

This Williams sees as creating a specific form of consciousness inherent in the dominant mode of production, in and through which we define ourselves and our activities. Williams' position was not to celebrate or succumb to this capitalist triumphalism but to identify it as a deforming phenomenon and encourage reasoned resistance to it. This resistance includes the explicit recognition that, while it is a mistake to mystify the 'rural', it is also a mistake to marginalize the role of agriculture in the world as a whole.

Imperialism has played its part in making the realities of agricultural production invisible, since much of our raw material comes from exploited Third World countries. Moreover, socialists, in their modernizing 'progressive' way, had simply not thought through the continuing and interconnected importance of the rural economy to the city. Indeed, *The Country and the City* can be seen as an original attempt to come to terms with the Marxist project of overcoming the division of labour:

> For we really have to look, in country and city alike, at the real social processes of alienation, separation, externality and abstraction. And we have to do this not only critically in the necessary history of rural and urban capitalism, but substantially by affirming the experiences which in many millions of lives are discovered and rediscovered, very often under pressure: experiences of directness, connection, mutuality, sharing, which alone can define, in the end, what the real deformations may be.
>
> (ibid.: 358)

We can see, then, that from a strategic point of entry, the rereading of pastoral poetry, Williams moves on to map on a grand scale the significance of capitalism for both town and country. Neither, for that matter are state socialist societies excluded from the analysis, since they are part of the process: 'Look at socialism or communism: historically the enemies of capitalism, but in detail and often in principle, in matter of the country and the city, continuing and even intensifying some of the same fundamental processes' (ibid.: 363). The reworking of the idea that the division of labour can be transcended, relatively neglected in Marxism so far as country and city are concerned, is grounded in the view that for all its strength and power capitalism will come to grief under the pressure of its own contradictions.

This can sound like whistling in the dark to keep one's courage up. Yet if the system is intolerable because of its exploitative character, the alternative values of common effort and community must be sought, to overcome the existing divisions. This, for Williams, is the difference between negative politics and the politics of affirmation. As he makes clear in another place ('The importance of community' in Williams 1989c), if politics is to be defined only in terms of the capitalist interplay of interests, that, for him, would be the end of politics in any sense which would be understandable to him as a political thinker and activist. This, we may add, is a call not for a retrospective but for a prospective politics. It requires identifying the weaknesses, the contradictions, the instabilities of capitalism, notwithstanding all its dynamic strength and pervasiveness. It also requires the affirmation of different values, some of which will be located in alternative movements, in some aspects of socialism, feminism and ecology, for example. As with *Culture and Society*, the basic choice is between ways which contain the seeds of life and those which contain the seeds of death. Yet the seeds of both, like wheat and chaff, are within us: 'Right back in your own mind, and right back inside the oppressed and deprived community, there are reproducd elements of the thinking and feeling of that dominant centre' ('The importance of community', in Williams 1989c: 117).

In the essay from which this quotation is taken special attention is given to the possibilities for renewal and affirmation within the context of Welsh materialism. Why does the idea of community retain its importance despite Williams' own hesitations, as expressed in *Politics and Letters*? It is surely, in part, because some of the communities which he knows from experience were the carriers of alternative values of mutuality, neighbourliness and sharing, in opposition to capitalist values of profit and exploitation. The prospective claim – and hope – is that those values can be reaffirmed on a different scale, in the development of organizations and movements grounded in alternative values, with appropriate and accessible means of technology and communication to ensure that capitalism is not the last and destructive word to our planet. This is anything but nostalgia. It is a vision of new times. Working for such new times was, Williams recognized, a complicated business. Yet he also knew that without vision the people perish.

Chapter 10

Politics
Shifts and continuities

Among the most explicitly political writings of Raymond Williams is *May Day Manifesto 1968*. This was in fact a collaborative work produced under Williams' editorship. The Penguin edition was a revised and enlarged version of a 1967 manuscript which had been published under the auspices of the May Day Manifesto Committee. It was explicitly a product of the New Left and the 1967 version was co-edited with Stuart Hall and Edward Thompson. As pointed out in the Preface of the Penguin edition, the 1967 version had already been translated into other languages. *Le Monde* commented that it was 'distinguished by the rigour of the analyses presented, the lucidity of the judgements made on contemporary Britain, the realism of its proposals' (Williams 1968b: 10). According to the front cover of the Penguin edition the *Manifesto* was 'a socialist alternative to Labour government policies. The New Left analyses the British crisis, in a world perspective, and gives fresh definition and directions in the fight against capitalism.'

We can treat the *Manifesto* as a hinge or pivot to open up a number of Williams' political concerns. The *Manifesto* itself was born out of a sense of disillusionment with the Labour Party in power. The first post-war Labour government under Attlee ended in 1951, to be followed by thirteen years of Conservative government under Churchill, Eden, Macmillan and Home. Harold Wilson became the second post-war Labour Prime Minister in 1964, no doubt to the surprise of commentators who had begun to wonder whether Labour could ever again return to power. Much of that had been associated with views about the changing class structure, the 'embourgeoisement' of the working class and the increasing affluence assumed in Macmillan's famous phrase, 'Most of our people have never had it so good.' The Wilson administration offered new opportunities for the left in Britain; yet here in 1967–8 (indeed, meeting a few months after Wilson's second election victory in 1966, which gave him a majority of 100 in the House of Commons thus augmenting the very slender majority of 1964) disappointment was writ large.

In *Politics and Letters* Williams gives a personal reaction to what he experienced at that time which had motivated him to become involved with the *Manifesto*. He cites the seamen's strike of 1966, which Wilson had denounced as being run by a small group of politically motivated men; the sterling crisis of the same year which resulted in deflation and cuts in social services to defend the exchange rate. This led him to conclude (though we should also remember his growing reservations about the Attlee administration) that the Labour Party was not for socialism but was actively collaborating in the continuing reproduction of a capitalist society (see Williams 1981a: 373). The strength of these convictions is soon revealed in the *Manifesto*, where the paradox of a Labour government setting the priorities of power and money against people is stated and then elaborated as a series of connected paradoxes;

> While thousands of our people are without homes, while our schools are overcrowded and our health service breaking under prolonged strain, we have watched the wives of Labour Ministers protected by police, launching Polaris nuclear submarines. In a prolonged economic crisis, which has consistently falsified orthodox descriptions and remedies, a Labour Government has stuck to old and discredited policies; cutting ordinary people's living standards, and putting the protection of a capitalist economic and financial system before jobs, care and extended education. At City banquets, at the centre of a society that still flaunts private wealth, places are set for Labour Ministers to describe the historic objectives of their own party – the defence and advancement of the working people – as selfishness and indiscipline. The limited provisions of the welfare state are called sacred cows, and are cut, in a false equation with a still intolerable military expenditure. More than half a million people are left to stand and wait without jobs, and in this new language are called spare capacity. The new generations are generations of weapons.
>
> (Williams 1968b: 13)

The strong feelings expressed about the half a million people without jobs remind us that this was twenty-five years ago, when in the 1990s unemployment is anything between 3 and 4 million depending on how the figures are counted. But the paradoxes were so because a Labour government was in power: the *Manifesto* sensed failure in the midst of electoral success. It was a socialist critique grounded in the conviction that it was necessary to rethink the ways in which single issues were interconnected. To understand the connectedness between the industrial and the political, the international and the domestic, the economic and the cultural, the humanitarian and the radical, was the necessary step to take if the fragmentation of consciousness was to be resisted.

The approach of the *Manifesto* was, then, to re-examine the position Britain found itself in and challenge some of the conventional wisdom in which policy was grounded. Early on, for example, the issue of poverty was addressed. In 1964, 14 per cent of the population were living on incomes 40 per cent below the basic National Assistance rate or less, which included large numbers of the unemployed, the old and the chronically sick, and the single-parent families. Such poverty is a structural matter and not a matter of personal characteristics or failings. Indeed the argument was advanced that despite the myth that poverty was disappearing in an affluent society there were signs of a structural increase in the proportion of the population subject to poverty, even using the official bases for calculating, which were arguably modest. Poverty and social inequality were seen as inherent in the structure of British society. Income and employment inequalties were central to this. Thus the poorest 30 per cent received 12 per cent of total income after tax. Moreover there were continuing inequalities of pay between men and women, as well as in legal status and educational opportunity.

Interestingly there is a criticism of what has later come to be termed 'trickle-down economics'. The argument advanced that increases in social services depend on economic growth, which was constantly reiterated by the Labour government, was challenged:

> We have only to look to the United States, with a per capita income twice as high as in this country, to see that economic growth in no way automatically solves any of these difficulties. We need a clear identification of the mechanisms which in capitalist society generate this inequality which we so bitterly

oppose. The problem must be tackled at its roots, and these are fundamentally in the ownership and control of the economic system.

(1968b: 28)

The *Manifesto* went on to consider issues of housing, health and education. Here, as in some other parts of the book, the effect is rather like discovering that the electricity system in an old, disused house is still working. There is the recognition that real housing needs can be lost between speculative private interests and bureaucratic local government interests. While local authority tenants were often getting a bad deal, only the better off could buy into the private housing market. This left a great deal of unmet housing need and contributed to the decay of inner city areas, with all their attendant social problems, where the poorest struggled against the odds to survive with any dignity.

What about the National Health Service, which had been established by the first post-war Labour government to establish a new standard of civilized community care? The *Manifesto* referred to dilapidated hospitals, bad pay and conditions for staff and a draining of the public sector for private medical provision:

> What is now happening is a fight to keep even this service going, against powerful pressures to revert to a more primitive correlation of care and money. . . . To return the health service to its true status, at the centre of any humane society, is to demand the resources which would make possible not only the reconstruction of the most threadbare parts of the service, but also the radical remaking of existing structures in a new emphasis on community care.

(ibid.: 33)

The arguments in the 1990s about 'privatization' of the Health Service, concerns about a two-tier health service, and a general recognition that rhetoric around community care does not connect with the reality of inadequate resources – all of these are prefigured in the *Manifesto*.

The comments on education dwelt not only on the social division created by the private educational provision available to those who could afford it but also on the inequalities in the state system between different regions and local authorities. The *Manifesto* advocated a genuinely comprehensive system of education from nursery to tertiary levels. It did in fact call for a basic common curriculum, 'which relates all learning to the centres of human need, rather than to prospective social and economic grades' (ibid.: 35). This, however, was not developed.

Harold Wilson had coined the phrase 'the white heat of the technological revolution' to portray a Labour Party on the move, with a commitment to modernization to deal with Britain's economic decline. Clearly, it was not the need for change that the *Manifesto* contested but what was actually being done in the name of modernization. It could be seen as a kind of working out of the 'end of ideology' thesis, which masked the real effects of change on specific groups of people. Issues of values were not pinned down and questions of interests, other than some vague notion of national interest, were not put. Here we come to the heart of the disagreement between the writers of the *Manifesto* and the Labour government:

> Modernisation is, indeed, the 'theology' of a new capitalism. It opens up a perspective of change, but at the same time it mystifies the process and sets limits to it. Attitudes, habits, techniques, practices must change: the system of economic and social power, however, remains unchanged. Modernisation fatally short-circuits the formation of social goals. Any discussion of long-term purposes is made to seem utopian, in the down-to-earth, pragmatic climate which modernisation generates. The discussion about 'modernised Britain' is not about what sort of society, qualitatively, is being aimed at, but simply about how modernisation is to be achieved. All programmes and perspectives are treated instrumentally. As a model of social change, modernisation crudely foreshortens the historical development of society. Modernisation is the ideology of the never-ending present. The whole past belongs to 'traditional' society, and modernisation is a technical means for breaking with the past without creating a future. All is now: restless, visionless, faithless: human society diminished to a passing technique. No confrontation of power, values or interests, no choice between competing priorities, is envisaged or encouraged. It is a technocratic model of society, conflict-free and politically neutral, dissolving genuine social conflicts and issues in the abstractions of 'the scientific revolution', 'consensus, 'productivity'. Modernisation presumes that no group in the society will be called upon to bear the costs of

the scientific revolution – as if all men have an equal chance of shaping up the consensus, or as if, by some process of natural law, we all benefit equally from a rise in productivity. 'Modernisation' is thus a way of masking what the real costs would be of creating in Britain a truly modern society.

(ibid.: 45)

What then did this lack of vision for a future, as opposed to an instrumental rejection of tradition without any named value content, really mean? Crucially, it is expressed in what the *Manifesto* calls 'managed politics'. What is done in the name of consensus is in practice anti-democratic manipulative politics. It is a partnership of public and private bureaucracies in defence of established political and economic interests, which, by and large, had control of the means of communication, such that dissent is marginalized or tolerated within controlled limits. So it is that very specific interests – like the banks, the City and large corporations – shape what is defined as the 'national interest'. This is not, however, to be equated with the public interest, which in a democratic society would need to take account of the poor, the disadvantaged and the victims of market forces. Historically, the Labour Party had been set up to speak for and defend such groups against the powerful. But Labourism now was part of the new capitalism. On a more extended canvas this meant that cold war politics was sustained, that aid to the poor countries in the world put them in ever further debt as new loans were taken in order to repay the old ones, and it resulted in a capitalist market that failed to respond to public needs.

The *Manifesto*'s illustration of the treatment of interconnectedness not always recognized because of an emphasis on short-term company interests, to the exclusion of other things, was the mining industry. In the light of later and continuing conflicts it remains of relevance even though new considerations, notably the privatization of the electricity supply industry, have entered in:

The correct response . . . to the decline of the mining industry is not the present policy of accepting the priorities of the international oil companies, both in fuel oil and in their stake in what should be our national resources of North Sea Gas, and then leaving the colliery areas to a process of persuading private firms to set up there on grants. It should be, first, a clear re-working of real costs in fuel; not just the immediate costs, at the point of market delivery; but also the consequent costs, in a financial system dominated by institutions based outside Britain; in the military and political support, now so expensive to Britain, on which those international firms, and especially the oil companies, now rely; and in the consequences, at every level from transport to housing, of the social dislocation and distortion of an economy planned only in the companies' interests.

(ibid.: 136)

The point is then broadened out:

Everywhere, now we are faced with what looks like a realistic, practical accounting, even when it somehow produces the selling of carrots from Texas in the middle of an English horticultural region. The reason is that the accounting follows the internal convenience of the system, and pushes all consequent costs off to another, apparently irrelevant account. It is this that must be challenged over the whole range.

(ibid.)

But let us return to the miners. Some fifteen years later, in the wake of the 1984–5 miners' strike, Williams wrote a piece which combined his academic interest in language with his socialist politics – 'Mining the meaning: key words in the miners' strike' (reprinted in Williams 1989c). The purpose of the article was not to make judgements on the tactics, timing or personalities of the strike. Rather he looked at four terms – management, economics, community and order – and what the contest over their meaning signified. Management, as a concept, becomes transmuted into 'the right to manage'. Even nationalization had not stopped the National Coal Board from becoming in effect a corporate employer. Elaborate procedures of joint consultation had been established in the mining industry, but all this was overridden so that the 'right to manage' short-circuits the processes of information and negotiation and becomes an arbitrary claim. Typically Williams generalizes from the experience of the miners:

For this now is the general interest: that people working hard at their jobs should not be exposed to these arbitrary operations of capital and the state, disguised as 'the right to manage'. In a period of very powerful multinational capital, moving its millions under various flags of convenience, and in a period also of rapid and often arbitrary takeover and merger by financial groups of all kinds, virtually everyone is exposed or will be exposed to what the miners have suffered.

(Williams 1989c: 122)

As we may recall, much of the argument during the strike revolved around what was and what was not an uneconomic pit. There may be technical and commercial calculations and accounting procedures which undergird the official position. Here Williams makes two points. One is that even in economic terms the interest has to be defined in terms of general energy policy. This is not just a matter of the short-term profitability of individual pits but must be related to the consideration of long-term reserves. The second point has to do with social costs:

Houses, schools, hospitals, and roads in these areas compose a huge economic investment which dwarfs the trading calculations of any particular industry. It is here, at the most fundamental level, that the miners have begun to define the real issues and problems of a socialist economy, and to expose the long term and destructive character of a capitalist economy.

(ibid.: 123)

This, of course, links up with the third concept, community, to which Williams had devoted so much attention in his writings. He holds before us an image of the larger society which has to show care for the actual and diverse communities it contains. If it does not, then, for Williams, it is destroying actual communities in the name of the 'community' or 'public'. This he castigates as 'evil as well as false'. How does it happen? Williams speaks of the 'alien order of paper and money', and the logic of a new nomad capitalism. These nomads simply move from place to place in search of profits. Yet coal is a given resource in the country and this fact itself should challenge ruling definitions of wealth and profit.

An economic policy which would begin from real people in real places, and which would be designed to sustain their continuing life, requires a big shift in our thinking, but a shift which in their arguments about pits and communities – their refusal to separate economics from a people and a society – the miners have begun to indicate.

(ibid.: 125)

So the resistance to nomad capitalism was important in human terms but it was also important because such predatory activities could threaten, in the end, the existence of a whole society. This, we can reasonably suppose, helps to explain the national resistance to the announcement of the closure of thirty-one pits by the Conservative government in 1992. .... If 30,000 jobs could go at the stroke of a pen, where would it stop?

This brings together, quite naturally, the concept of community and the concept of order. Here Williams inverts the conventional 'law and order' rhetoric deployed against the miners to define the political and economic offensive as dislocating and destructive of the social order. Late capitalism is a problem rather than a solution:

> Capitalist policy, which is still one of buying in the cheapest market and selling in the dearest, has in recent decades been profoundly subversive of what is still the most freely chosen social order of our people: that is, existence as an independent and self-sustaining nation. The continued legitimacy of appeals to either *law* or *order* rests primarily upon this identity. Thus when supposedly public corporations in steel, or electricity, or now coal, openly subordinate the interest of this true national to their own market calculations – hauling coal, for example, across the seven seas to undercut, reduce or close down any supposedly national industry – a profound social crisis has begun.
>
> (ibid.: 126)

Each of these concepts – management, economics, community and order – as applied to the mining industry and its problems serves to remind us that there are alternative ways of thinking about society which, however complex, begin with human need. This takes us back to the critique of modernization which the *Manifesto* saw as a technical means for breaking with the past without creating a future. To do that was a failure of vision and therefore a betrayal of hope. In particular it failed to deal with the complex issue of continuity and change in terms of human interests and human needs. This was to be explored much further by Williams in *Towards 2000*. We will return to this but for the moment we can note a typical comment:

> There is no useful way of thinking about the future which is not based in these values of close continuity in life and the means of life. All the practical problems begin when these have to be

related to other lives and other means, in an unavoidable and necessary diversity, and under the stresses of actual change. Many ways of thinking about the future jump from this practical level, where substantial feelings are deeply engaged, to what seem more realistic objective assessments, based on selected versions, often in fact contradictory, of these primary needs and desires.

(Williams 1985b: 6)

If this was so for economic matters of work and employment, it was also necessary to see how human needs and aspirations could be affected by the conduct of politics which continued to exploit the poorer countries of the world and threatened the very survival of the species through the ever-intensifying nuclear arms race.

The *Manifesto* expressed a view about the cold war and the nuclear arms race that was central to much New Left thinking about international relations. There were the two power blocs – the West, under the leadership of the USA, and the East, controlled by the Soviet Union – representing capitalism and communism. Their antagonistic relationship spiralled into the nuclear arms race from 1945 onwards. The West's exclusive possession of nuclear weapons was broken by the Soviet Union and thereafter the nuclear arms race accelerated in the name of strategic parity: both sides claimed they had to keep developing their nuclear weapons programme in order to catch up with the other. Consequently, there was build-up but never build-down.

The *Manifesto*, an explicitly socialist document, was deeply anti-Stalinist.

For, even if the role of United States imperialism could be clearly seen, it was never possible to give simple assent to Soviet communism as the protagonist of socialist policies. The actual progress of Russian communism, under severe pressures – internally, in the rapid fight out of backwardness; externally, in the invasion and hostility of the old powers – had long been of a character to check all easy, utopian assumptions. Many features of this communism could not be recognised as anything but hostile to socialist ideas nurtured in a more temperate historical experience. Long before the Cold War commenced the communist parties outside Russia had passed from the role of defender of the first socialist state to that of apologist for some of its most indefensible authoritarian features.

(Williams 1968b: 89)

Indeed, because the Soviet Union was concerned with its national interests, rather than the promulgation of socialism, it did not usually support indigenous revolutionary movements in other countries. Whether one thinks of the Greek resistance against the monarchy (reimposed by British troops immediately after the Second World War), the Chinese revolution under Mao, or the communist parties of Italy, France and Britain dominated by the Moscow line on political correctness, it was not socialism that was being supported. Rather it was superpower politics, with its spheres of influence that subordinated the communist parties of the West to the demands of Soviet diplomacy. Thus were they compromised and discredited by their Stalinist apologetics.

However alienated from Stalinism the contributors to the *Manifesto* were, this did not lead them to the conclusion that the Soviet Union was engaged in expansionist policies. It had been deeply damaged by the war, in which some 20 million had died, and had of necessity to be preoccupied with reconstruction. It worked with the spheres of influence parameters of the Yalta agreement. So not only was the concept of Soviet-inspired subversion a falsification of actual international power politics but the belief that the Soviet Union constituted a direct military threat was a myth. Yet it was these two assumptions that governed the conventional wisdom of Western military thinking (or at least its public presentation). The arms build-up – conventional and nuclear – was a necessary defence against Soviet imperialism. The doctrine of MAD – Mutually Assured Destruction – became the established version of nuclear deterrence theory at this time. It was in this political and military context that the New Left in Britain supported unilateral nuclear disarmament:

> By the mid-1950s the Cold War, through sheer weight of matching nuclear terror, had fought itself to a standstill in Europe, bringing with it a general deadlock of all popular political initiatives. We believe that we were right, in that situation, to identify nuclear weapons as the immediate and major danger to civilisation and indeed to human existence. We were right to demand British withdrawal from a nuclear strategy, and to offer this as a positive political and moral initiative. We had to choose, and had always needed to choose, even in the worst period of Stalinism, between rival world political orders which, in the sheer weight of their military power, made any unambiguous choice

virtually unbearable. This was the instinct of the simple call for
unilateral nuclear disarmament: to establish a human choice
where no fully supportable political choice existed.

(Williams 1968b: 89)

To call a plague on both houses, East and West, was of course
to espouse an active neutralism. Such a position was likely to, and
did, evoke a response from political leaders in the West that this
was subversive and, at best, woolly-minded idealism; and from the
East that it was anti-Soviet. What, after all, was being challenged
was what C. Wright Mills had called the 'crackpot realism of the
military metaphysic' (Mills 1960). Mills, in *The Causes of World
War III*, was writing primarily for an American readership. The
book was a counterblast against cold war journalism. He saw part
of his task as drawing attention to facts or events which his fellow
Americans might scarcely know, such as the fact that the Soviets
had already stopped nuclear tests unilaterally and made a number
of specific disarmament proposals. While this might redress the
balance of blame, his fundamental argument was that it was the
lethal symmetry of action that provided the dynamic of the move
towards a third world war. In the *Manifesto* Mills is indeed briefly
referenced (1968b: 96) but the closeness of the shared analysis is
well brought out in the following comment:

> Since 1962 the network of missile, satellite and anti-satellite
> weapons has become more dense, and the time for decision more
> hair's breadth. Thus the Cold War contains within itself, simply
> in terms of its own rationale and technology, dangerous hysteric
> tendencies.

(ibid.: 91)

In his analysis Mills had written of the drift and thrust towards
nuclear war. This was a way of trying to deal with the difficult topic
of structure and agency in social theory. Mills was crucially
concerned to distinguish between 'fate' understood as a consequence
of inescapable structural forces and 'fate' as a social construct, when
authorities claim that nothing else can be done, that present policies
are 'necessary' and 'realistic' and that there is no alternative which
is 'practical'. While we may be persuaded or manipulated into
believing that what these authorities say is true, 'inevitably' is a
social construct: it is therefore open to challenge and to a strategy
of resistance that can change our 'fate'. For Mills, 'drift' carried

with it the first meaning of 'fate' – in this case innumerable decisions which have coalesced, sometimes in unforeseen ways, and moved the world into cold war. 'Thrust' related to actions which people take or refuse to take. Mills' point was that drift and thrust were intertwined in a way that was leading the great powers closer to the abyss of a third world war. But since human agency, individual and collective, is intertwined in this process, Mills argued that we do have the responsibility to bring the significance of that to the fore and work for alternatives, rather than accept our powerlessness. This included a challenge to the doctrine of nuclear deterrence. As Jonathan Schell was to write, a generation later, in *The Fate of the Earth*:

> This is the circularity at the core of the nuclear deterrence doctrine: we seek to avoid our self-extinction by threatening to perform the act. According to this logic, it is almost as though if we stopped threatening ourselves with extinction, the extinction would occur.

(Schell 1982: 201)

Re-establishing the importance of human choice, in a world where the majority appeared powerless to affect the nuclear arms race, was always going to be a difficult task. Given the nature of the power structure, hope was always liable to be overwhelmed by despair. In the end, after all, human choice had to be exercised in political action if the activities of what Mills had termed the power elites were to be curbed or transformed. So it was crucial to establish some political space and then to extend it. There were moments in post-war history when this seemed a forlorn hope.

Edward Thompson, one of the contributors to the *Manifesto*, had from the earliest post-war period pressed the case for nuclear disarmament. He it was who in the late 1970s and early 1980s became a significant figure in the campaign known as END – European Nuclear Disarmament. This arose with the growing recognition that the doctrine of Mutually Assured Destruction was being effectively displaced by concepts of flexible response. This meant that in the event of nuclear war – and NATO refused to give up its commitment to first strike with nuclear weapons – Europe would have become the battlefield for intermediate and short-range nuclear weapons. So it was that the British Campaign for Nuclear Disarmament was put into a European-wide context and very effectively challenged the conventional wisdom the nuclear deterrence could provide collective security. But Thompson himself, who in his theoretical writings had always stressed the role of human agency in change, albeit not in circumstances of our choosing, did come close to despair. Early in 1989 he published a paper in the *New Left Review*: 'Notes on exterminism, the last stage of civilisation'. This was reprinted by *New Left Review* in a collection of essays responding to Thompson in a book entitled *Exterminism and Cold War* (Thompson 1982). Thompson's essay was a chilling one. With an ironic gesture towards familiar Marxist categories he suggested that if the hand-mill gives feudal society, the steam mill industrial capitalism, the nuclear bomb society gives us exterminism. Consciously echoing Wright Mills, he portrays the logic of exterminism in terms of two interlocking processes. While the East and the West were apparently pursuing rational self-interest, the reality of the process was to move the world closer to destruction. What particularly concerned him was that political space was being squeezed almost out of existence by technology creep and the bureaucratic apparatus that surrounded it: 'Today's hair trigger military technology annihilates the very moment of "politics". One exterminist system confronts another, and the act will follow the logic of advantage within the parameters of exterminism' (Thompson 1982: 8). Describing the scenario of impending superpower collision and ideological instability he concluded that it was 'not likely that "we" – with our poor resources, our slight political preparation, our wholly inadequate internationalist communications – can succeed. *It is probable that exterminism will reach its historical destination*' (ibid.: 25; emphasis added).

This looked very much like pessimism of the intellect and of the will. Yet it was greatly to Thompson's credit that he continued to look for ways of acting in broad alliances, across the cold war fronts of East and West, that would open up a new space for politics. Williams was one of the contributors to *Exterminism and Cold War*. His essay 'The politics of disarmament', was also in large part reprinted in *Towards 2000* in the chapter entitled 'War: the last enemy'. What he characteristically challenged was what he regarded as the technological determinism of Thompson's position. Such determinism is, he argued, when taken seriously,

> a form of intellectual closure of the complexities of social process. In its exclusion of human actions, interests and intentions in favour of a selected and reified image of their causes and results,

it systematically post-dates history and excludes all other versions of cause. This is serious everywhere, but in the case of nuclear weapons it is especially disabling. Even when, more plausibly, it is in effect a form of shorthand, it steers us away from originating and continuing causes, and promotes (ironically, in the same mode as the ideologies which the weapons systems now support) a sense of helplessness beneath a vast, impersonal and uncontrollable force. For there is then nothing left but the subordinated responses of passivity or protest, cynical resignation or prophecy. That the latter response in each pairing is infinitely better, morally and politically, goes without saying. But that the tone of a campaign can be radically affected by the initial assumption of so absolute and overpowering a system is already evident, mixed incongruously as it also is with the vigorous organisation and reaching out to others which follow from different initial bearings.

(Thompson 1982: 68)

We can see in this response a characteristic Williams' critique of the connection between technological determinism and cultural pessimism. So he concludes his essay by writing: 'It is then in making hope practical, rather than despair convincing, that we must resume and change and extend our campaigns' (ibid.: 85). In his reflections on the contributors to *Exterminism and Cold War* Thompson acknowledged the criticism of Williams and others that he had been too pessimistic and deterministic in his analysis ('I ought to have known better than to have gestured at Marx's suggestive image of the hand-mill and the steam-mill') (Thompson 1982: 330).

But there are other things of interest in Williams' essay. The 'logic of exterminism' reminds him explicitly of Orwell's *Nineteen Eighty-Four*. While this correctly portrayed, albeit in fictional anti-utopian terms, the emergence of superstates, Williams argues that actual developments in world history have been much more complex. So it is not just a matter of superstates technologically determining, through military competition, what happens in the rest of the world. This is because political and economic struggles do not wholly mirror or reinforce that activity; and also because secondary states can export other kinds of arms to various parts of the world. This has led to many millions of deaths around the world at a time when nuclear weapons are supposed to be determining and deterring. Williams then reconsiders the notion of deterrence and makes the central claim that we should distinguish between deterrence as strategy and deterrence as ideology. He reminds us that the USA was the first to possess the atomic bomb and that during that period there were active policy proposals to use it to destroy the world centre of communism before the Soviet Union could also develop such weapons. There was, after all, a view expounded by the then influential writer James Burnham in *The Struggle for the World* (1947) that once both sides obtained the nuclear weapon, war with these weapons would be inevitable since possession implied inevitable use. This, however, did not happen and Williams argues that, while there were many reasons for this, including public revulsion against the first use of nuclear weapons and the unpredictable effects of fallout, in its limited, direct context, deterrence was effective. Yet it is one thing to seek security against attack – a reasonable desire of any nation – but another to become a pawn in the game of world political struggle. This is precisely where Williams makes his support for END clear. For it is through his understanding of the world political struggle that he sees deterrence as ideology taking over from deterrence as a strategy. So the ugly paradox is manifest: the European 'theatre' is seen as a 'controlled' part of the global struggle. Not only is this a questionable military calculation but the subjects of deterrence

> have become the objects in an ideology of deterrence determined by interests wholly beyond us as nations or as peoples, though significantly not beyond our frontiers as the interests of existing ruling classes. Whatever the scenario might be for others, for us, as peoples, it is from the opening scene the final tragedy. Global deterrence would have achieved a Europe in which there was nobody left to deter or to be deterred.
>
> (ibid.: 74)

For these reasons Williams insists that it is not a matter of academic nicety but of practical politics to reconsider the use of the terms 'multilateralism' and 'unilateralism'. Once the distinction is made between deterrence as strategy and as ideology it is possible to see that multilateralism in relation to the first can be a reasonable and sensible approach to disarmament. Yet when deterrence is treated as ideology, multilateralism becomes a code word for weapons modernization and rearmament. Indeed multilateralism becomes, in practice, bilateralism in which the rest of the world in general and Europe in particular are spectators. But where does this leave unilateralism? Apart from the absolutism of the pacifist case Williams argues that British anti-nuclear policy has to be politically coherent. This has to take into account that Britain is locked into an alliance with advanced capitalist societies with interrelated military, economic and political elements. This is why developing a campaign on a European scale becomes so important.

Writing explicitly as a socialist, Williams identified seven areas in which progress towards a politically coherent anti-nuclear campaign could be made. In summary, these were: heightening public consciousness about the dangers of modern weapons systems; exposing the deceit of civil defence campaigns in relation to security against nuclear attack; organizing public pressure for arms control and negotiated disarmament; explaining the nature of changing weapons systems and their relation to actual negotiations on arms control; opposing arbitrary secrecy and security controls within individual states; showing the real links between nuclear energy and nuclear weapons programmes; and opposing the naturalization of arms production and export as part of the economic strategy of the advanced industrial world (see Thompson 1982: 79).

In the light of the events of 1989 and beyond – the dissolution of the Soviet Union, the dismantling of communist states in Eastern Europe and the reunification of Germany – which Williams did not live to see, there are two points which are still worth noting in his analysis. First, there was his recognition of the problematic relationship between the military-industrial complex and the economic and political spheres. In the centralized socialist systems, he pointed out, the scale of military spending was economically crippling and unproductive. In the case of capitalist societies support for the arms industries is not unconditional, since taking vast sums from public revenue can disrupt other potential investment programmes and generate socioeconomic discontent, especially when manufacturing industry is in recession. This, indeed, is why Williams concludes that there is no inevitability that the military sector will dominate all other considerations: for both social systems, capitalist and communist, there were dysfunctional features about the arms race. It is this that moves one away from the logic of exterminism, whilst recognizing the real dangers of the arms race, and readmits the role of struggle in politics – a struggle against the culture and politics of violence.

The second point has to do with what Williams unashamedly referred to as the imperialist economic system of capitalism and the role of military intervention. What happens when there is a crisis of resources? In the light of the Gulf War, the following passage leads, surely, to sober reflection:

> It has become an absolute duty for Western socialists to prepare, in good time, the position from which we can oppose and defeat attempts to secure scarce resources – the case of oil is the most urgent example – by military interventions, whether direct or indirect. Such interventions will of course attempt to recruit popular opinion by appeals for the protection of our (privileged) 'way of life'. Given the effects of the simultaneous crisis of imposed unemployment and deprivation on the working peoples of the West, no socialist can suppose that these attempts will be easy to defeat.
>
> (Thompson 1982: 84)

WHAT KIND OF POLITICS?

Was Williams a utopian? With some surprise one observes that there is no entry for this word in *Keywords*. We can, however, be guided by two extended discussions of the term elsewhere in his writing. In 'Utopia and science fiction' (reprinted in Williams 1980), he characteristically tells us that the relationship between the two concepts is 'exceedingly complex'. He offers a neat, if overlapping, fourfold distinction concerning fictional utopias: 1) the paradise – where a happier life exists elsewhere; 2) the externally altered world – where a new kind of life is made possible by unlooked-for natural events; 3) the willed transformation – where a new kind of life has been achieved by human effort; and 4) the technological transformation – where technical discovery makes a new kind of life possible. All of these can also be thought of in negative terms to produce characterizations of dystopias. The use of the concept of utopia was, of course, famously questioned by Engels in his contrast between utopian and scientific socialism. But there have been some strange twists to this, as Williams points out, such that the notion of scientific socialism can be regarded as utopian, using Engels' own pejorative sense of the term. Moreover, there is another perspective that stresses the importance of 'desire' which can give direction and substance to images of the future. But, claims Williams, 'we cannot abstract desire. It is always desire for something specific, in specifically impelling circumstances' (Williams 1980: 208).

Developing this point Williams draws upon a further distinction between utopian modes of thinking: those that emphasize systematic and those that stress heuristic futures. The first concerns itself with the systematic building of alternative organizational models and the second with a more open discourse about alternative values. It is the second which allows more scope for the 'education of desire'. Even so, it is not a question of asking which is better or stronger:

> The heuristic utopia offers a strength of vision against the prevailing grain; the systematic utopia a strength of conviction that the world really can be different. The heuristic utopia, at the same time, has the weakness that it can settle into isolated and in the end sentimental 'desire', a mode of living with alienation, while the systemic utopia has the weakness that, in its insistent organisation, it seems to offer little room for any recognisable life. These strengths and weaknesses vary, of course, in individual examples of each mode, but they vary most decisively, not only in the periods in which they are written but in the periods in which they are read. The mixed character of each mode then has much to do with the twentieth century dystopias which have succeeded them. *For the central contemporary question about the utopian modes is why there is a progression, within their structures, to the specific reversals of a Zamyatin, a Huxley, an Orwell – and of a generation of science-fiction writers.*

> (ibid.: 203–4; emphasis added)

The well-known cases of Huxley's *Brave New World* and Orwell's *Nineteen Eighty-Four* remain important reference points for Williams, and for good reasons. Huxley takes the word 'community', a central concept in utopian thinking (and, of course, for Williams throughout his work) and applies it to the repressive system: 'Community, identity and stability' is the motto of the brave new world. The contrast with William Morris' *News from Nowhere* could not be more strong with its sense of a revolutionary struggle – albeit long and uneven in its development – towards new social relations and feelings, with all the energy that entails. Yet, instructively, Huxley in the Foreword to the 1946 edition of his novel, does envisage in the real world the possibility of a utopia beyond his dystopia. It is, as Williams points out, not so different from Morris' vision of a self-governing and balanced community. But it is elitist in its conception, belonging to the 'exiles and refugees' from the dominant system. Williams finds this significant because

> This is the path travelled, in the same period, by bourgeois cultural theory: from the universal liberation, in bourgeois terms, through the phase in which the minority first educates and then regenerates the majority, to the last sour period in which what is now called 'minority culture' has to find its reservation, its hiding place, beyond both the system and the fight against the system.
>
> (Williams 1980: 207)

Although the utopian mode emerges almost unbidden from Huxley's reflections, it is a displacement that has no historical grounding. The case of Orwell here, as elsewhere, troubles Williams. Although *Nineteen Eighty-Four* is a fiction, its emphasis on the repression of autonomy and cancellation of variations and alternatives carries with it a bitter sense of the inevitable hopelessness of the human condition such that even oppositional forces can be converted into agencies of subjection. Even its satirical intentions are submerged. The possibility of human struggle to achieve new kinds of society, even if no certainty of the outcome can be given, is crucial for Williams.

What Williams usefully does is to remind us of the connection between utopian or dystopian writing and the times in which it was written. While he wants to contest the despair, sourness and even cynicism that provides the structure of feeling for anti-utopias, he also recognizes that by the time we reach the 1960s and 1970s the utopian impulse has surfaced again. But – and here he refers to Le Guin's *The Dispossessed* (1974) as an example – it is an impulse that is treated warily. This he sees as applying to radical thought about society and social change among Western radicals:

> It belongs to a general renewal of a form of utopian thinking – not the education but the learning of desire – which has been significant among Western radicals since the struggles and also since the defeats of the 1960s. Its structures are highly specific. It is a mode within which a privileged affluence is at once assumed and rejected: assumed and in its own ways enjoyed, yet known, from inside, as lying and corrupt; rejected, from in close, because of its successful corruption; rejected, further out, by learning and imagining the condition of the excluded *others*.
>
> (Williams 1980: 221)

So he concludes that in a world dominated by capitalism it is not appropriate to have utopian concepts that are static, based on images of perpetual harmony and rest, but rather those that challenge social injustices and corruption without succumbing to defeatism. This allows for the possibility of social transformation without assuming that history is on 'our' side and for the recognition that technological advances can have an enabling as well as a repressive potential. Williams' utopianism is of a specific kind. It is where, 'within a capitalist dominance, and within the crisis of power and affluence which is also the crisis of war and waste, the utopian impulse now warily, self-questioningly, and setting its own limits, renews itself' (ibid.: 212).

This is the perspective which directly informs *Towards 2000*. Although Williams does not reference Popper's critique of utopianism (Popper 1961a, 1961b) it is precisely the idea that systematic utopias, however humane and rational their intentions, in practice lead to inhuman, repressive social orders, that is, systematic dystopias, which Popper emphasized. The unplanned and unintended consequences of planned social change were seen by Popper as inimical to freedom and leading in practice to tyranny. Williams argues that this kind of critique, in so far as it is related to the Bolshevik revolution, is somewhat misplaced because Bolsheviks rejected utopian thinking as idle dreaming. In any case, while he admits that thinking about systematic utopias can fail to come to terms with the world as it is they can still have value:

> what the systematic utopia offers, at its best, is an imaginative reminder of the nature of historical change: that major social orders do rise and fall, and that new social orders do succeed them. . . . There can be idle dreaming either way: the systematic nightmare no less idle than the rosy fantasy. But the value of the systematic utopia is to lift our eyes beyond the short-term adjustments and changes which are part of the ordinary material of politics, and thus to insist, as a matter of general principle, that temporary and locally incredible changes can and do happen.
> (Williams 1985b: 13)

And heuristic utopias? Although they might be reduced to a vague impulse that things could be different they can find expression in small-scale communal groups and attempts at alternative lifestyles. As such they have the seeds of hope within them and can challenge what Williams sees as the incorporated and marketed versions of capitalist cornucopia.

Aware of the weaknesses of utopian thinking, whether systematic or heuristic, whilst pressing the case for going beyond short-term thinking and taken-for-granted assumptions, Williams makes what is at first sight a surprising connection between cultural analysis and the approach illustrated in the Club of Rome's trend report *Limits to Growth* (1972). One of the strengths of cultural analysis has been that it has not been bounded by any area of society or specialist discipline. Hence, through cultural analysis we are able to obtain a lively sense of interconnections and interactions. But, once dogma goes out of the window, its claims to establish the real order of determination between different forms of activity are surrounded with uncertainty:

> That there always is such an order of determination cannot be doubted from the historical evidence, though that it is not always the same order is equally clear. This is the necessary theoretical base for the recognition of genuinely different social orders. This point bears especially upon the possible development of cultural analysis (always in practice pulled towards the manageable past) into constructive analysis of the present and of possible and probable futures, where its methods are especially necessary and where new practical formations might be found. For it is only by continuing to attend to a whole lived social order, and at the same time identifying the primary determining forces within it, that this kind of general humanist analysis can significantly contribute to thinking about the future.
>
> (Williams 1985b: 15)

Why does Williams think the approach developed in the *Limits of Growth* connects with this? First, because it represents a shift in time-scale, compared to the short-term thinking of much day-to-day politics. Secondly, because, like cultural analysis, it too is concerned with dynamic interactions rather than piecemeal analyses. Although Williams does not say so, in effect the approach also draws our attention to non-cultural factors: population, food, capital, industrial production, mineral resources. The idea of feedback in the two forms of analysis also suggests an instructive parallel. If the dangers of pollution to which a systems-dynamics approach may point are not responded to, then at some stage the effects on nature may be irreversible. It is a question of identifying the signals

and taking appropriate action. How we choose to read these
messages that have to do with long-term concerns about the physical
well-being of the planet is itself a cultural matter. Yet to have the
discernment to recognize the gravity of the ecological problems
facing the planet, is to appreciate that these problems are not yet
out of control, and that through the development of adequate social
and political agencies the intelligence and information is available
to deal with them creatively. But is anybody, or are enough people,
listening? This, for Williams, is a disturbing concern:

> What kind of culture is it, when some serious analysis appears
> and is almost at once placed as another instalment of 'doom and
> gloom'? What kind of culture is it, which pursues distraction,
> in its ordinary selection even of news, to the point where there
> is hardly any sustained discussion of the central and inter-
> locking issues of survival? There are times, in the depth of the
> current crisis, when the image materialises of a cluttered room
> in which somebody is trying to think, while there is a fan-dance
> going on in one corner and a military band blasting away in
> the other. It is not the ordinary enjoyments of life that are
> diverting serious concern, as at times in a natural rhythm, they
> must and should. It is a systematic cacophony which may indeed
> not be bright enough to know that it is jamming and drowning
> the important signals, but which is nevertheless, and so far
> successfully, doing just that.
>
> (Williams 1985b: 18)

Even so, by the time we get to the concluding chapters of *Towards
2000* Williams is pointing out that there are those who are listening to the signals and thinking about the future but in ways which
he wants to contest. What he has in mind is not so very different
from the version of managed politics which was criticized in the
Manifesto. In *Towards 2000* he labels it Plan X, acknowledging that
it is a plan as distinct from the unthinking reproduction of distinction. But the focus on strategic or competitive advantage, which
exemplifes Plan X, is, in Williams' view, dangerous because its
proponents do not seriously believe that the crises facing the planet
can be effectively dealt with:

> Thus, while as a matter of public relations they still talk of
> solutions, or possible stabilities, their real politics and planning
> are not centred on these, but on an acceptance of an indefinite

continuation of extreme crisis and extreme danger. With this harsh perspective, all their plans are for phased advantage, an effective even if temporary edge, which will always keep them at least one step ahead in what is called, accurately enough, the game plan.

(ibid.: 244)

This is a thinking about the future which is neither utopian nor anti-utopian: it is a *realpolitik* that has no concern for human welfare or the future of the planet and should not be seen as a conspiracy theory. On the contrary, it becomes part of the open common sense of high-level politics and it can be found on the left as well as on the right of the political spectrum:

from the long experience of capitalist society, there is a widespread common sense that we always have to look to our own advantage or we shall suffer and may go under. This daily reality produces and reproduces the conditions for seeing Plan X as inevitable. It has then made deep inroads into the labour movement which was basically founded on the alternative ethic of common well-being. When a trade-union argues for a particular wage-level, not in terms of the social usefulness of the work but, for example, in terms of improving its position in the 'wages league table', it is in tune with Plan X.

(ibid.: 246)

This comment on the labour movement gives pause for thought. As far back as the writing of *The Long Revolution* Williams had identified these contradictions in the labour movement. No one, after all, should be too surprised that the institutions of labour could embody capitalist as well as socialist elements. Since then he perceived the pressures on the labour movement as greater rather than less, with the breakdown of working-class communities, the crises of capitalist profitability and the international relocation of industry:

What will happen now is either the final incorporation of the labour movement into a capitalist bargaining mechanism, with socialism left stranded as a theory and as a sect, or the wide remaking of a social movement which begins from primary human needs. These needs are for peace, security, a caring society and a careful economy. They are needs which the capitalist social order cannot adapt itself to. But which equally the narrowed interests of maximum wage-earning in any kind of employment (the now dominant definition of what was once the whole labour movement) cannot define or support.

(Williams 1985b: 173)

Given his own background and sympathies with the labour movement, Williams recognizes the personal difficulty he has in making such criticisms:

But it is better to say them than to go on acquiescing in the limited perspectives and the outdated assumptions which now govern the movement, and above all in its sickening self-congratulatory sense of a taken-for-granted constituency. The real struggle has broadened so much, the decisive issues have been so radically changed, that only a new kind of socialist movement, fully contemporary in its ideas and methods, bringing a wide range of needs and interests together in a new definition of the general interest, has any real future.

(ibid.: 174)

This is surely where we can encounter Williams' wary utopianism: in the recovery of an understanding of the general interest – the common good. And it is in this context that he writes of social movements as providing resources for hope. He has in mind the peace movement, the ecology movement, the women's movement, human rights agencies, campaigns against poverty and homelessness and groups seeking to raise awareness about the Third World and the North–South divide. Typically, as he points out, these groups have started from outside organized class interests and institutions. They are contrasted with the defensive labour institutions of the West and the evident failure of 'actually existing socialism' of the East, moving from common economies to competitive accumulation. What impressed Williams about the new social movements was, in part, the communal nature of their organization, but crucially their ability to identify disabling features of the modern situation and their interconnections. Moreover, they contained within their ranks people who were able to combat conventional wisdom with informed, rational argument, as well as with humane passion. But, whether thinking of such movements or of oppositional cultural developments in film, theatre and writing, the question of how this relates in the end to the political process has to be confronted. Always there is the risk that new movements may be incorporated or marginalized; so the relations between small-group potentials and the dominant system are at the heart of the problem. The resources of hope have to be tested and deployed against this dominant system; Williams is not sanguine about this or about the magnitude of the task:

> it has been possible to move relatively large numbers of people on popular versions of the issues of disarmament, protection of the environment, the rights of women. There is then an apparent asymmetry between these real advances and persistent majorities of a different kind: conservative (in more than one party); nationalist; consumerist. Some people make desperate attempts to prove that this is not so, seizing on all the exceptions, all the local breaks, all the local resistances. But while these of course must be respected, there is no real point in pretending that the capitalist social order has not done its main job of implanting deep assent to capitalism even in a period of its most evident economic failures. On the old assumptions it would have been impossible to have four million unemployed in Britain, and most of our common services in crisis or breaking down, and yet for the social order itself to be so weakly challenged or political support for it so readily mobilised. Yet that is where we now are.
>
> (ibid.: 254)

At the end of *Towards 2000*, set against what he had identified as Plan X, Williams offers an outline for an alternative social theory. It is based upon what he terms three changes of mind, which is in effect to advance his own self-questioning utopianism. It is as though he invites us to share in his own dialogue with himself, as he contemplates the magnitude of what is required for change, while advancing the possibility that it can be so.

First there is the need to rethink the connection between the forces and the relations of production. We are not surprised to see, again, the rejection of technological determinism, which is, after all, a motif throughout his work. But relations of production also, in both capitalist and 'actually existing socialist' economies, with their notions of necessity, also have to be challenged. The product of these interrelations has led in practice to defining the world in terms of possibilities for its profitable exploitation rather than seeing the intricate interdependence of life and land. The present situation had its weaker precedents in earlier systems of slavery and serfdom, and the exploitation of people themselves as raw material through

military political, economic and ideological means is not peculiar
to capitalism. But:

> In the development of much more powerful technologies, and
> in their capture by a class which defined its whole relationship
> to the world as one of appropriation, what was once selective
> and guided by conscious affinities with natural processes has been
> replaced by a totalitarian and triumphalist practice in which,
> to the extent that it succeeds, there is nothing but raw material:
> in the earth, in other people, and finally in self.
>
> (ibid.: 262)

Clearly the human presence in the world involves interventions
in constituted nature. What we are now able to do, if we choose,
is to elect, monitor and control the kinds of interventions we make.
Yet however strong the argument on ecological grounds, only if
the connection with politics and economics is made can effective
change be made. This requires understanding what dominant forms
of politics and economics do to the human personality: we become
accustomed to treating others as objects, raw material to be
exploited. In the end this also extends to the self. So, Williams
comments, in this way sexual relationships can be interpreted as
a way of using another person as the raw material for private
sensations. This can be institutionalized for the purposes of profit
in pornography and in the violence visited on the vulnerable, usually
women and children. There then follows a passage which takes us
to the heart of Williams' position:

> Failure in such versions of relationship is wholly predictable since
> relationship is precisely an alternative to the use of others as raw
> material. But what is most totalitarian about this failure is that
> it extends not only to the cruel punishment of others, who indeed
> in these terms cannot yield the lasting satisfactions that are
> sought, but also to the cruel punishment of the self: in alcoholism,
> in addiction to damaging drugs, in obesities and damaging
> asceticisms. For the very self is then only the raw material in
> the production of sensations and identities. In this final reach
> of the orientation, human beings themselves are decentred.
>
> (ibid.: 263)

Although he does not say so, we can see here affinities with
Durkheim's concept of the self in conditions of anomie, wherein
greed is aroused and insatiable; nothing can calm it (Durkheim

1952). There is an instrumentality which is not capable of fulfilment, as utilitarianism might suppose. But there is also meaninglessness, a point well developed in Charles Taylor's important study, *Sources of the Self* (1989). The loss of meaning can be formulated in terms of division or fragmentation.

> To take an instrumental stance to nature is to cut us off from the sources of meaning in it. An instrumental stance to our own feelings divides us within, splits reason from sense. And the atomistic focus on our individual goals dissolves community and divides us from each other.
>
> (Taylor 1989: 500–1)

This theme, Taylor observes, was articulated by Schiller, the early Marx, Lukács, Adorno and Horkheimer, Marcuse, and also in the student movement of 1968. This, it seems to us, is the company Williams is keeping in this crucial aspect of his thinking.

Secondly, and provocatively from the standpoint of Marxist orthodoxy, Williams argues that the concept of the 'mode of production' needs to be reconsidered. The reasoning is linked to the first point. While this kind of analysis has been successful in identifying the different ways in which production has been organized in the course of human history, it cannot look beyond itself:

> For all that follows from one mode of production is another, when the real problem is radical change, in hard social and material terms, in the idea of production itself. For the abstraction of production is a specialised and eventually ideological version of what is really in question, which is the form of human social relationships within a physical world.
>
> (Williams 1985b: 264)

This, again, involves a radical reorientation: it is precisely the idea of raw material for production that is being rejected and, in its place, 'there is the new orientation of livelihood: of practical, self-managing, self-renewing societies, in which people care first for each other, in a living world' (ibid.: 266).

This leads to the third, and again interconnected, point. We must replace the idea of 'society as production' with an understanding of human relationships within the physical world as a way of life. To point to the need to shift from production to livelihood as the central guiding concept is to rediscover the importance of developing co-operative relationships. This is not to replace rationality by sentiment but to combine reason and emotion to generate the energy and means for an alternative social order. There is no doubt in Williams' mind or, we may venture, for most of us, that we live in unsettling, bewildering and confusing times. There is no necessary reason why his commitment to the long revolution will be vindicated. But it is the openness to alternative and not inevitable futures that encourages him to draw our attention to these resources for a journey of hope:

> It is not some unavoidable real world with its laws of economy and law of war, that is now blocking us. It is a set of identifiable processes of *realpolitik* and *force majeure*, of nameable agencies of power and capital, distraction and disinformation; and all these interlocking with the embedded short-term pressures and the interwoven subordination of an adaptive commonsense. It is not in staring at these blocks that there is any chance of movement past them. They have been named so often that they are not even, for most people, news. The dynamic movement is elsewhere, in the difficult business of gaining confidence in *our own* energies and capacities.
>
> (ibid. 268)

Bibliography

The Bibliography is divided into two sections: work by Raymond Williams cited in the text and secondary literature. The dates of the works we cite are those of editions used for quotations. If the date of the first publication differs from this, it is given in square brackets after the title. The most extensive bibliographies of Williams' work can be found in O'Connor (1989) and Eagleton (1989).

WORKS BY RAYMOND WILLIAMS

Axton, Marie and Williams, Raymond (eds) (1977) *English Drama: Forms and Development: Essays in Honour of Muriel Clara Bradbrook*, with an Introduction by Raymond Williams, Cambridge and New York: Cambridge University Press.

Orrom, Michael and Williams, Raymond (1954) *Preface to Film*, London: Film Drama Limited.

Williams, Joy and Williams, Raymond (eds) (1973) *Lawrence on Education*, Harmondsworth: Penguin.

Williams, Raymond (1950) *Reading and Criticism*, London: Frederick Muller.

—— (1959) 'Arguing about television', *Encounter*, June: 56–9.

—— (1961) *Culture and Society 1780–1950* [1988], Harmondsworth: Penguin.

—— (1964) *Drama from Ibsen to Eliot* [1952], Harmondsworth: Penguin.

—— (1965) *The Long Revolution* [1961], Harmondsworth: Penguin.

—— (1966) *Modern Tragedy*, London: Chatto & Windus.

—— (ed.) (1968) *May Day Manifesto* [1967], Harmondsworth: Penguin.

—— (1973) *Drama from Ibsen to Brecht* [1968], Harmondsworth: Penguin.

—— (1974) *Television: Technology and Cultural Form* [revised edn 1990], Glasgow: Fontana.

—— (1975a) *The Country and the City* [1973], St Albans: Paladin.

—— (1975b) *Orwell* [1971], Glasgow: Fontana.
—— (1976) *Communications* [1962], Harmondsworth: Penguin.
—— (1977) *Marxism and Literature*, Oxford: Oxford University Press.
—— (1980) *Problems in Materialism and Culture*, London: Verso.
—— (1981a) *Politics and Letters: Interviews with New Left Review* [1979], London: Verso.
—— (1981b) *Culture*, Glasgow: Fontana.
—— (1982) 'This Sadder recognition', Interview with Sue Aspinoll, *Screen*, 23: 3–4.
—— (1983a) *Keywords: A Vocabulary of Culture and Society* [1976], Glasgow: Fontana.
—— (1983b) *Cobbett*, Oxford: Oxford University Press.
—— (1984) *The English Novel from Dickens to Lawrence* [1970], London: Hogarth Press.
—— (1985a) *The Volunteers* [1978], London: Hogarth Press.
—— (1985b) *Towards 2000* [1983], Harmondsworth: Penguin.
—— (1987) *Country and City in the Modern Novel*, Swansea: University College of Swansea.
—— (1988a) *Border Country* [1960], London: Hogarth Press.
—— (1988b) *Second Generation* [1964], London: Hogarth Press.
—— (1988c) *The Fight for Manod* [1979], London: Hogarth Press.
—— (1988d) 'Art: Freedom as Duty', *Planet*, April/May: 7–14.
—— (1989a) *Loyalties* [1985], London: Hogarth Press.
—— (1989b) *People of the Black Mountains I: the Beginning*, London: Chatto & Windus.
—— (1989c) *Resources of Hope: Culture Democracy and Socialism*, Robin Gale (ed.), London: Verso.
—— (1989d) *The Politics of Modernism, Against the New Conformists*, Tony Pinkney (ed.), London: Verso.
—— (1990a) *People of the Black Mountains II: The Eggs of the Eagle*, London: Chatto & Windus.
—— (1990a) *What I came to say*, Neil Belton, Francis Mulhern and Janny Taylor (eds), London: Century Hutchinson.
—— (1991a) *Drama in Performance* [1954], Milton Keynes: Open University Press.
—— (1991b) *Writing in Society* [1983], London: Verso.

SECONDARY LITERATURE

Anderson, B. (1983) *Imagined Communities: Reflections on the Origins and Spread of Nationalism*, London: Verso.
Anderson, Perry (1976) *Considerations on Western Marxism*, London: New Left Books.
—— (1980) *Arguments within English Marxism*, London: New Left Books.
Arnold, Matthew (1869) *Culture and Anarchy*, Edinburgh: Murray.
Avineri, Shlomo and de-Shalit, Avner (eds) (1992) *Communitaranism and Individualism*, Oxford: Oxford University Press.

Bahro, Rudolf (1978) *The Alternative in Eastern Europe*, London: New Left Books.
Barnett, Anthony (1976) 'Raymond Williams and Marxism: A rejoinder to Terry Eagleton', *New Left Review*, 99: 47–64.
—— (1988) 'The Keywords of a Key Thinker', *The Listener*, 4 February: 15.
Bell, Colin and Newby, Howard (1971) *Community Studies*, London: Allen & Unwin.
Benedict, Ruth (1935) *Patterns of Culture*, London: Routledge & Kegan Paul.
Bigsby, C.W.E. (ed.) (1976) *Approaches to Popular Culture*, London: Edward Arnold.
Bratlinger, Patrick (1990) *Crusoe's Footprints: Cultural Studies in Britain and America*, London: Routledge.
Brennan T., Cooney, E.W. and Pollin, H. (1954) *Social Change in South West Wales*, London: Watts.
Burke, Edmund (1950) *Reflections on the Revolution in France*, London: World Classics.
Carey, James, W. (1989) *Communication as Culture*, London: Unwin Hyman.
Carey, John (1992) *The Intellectuals and the Masses: Pride and Prejudice among the Literary Intelligentsia*, London: Faber & Faber.
Caudwell, Christopher (1938) *Illusion and Reality*, London: Lawrence & Wishart.
Clarke, John, Critcher, Chris and Johnson, Richard (eds) (1979) *Working Class Culture*, London: Hutchinson.
Collins, Richard, Curran, J., Garnham, Nicholas, Scannell, P., Schlesinger, P. and Sparks, C. (eds) (1986) *Media, Culture and Society: A Critical Reader*, London: Sage.
Durkheim, Emile (1952) *Suicide*, London: Routledge & Kegan Paul.
Dworkin, Dennis L. and Raman, Leslie G. (eds) (1993) *Views Beyond the Border Country: Raymond Williams and Cultural Politics*, London: Routledge.
Eagleton, Terry (1978) *Criticism and Ideology: A Study in Marxist Literary Theory*, London: Verso.
—— (1984) *The Function of Criticism: From Spectator to Post-Structuralism*, London: Verso.
—— (1988) 'Professor Raymond Williams', *Independent*, 29 January.
—— (ed.) (1989) *Raymond Williams: Critical Perspectives*, Cambridge: Polity Press.
Easthope, Anthony (1988) *British Post-Structuralism since 1968*, London: Routledge.
Eldridge, John (1971) *Sociology and Industrial Life*, London: Nelson.
—— (1983) *C. Wright Mills*, London: Tavistock, Horwood.
Eliot, T.S. (1939) *The Idea of a Christian Society*, London: Faber & Faber.
—— (1948) *Notes Towards the Definition of Culture*, London: Faber & Faber.
Featherstone, Mike (1991) *Consumer Culture and Postmodernism*, London: Sage.

Frisby, David and Sayer, Derek (1986) *Society*, London: Horwood/ Tavistock.

Fromm, Erich (1942) *Fear of Freedom*, London: Routledge & Kegan Paul.

Garnham, Nicholas (1990) *Capitalism and Communication*, London: Sage.

Gellner, Ernest (1992) *Reason and Culture*, Oxford: Blackwell.

Geoghegan, Vincent (1987) *Utopianism and Marxism*, London: Methuen.

Giddens, Anthony (1982) *Profiles and Critiques in Social Theory*, London: Macmillan.

Gorak, Jan (1988) *The Alien Mind of Raymond Williams*, Columbia: University of Missouri Press.

Gorz, André (1989) *Critique of Economic Reason*, London: Verso.

Gouldner, Alvin W. (1976) *The Dialectic of Ideology and Technology*, London: Macmillan.

Hall, Stuart (1986) 'Cultural Studies: two paradigms', in Richard Collins, J. Curran, Nicholas Garnham, P. Scannell, P. Schlesinger and C. Sparks (eds) *Media, Culture and Society. A Critical Reader*, London: Sage.

—— (1988a) 'Only connect: the life of Raymond Williams', *New Statesman*, 5 February: 20–1.

—— (1988b) *The Hard Road to Renewal*. London: Verso.

—— and Whannel, Paddy (1964) *The Popular Arts*, Boston: Beacon Books.

Hampshire, Stuart (1966) *Unhappy Families*, 29 July: 169–70.

Hare, David (1989) 'Cycles of hope and despair', *Weekend Guardian*, 3–4 June: 2–5.

Havel, Vaclav (1987) *Living in Truth*, London: Faber & Faber.

Hebdige, Dick (1988) *Hiding in the Light: On Images and Things*, London: Routledge.

Himmelweit, H., Oppenheim, A. and Vince, P. (1959) *Television and the Child*, Oxford: Oxford University Press.

Hoggart Richard (1992) *The Uses of Literacy*, Harmondsworth: Penguin.

Inglis, Fred (1982) *Radical Earnestness: English Social Theory 1880–1980*, Oxford: Martin Robertson.

—— (1988) 'Lost behind enemy lines', *The Times Higher Education Supplement*, 5 February: 7.

Jameson, Fredric (1992) *Postmodernism or the cultural Logic of Late Capitalism*, London: Verso.

Johnson, Lesley (1987) 'Raymond Williams: a marxist view of culture', in Diane J. Austin-Broos (ed.) *Creating Culture*, London: Allen & Unwin.

Johnson, R.W. (1990) 'Moooovement', *London Review of Books*, 8 February: 5–6.

Kermode, Frank (1966) 'Tragedy and Revolution', *Encounter*, 27 August: 83–5.

—— (1988) 'Professor Raymond Williams', *Independent*, 29 January.

Kettle, Arnold (1961) 'Culture and Revolution: A consideration of the ideas of Raymond Williams and others',*Marxism Today* 5: 301–7.

Kiernan, V. (1959) 'Culture and Society', *New Reasoner* 9: 74–83.

Kormhauser, William (1960) *The Politics of Mass Society*, London: Routledge & Kegan Paul.

Kumar, Krishan (1987) *Utopia and Anti-Utopia in Modern Times*, Oxford: Blackwell.

Leavis, F.R. (1930) *Mass Civilisation and Minority Culture*, Cambridge: Pamphlet.

—— (1962) *The Great Tradition* [1948], Harmondsworth: Penguin.

Levitas, Ruth (1990) *The Concept of Utopia*, Hemel Hempstead: Philip Allan.

Lovell, Terry (1989) 'Knowable pasts, imaginable futures', *History Workshop* 27, Spring: 136–40.

Lyotard, Jean François (1986) *The Post-Modern Condition: A Report on Knowledge*, Manchester: University of Manchester Press.

Lynd, R.S. and Lynd, H.M. (1929) *Middletown: A Study in Contemporary American Culture*, New York: Harcourt Brace.

—— (1937) *Middletown in Transition*, New York: Harcourt Brace.

MacDonald, D. (1961) 'Looking backward', *Encounter*, 16 June: 79–84.

McGrath, J. (1981) *A Good Night Out: Popular Theatre: Audience, Class and Form*, London: Methuen.

McIlroy, John and Westwood, Sallie (eds) (1993) *Border Country: Raymond Williams in Adult Education*, Leicester: National Institute of Adult Continuing Education.

Mattelaut, Armand (1991) *Advertising International*, London: Routledge.

Mellencamp, Paricia (ed.) (1990) *Logics of Television*, London: British Film Institute Press.

Miller, Jane (1990) *Seductions: Studies in Reading and Culture*, London: Virago.

Mills, C.W. (1960) *The Causes of World War III*, New York: Ballantine Books.

—— (1967) *The Sociological Imagination* [1959], Oxford: Oxford University Press.

Morgan, Kenneth O. (1992) *Labour People: Hardie to Kinnock* Oxford: Oxford University Press.

Morris, William (1962) *News from Nowhere* [1891], Harmondsworth: Penguin.

Muker, Chandra and Schudson, Michael (eds) (1991) *Rethinking Popular Culture: Contemporary Perspectives in Cultural Studies*, Berkeley: University of California Press.

Murdoch, Rupert (1989) 'Freedom in broadcasting', *McTaggart Lecture*, Edinburgh: News International Corporation.

Nisbet, Robert (1966) *The Sociological Tradition*, New York: Basin Books.

O'Connor, Alan (1989a) *Raymond Williams on Television, Selected Writings*, London: Routledge.

—— (1989b) *Raymond Williams: Writing Culture Politics*, Oxford: Basil Blackwell.

Orwell, George (1954) *1984*, Harmondsworth: Penguin.

Parrinder, Patrick (1984) 'The accents of Raymond Williams', *Critical Quarterly* 26: 47–57.

Pinkney, Tony (1991) *Raymond Williams*, Cardiff: Poetry Wales Press.

Popper, Karl (1961a) *The Poverty of Historicism*, London: Routledge & Kegan Paul.
—— (1961b) *The Open Society and its Enemies*, London: Routledge & Kegan Paul.
Rees, A. (1950) *Social Life in a Welsh Countryside*, Cardiff: University of Wales Press.
Richards, I.A. (1924) *Principles of Literary Criticism*, London: Kegan Paul, Trench & Trubner.
—— (1926) *Science and Poetry*, London: Kegan Paul, Trench & Trubner.
Rustin, Michael (1985) *For a Pluralist Socialism*, London: Verso.
—— (1988) 'Raymond Williams (1921–1988)', *Radical Philosophy* 49, Summer: 46–7.
Samuel, R. (1989) 'Philosophy teaching by example: positions present in Raymond Williams', *History Workshop* 27, Spring: 141–53.
Schell, Jonathan (1982) *The Fate of the Earth*, London: Jonathan Cape.
Scannell, P. (1990) 'Public service broadcasting: the history of a concept', in A. Goodwin and G. Whannel (eds) *Understanding Television*, London: Routledge.
Stein, M. (1960) *The Eclipse of Community*, Princeton, N.J.: Princeton University Press.
Stein, Walter (1969) *Criticism as Dialogue*, Cambridge: Cambridge University Press.
Stuart, G. (1975) *The Reith Diaries*, London: Collins.
Tawney, R.H. (1921) *The Acquisitive Society*, London: Allen & Unwin.
—— (1931) *Equality*, London: Allen & Unwin.
Taylor, Charles (1989) *Sources of the Self: The Making of Modern Identity*, Cambridge: Cambridge University Press.
Thompson, Denys (ed.) (1964) *Discrimination and Popular Culture*, Harmondsworth: Penguin.
Thompson, E.P. (ed.) (1960) *Out of Apathy*, London: New Left Books.
—— (1961) 'The Long Revolution', *New Left Review* 9 and 10: 24–33, 34–9.
—— (1965) *The Making of the English Working Class* [1963], Harmondsworth: Penguin.
—— (1977) *William Morris: Romantic to Revolutionary* [1955], London; Merlin Press.
—— (1981) 'The politics of theory', in R. Samuel (ed.) *People's History and Socialist Theory*, London: Routledge & Kegan Paul.
—— (1982) *Exterminism and Cold War*, London: Verso.
Vidich, Arthur J., Benjamin, Joseph and Stein, Maurice R. (1964) *Reflections on Community Studies*, New York: John Wiley.
Wainwright, Hilary (1987) *Labour: A Tale of Two Parties*, London: The Hogarth Press.
Ward, J.P. (1981) *Raymond Williams*, Cardiff: University of Wales Press.
Warner, W. Lloyd and Low, J.O. (1941) *The Social Life of a Modern Community*, New Haven: Yale University Press.
—— (1942) *The Status System of a Modern Community*, New Haven: Yale University Press.

—— (1947) *The Social System of a Modern Factory*, New Haven: Yale University Press.

Weber, Max (1930) *The Protestant Ethic and the Spirit of Capitalism*, London: Allen & Unwin.

Wiener, Martin J. (1985) *English Culture and the Decline of the Industrial Spirit 1850–1980*, Harmondsworth: Penguin.

Williams, W.M. (1956) *The Sociology of An English Village: Gosforth*, London: Routledge & Kegan Paul.

Willmott, P. and Young, M. (1957) *Family and Kinship in East London*, London: Routledge & Kegan Paul.

Young, B. (1990) 'Programmes above profit', *Airwaves*, Summer: 8–9.

Index

sadell, Co. Sligo was seven miles long; his proud boast that he could travel all the way to Sligo town without once leaving his own land. A local newspaper taking a poke at the 'Emperor's clothes', wrote this satirical piece when, in 1839, Sir Robert drove his latest toy, a full size mail coach, all the way into Sligo. This was the same year he evicted all of the tenants of the townland of Ballygilgan, sixty-three families, to make a bigger lawn:

> '…This useful and distinguished member of society drove his newly acquired mail coach into Sligo, the top of which was crowned with various bilious looking individuals who were, no doubt, worthy scions of our useless aristocracy. The respected Baronet seemed very ambitious to be looked upon by the wondering multitudes as an accomplished whip.
> He imitated the scream or yelp of the professional jarvey admirably. He wore on the occasion (we like to be minute even in dress when a great man is in question) a small glazed hat, large pilot cloth-box coat and belecher handkerchief and ever and anon gave a graceful whoop resembling an Indian war cry.
> In short, he looked the part in life, and when one gazed at his little brandy face and undignified figure he could not help but regret that Dame Nature did not really make him a coachman, as it was just the position in society that he appeared to be cut out for. A few more words about this aristocratic jarvey: Mr. Dukes complained in the jury room last Assizes that he had to relieve several of Sir Robert Gore-Booth's tenants that were reduced to a state of destitution. Now if this statement were true, and we see no reason to doubt it, would it not, we ask, be more becoming of him as a landlord, as a man, and as a Christian to provide for the wants of his people than to spend his loose cash on such useless frippery as a mail coach…'

Despite the harsh conditions in which they lived every locality

had its local champions who fought, and sometimes won, small
battles with their 'masters'. Even when they lost it was thought a
heroic loss and they were lauded as heroes: small town Davids
in a hopeless battle against a monolithic Goliath. Famine and
failed rebellions had broken their bodies but not their will. The
last futile attempt to revolt, in 1867, only confirmed in the minds
of the people that any attempt to overthrow English rule in Ireland by military means could only end in disaster. With nothing
left to them but their wits they proceeded, having Michael Davitt
and Captain Boycott as their inspiration, on a campaign of civil
disobedience and mockery.

Local newspapers joined in describing the local justices of the
court, political appointees drawn from the ascendancy classes,
as 'just-asses, and 'doughty and gouty' dispensers of the law. The
law had been dictated for hundreds of years, 'by a small minority, differing in race, religion and outlook, holding nothing in
common with the great majority of the people. Placed in position
here and given over the lands and natural resources of the country, of which the people had been robbed, this minority, sustained by British bayonets, ruled and dispensed the law in the
interests of themselves and their class.'[23]

Even so there were the proud and the defiant provoked beyond
endurance that, as we shall see in the next chapter, risked freedom and even life itself daring to challenge their masters.

[23] Fennel, Thomas: *The Royal Irish Constabulary* p78

14

THE CHALLENGE OF DAVID

The history of a nation is, not in parliaments and battlefields but in what the people say to each other on fair days and high days, and in how they farm and quarrel, and go on pilgrimage.

W.B. Yeats

In September 1881 a large and noisy crowd had gathered at Grange Petty Sessions, Co. Sligo. They had come to support Patrick Boyce of Mullaghmore, a tenant of Lord Ashley's, who was up before the court charged with assault. Outside the court-house armed police patrolled the crowd who had gathered to jeer and shout abuse at the R.I.C. and landlord's agents. The authorities feared a riot as the case had attracted huge attention in the countryside

Boyce, the prosecution claimed, had attacked a party of shooters headed by Lord Ashley as they crossed the fields in search of game. Charles Barker, the agent on behalf of Ashley, told the court that Boyce was mowing in a field when the huntsmen crossed the fence in pursuit of game. Boyce had confronted the party as they attempted to pass blocking their path; he had first threatened them and then attacked the party with his scythe.

Boyce denied the charge saying that he had just tried, in a peaceful manner, to prevent the party from crossing his field. His meadow and potato crop would be trampled and destroyed by the horses and hounds. His pleas falling on deaf ears the judge decided the case against Boyce and committed him to prison for six weeks. The crowd outside were batoned and dispersed by the R.I.C. while Boyce was taken away and lodged in Sligo jail. Crowds gathered and bonfires blazed throughout the countryside to welcome the still defiant Boyce when he was released some weeks later.

The Healy brothers, Pat and Owen, and their mother lived in a little two-roomed, thatched house with earthen floors across the road from the Classiebawn estate. While owning little themselves they were kings by their own fireside — and a constant thorn in the side of authority. Fishing a Greencastle yawl to earn an uncertain living, a small plot of land behind the house provided them with the essentials: potatoes, vegetables, hay, oats and rye. Although lacking in formal education they were very well versed in natural lore and local history. Pat, the last native Irish speaker in Sligo, was ninety-one years old when he passed away in 1951. In addition to Irish he spoke English and French, or at least enough French to impress his peers who had no French at all. He had great respect and love for nature at a time when people paid no attention to such things and whose efforts were often bent to trapping thrushes and blackbirds for the dinner table.

The family matriarch Mrs Healy lived to be 100 years old. A native Irish speaker, she had not a word of English and often told Pat of a tragedy that befell the family during the famine years. Pat told the story to his neighbours and to a collector from the Department of Irish Folklore in 1950. He was over 90 years old at the time.

In order to alleviate the effect of the blight Pat's father and his neighbours cut down the contaminated foliage, plus a ridge or two of those adjoining, and removed the stalks to a corner of the field. Smallholders lit fires to purify the air, all to no avail as, 'the big potatoes melted', leaving nothing but rotten shells and 'poheens' (tiny potatoes). A small patch of Healy's ground remained blight free so with great delight the family gathered these potatoes into a pit, a clay-covered heap, to keep for the spring. When the winter passed they went to bring the potatoes into the house only to discover they were gone. The outward appearance of the heap remained the same as the pit had been shored up on the inside with stones to conceal the theft. Pat recalled his mother telling him that, 'the household cried in despair when they discovered the cruel wrong they had come to.'

My father and other neighbours spoke well of the brothers and, indeed, sometimes admiringly. Pat was a gentle man, no one 'ever heard him cursing or swearing'. Although having no children of his own he was good to youngsters of the village, they said. He gave them pennies, imitated the blackbird's song for them and encouraged them to talk the Irish they learned in school. Stories of Pat and his brother's exploits passed many a pleasant hour around winter firesides:

'Y'know the hÉalais were th'only ones in Mullagh that didn't sign up their rights to the crowd up in the castle,' they'd say with a smile and a hint of pride.

'If th'oul landlords shot a pheasant and it landed on the hÉalais land they couldn't go in after it. They tried it one time an' Owen chased them with the pitchfork! Ashley took him to Grange court but damn the hate they he could make of him!'

There was no limit to the variety of ways in which the Healy's outwitted the castle and their agents. Owen, having once decided on a modest expansion of his property, requested permission from Lord Ashley to move his boundary wall a bit closer to the road. He explained that he wanted to plant an extra ridge or two of potatoes. Having so little land it would mean a lot to him. On being refused he was quite indignant. After all, he complained to anyone that would listen, the landlord's entire wall was close to the road and he had thousands of acres. So why couldn't Owen move his fence out that had only two! Having failed to get permission fair and square he decided to skin a cat by other means.

When cropping time came, access to the field was gained by opening a gap in the stone fence to admit the ass and cart. Now, each year, he made an opening in a different place; rebuilding the wall a few feet at a time he moved it out, little by little each year. Ashley's agents eventually noticed. They came to chastise

Owen, ordering him to move the ditch back to where it was. Owen held his ground and made what he felt was a reasonable case: 'Why don't you move your ditch back? Haven't you more land than me?'

In time the entire wall was moved: a small victory, but a victory nevertheless. The wall's irregular contours can yet be seen, a monument to the past and to the spirit of Pat and Owen Healy.

Out in front of Healy's home, across a little grassy lane, was a plantation of sycamore trees belonging to the 'Rt. Hon. Wilfrid Ashley'. Pat and Owen saw possibilities for expansion there too. There would be an awful fuss if they went out and cut the trees down so, according to local lore, they quietly bored holes in the trunk, inserted nitre, plugged the holes and waited. The trees soon died and had to be cut down. Pat applied to the estate manager and had no trouble acquiring the trees for firewood.

The plan was going well so the brothers pitted their potatoes on the now open space where the trees once stood. It seemed a harmless enough move, but, through time, by virtue of using the property, they established a legal claim to it. If left undisputed for a number of years the ground was going to go by default to the 'trespassers'. After a while they thought they might hurry things up a bit so they asked Ashley to cede or sell the piece of land to them. Stung to action by another refusal they called a meeting of adjacent plot owners who, under the leadership of the dauntless brothers, decided to take the initiative. They would fence in and take control of the whole plantation, an area of about twenty acres.

This plan went well — until it came time to put the confiscation into effect. This required the Healys and their accomplices to go into open defiance of the authorities. As time went on people thought about the inevitability of legal retribution and the consequences of failure. They dithered and dallied. When it came time to buy the fencing wire they fell away and the plan came to nothing. Years afterwards the committee, older and wiser and with benefit of hindsight, regretted they didn't follow through. They saw the wisdom of the Healy's plan and lamented a missed opportunity that just might have succeeded. The open space in the wood, where the Healy's pitted their potatoes, can still be seen across from where their house once stood.

Letters discovered on a visit to the landlord's archives in the Hartley Library in Southampton, England, revealed another side to Pat Healy. It showed a man who was prepared to play the two sides of the fence and use whatever guile was necessary to achieve his ends. We can only speculate as to whether Pat's admirers knew he was buttering up the landlord in such a seemingly servile manner. This letter was probably sent prior to their attempted annexation of the woods:

Pat Healy Mullaghmore, March 10th 1928

Dear Mr Wilfrid Ashley,
I write to you these lines hoping to find you well and in good health as the departure of this leaves us well at present, thanks be to God.
I am asking your Honour if your Honour would be pleased to sell the bit of a plantation that is pending on at our door. I would pay your Honour by the year or else the money down, but by the year it would fit me the best, the fishing has greatly failed in Mullaghmore but just for a while in Summer time. So this bit at the door would be for setting a little potatoes in it. It would do if your Honour would be pleased, my division of land is small and I feel it more since the fishing failed.
I will be obliged and thankful to your Honour for ever and ever so now I must say goodbye to your Honour for this time but I hope you will kindly answer this letter. As I have already said Mullaghmore is the same old way as just when your Honour seen it. It is very lonely looking since the houses was burnt [24]. That made it lonely and poor also, and put a great lot of earning out of the poor people's way. I lost very severe as I had the boating of some great families but great thanks to them they are very good to me all the time. I hope the great God will assist in goodness to them.

[24] The burnt houses referred to are the English owned Coastguard stations burned by the local I.R.A. in 1920 during the War of Independence.

I am your truly obedient servant,
Patrick Healy, Mullaghmore, Co. Sligo Ireland

Another story concerns the landlord's pheasants that roamed free and knew no man-made boundaries. They were always guaranteed a welcome and a tasty meal on Healy's plot where the brothers left down oats and small potatoes to tempt them. It was a trap! The potatoes had hooks inserted that were attached to a string that led down the potato drills to an outhouse. Any pheasant tempted by a free meal on Healy's land was in for an unpleasant surprise. It was promptly and unceremoniously reeled, in a flurry of feathers and loud squawks, to the waiting Pat who quickly despatched it.

The trail of oats was another false promise that ended in a concealed trap and another nutritious dinner for Pat and Owen and their aged parents. The Brackens, successors to Barker that prosecuted Patrick Boyce, knew what was going on but all they could do was bluster. They couldn't enter the property and could never catch the brothers in the act. This is all the more surprising, and a tribute to the men's cunning, when we realise that the gamekeeper's windows looked directly down on the Healy's land and cottage just one field away!

A different slant to the story emerges in another one of Pat's letters on deposit in the Hartley Library. Here there is no mention of poaching but a claim of quarrels with his neighbours in defence of Ashley's birds. He has managed to build up a big head of steam about the damage they are, ostensibly, doing to his crops:

Mullaghmore, January 6th, 1913

Dear Mr. Wilfrid Ashley,
I write your Honour these lines hoping to find you in good health as the departure of this leaves us in good health at present.

Thanks be to God I was speaking to your Honour at Classiebawn about the pheasants, and so also did Mr. Bracken offer 4 shillings to my mother which she did not take, and did not think it in any way honest or just for the damages and cares that me and my mother got from protecting them pheasants in our field. We were sure that we would get from your honour something fair and just and honest, as usual.

Now I stopped all people from firing stones in to my field at your pheasants and I got into a scrimmage about it from the effects of stopping them, and if I had permission or a pay from your honour I would make it dear on them. Your Honour knows well they have not far to come, your Honour knows the distance very well. No man can know it better.

The corn is not worth speaking about from the depredations of your fowl. So now I must say goodbye to your Honour. My mother says she should get in proportion to the damage.

I am, your obedient servant,

Patrick Healy, Mullaghmore

A dense fog of time and neglect has closed over these tantalizing glimpses of another era and we are left to fill in the gaps ourselves. Did Pat ever get his stipend for 'protecting' the pheasants? How much did the neighbours know of his attempts of a cosy relationship with the landlord? We will never know.

What we do know is that Pat never got the desired piece of plantation. It belongs today to an Irish landlord, who differs little in outlook from his English predecessors. We believe the story about the wall because it still maintains a crooked vigil on the margin of Pat's plot. The field that sustained life for the Healy family is not a field anymore but a parcel of sites and holiday homes. The little stone ditches demolition is imminent and few will regret it's passing or know its story. The only memorial to its existence and Pat's labours of defiance will be a few lines in this book.

It was not just their defiance that made the brothers special; they were a rich source of funny stories too. Pat, some neighbours said, changed his shirt once a year. This new shirt was bought at Mc Gowan's shop two miles out the road. It was one of those old fashioned shops of pre-supermarket days where you could buy groceries, tea, sugar, butter, etc; you could sell your eggs there too, to pay for the groceries. At another counter shoes, shirts, wellingtons, suits, overcoats and big squares of leather for the home cobbler were on offer. At the back there were big bags of Clarendo, 'Injun' meal, flour, bran and other cereals for home and cattle. When it came time that families needed a coffin and arrangements made for a funeral here too is where they came. From birth to death everything was taken care of in one shop.

Pat's new shirt was purchased, neatly wrapped in paper and tied with brown string. On the way home he passed by Lough Eala on one side and 'the Brook' — which wasn't a brook at all but another small lake — on the other side. As the story goes, Pat, who may have stopped at Tommy Hannon's Pub for a 'half one', or a pint or two, in order to celebrate the occasion, paused at the lakes, undid the string and took out the new shirt to inspect it. Taking off the old shirt and rolling it into a ball he threw it out as far as he could into the water declaring:

'There ye go and bad luck to ye. If ye sink it won't be for the want of a crew anyway!'

Another story concerned an old ass they had owned for many a year. It had seen better days. Its hooves were turned up, its coat mangy and its general demeanour something like a caricature of Don Quixote's Rosinante. Nevertheless, they were fond of it. They hated to see their old friend go, but they reluctantly decided it was time for a change. They would sell the beast, get the best possible price for him and purchase a younger, stronger ass.

Next fair day in Grange Pat was up with the lark. He set out on the road early and was delighted when he sold his charge first thing in the morning to one of the many sharp-eyed 'jobbers'